APHRODITE DESPERATE MISSION

JACK OLSEN was the award-winning author of thirty-three books published in fifteen countries and eleven languages. Olsen was a bureau chief for *Time* magazine. He wrote for such magazines as *Vanity Fair, People, Paris Match, Readers Digest, Playboy, Life, Sports Illustrated, Fortune, New York Times Book Review* and others. The *Philadelphia Inquirer* described him as "an American treasure." Olsen was the author of *Silence on Monte Sole,* an extraordinary study of a Nazi massacre of Italian civilians in the closing days of World War II. Olsen died at the age of 77 in 2002.

AVAILABLE NOW

Silence on Monte Sole
Jack Olsen

Guadalcanal: Decision at Sea
Ambush Valley
Six Days in June
By Eric Hammel

Helmet for My Pillow
The General
March to Glory
By Robert Leckie

Samurai!
By Saburo Sakai with Martin Caidin
and Fred Saito

Zero
By Masatake Okumiya and Jiro Horikoshi
with Martin Caidin

Fork-Tailed Devil: The P-38
The B-17: The Flying Forts
By Martin Caidin

Sink the Bismarck!
By C. S. Forester

The World War II Reader
By the Editors of *World War II* magazine

What They Didn't Teach You About World War II
By Mike Wright

The Sea Hawks
By Lt. Commander Edgar D. Hoagland, USN (Ret.)

Battle for Bataan
By Colonel Richard C. Mallonée, USA (Ret.)

Americans Behind the Barbed Wire
By J. Frank Diggs

APHRODITE
DESPERATE MISSION

JACK OLSEN

ibooks
new york
www.ibooks.net

DISTRIBUTED BY SIMON AND SCHUSTER

For Su

An ibooks, inc. Book

ibooks, inc.
24 West 25th Street
New York, NY 10010

The ibooks World Wide Web Site address is:
http://www.ibooks.net

ISBN: 0-7434-8670-6
First ibooks printing July 2004
10 9 8 7 6 5 4 3 2 1

Foreword

By

John D. Gresham

"So what do military analysts do with their time?" Folks in my business get that question from time to time, often leading to mumbled answers and thin answers as we try to justify our existence. However, the truth is that we are often looking for needles in haystacks, namely the little kernels of truth and knowledge that will give an edge to warriors in future combat. Our credibility comes from making good "finds" for our customers, frequently from obscure sources or forgotten manuscripts, assisted of course by our existing base of knowledge. That knowledge, more often than not, comes from years of reading.

It goes without saying that military analysts and authors like myself are ravenous readers, consuming a steady diet of email, Internet newsgroups, newspapers, and magazines with an ear and eye always attentive on a 24-hour television news channel. It is books though, that provide us with the foundations of our knowledge and expertise. Were you to walk into my home, you would find the walls covered with shelves and stacked with books, many older than myself. Some are treasured old companions, corners and slipcovers worn by continual use and frequent visits. Each represents a piece of the knowledge base that I fall back on time and again in my work as author, analyst, and American citizen.

So what makes a "really good book" that you might pick up in my home? It often varies, though "really good books" always have a timeless quality to them, even when more recent volumes have covered or replaced the same subject or time period. Often, they form the basis for an examination, or just represent the book interested amateurs should start with. Sometimes, these books are just what you feel comfortable recommending to friends and family, in the hope that what you offer in advice will not bore or swamp the reader. There also are "little" books that provide readers with the historical basis for understanding more modern weapons systems or operational concepts. Such a book is *Aphrodite: Desperate Mission*.

Since 2002, following a wonderful experience helping ibooks put out a new edition of the classic book *Zero!*, I have worked to create a list of books that would be of particular interest or value to their readers of military history. Such lists are quite common within the major military service schools and academies around the world, each having their own set of choices. All share a common desire to provide student readers with a broad and solid foundation of military lessons to take with them into their careers. Some books however, make a lot of the lists. Robert Heinlien's science fiction classic *Starship Troopers* is on almost every American military reading list I know of from the Air Force Academy to the Naval War College. *Starship Troopers* encompasses many of the values and virtues desired for good military personnel of all levels, and is a universal favorite.

It was with this same desire to provide civilian readers of military history with a similar background that I began to make up my own reading list for the *John Gresham Military Library* at ibooks. This series is designed to give readers a list of book that will allow them to better understand military history from a "deckplates and ditches" point of view. Battles and campaigns, the real nuts and bolts of a victorious war, are rarely won in national capitols or command bunkers. Victories in battle go to the soldiers, sailors, airmen, and marines actually in the theaters of war. They also are won in laboratories and the minds of innovative people, who see things made possible by the march of time and technology. Often, initial attempts and efforts are unsuccessful and costly in lives and treasure: such is the cost of progress in producing new engines of war. Nowhere that I know of is this lesson more evident than a little book called *Aphrodite: Desperate Mission.*

In the dozen years since the end of the first Gulf War, warfare has undergone a fundamental short towards use of more precise, carefully targeted weapons and systems. For example, in the years between Desert Storm in 1991 and Iraqi Freedom in 2003, the use of precision-guided munitions (PGMs) actually replacing conventional unguided "iron" bombs in aerial warfare. In fact, PGM usage in Desert Storm was only around 10 percent of weapons dropped, while Iraqi Freedom saw that number grow to around 70 percent. Much of this shift was due to the political realities of modern war, which force military forces to limit non-combatant casualties and collateral damage. Another reason was efficiency: PGMs require fewer sorties and put fewer aircraft and aircrew at risk to take out a given target set. This however, was hardly the reason that PGMs were created. That reason, had to do with something that dated back to 1944.

June 1944 was perhaps the decisive month of World War II, as the Allies began their final drives on the empires of Nazi Germany and Japan. In Europe, the invasion of France began on June 6, with Operation Overlord, the largest amphibious operation in history. The massive air, sea, and land power of the Allies was mustered and committed, to put an expeditionary force into Normandy. The hope was that this force, composed of American, British, Free French, Canadian, and other Commonwealth ground units could be built up fast enough to overcome German counterattacks in Normandy. The problem was that the Germans were hardly going to let the Allies just walk into Europe. On the contrary, the forces under Hitler had fortified northern Europe into the most heavily defended bastion on Earth.

A very real part of *Festung Europa* was the deployment of a new generation of so-called "wonder weapons," designed to force the Allies to suspend their invasion attempt. These included the first jet fighters and bombers, along with a whole family of long-range strike weapons intended for use against England. It was these so-called *Vergeltungswaffe* (German for "revenge") weapons that became a near-obsession for Allied leaders in the spring and summer of 1944. The first of these, the famous V-1 "Buzz Bomb" (technically the Fieseler (Fi) 103), was primitive cruise missile, much like those in use today Designed to be built by unskilled labor and powered by a simple "pulse jet" engine, the V-1's were fired by the thousands at England, causing great damage and casualties. However, since the V-1 was launched either from an above ground launcher or dropped from bombers, and flew at a fairly slow speed, they could be countered. However, the other two *Vergeltungswaffe* were not so easily dealt with.

The V-2 (designated A-4) was the world's first ballistic missile to be used in combat. Designed to be fired by mobile launchers, the V-2 was the SCUD missile of its day able to deliver a ton of explosives onto targets in England with no possible countermeasure. There also was the V-3 *Hochdruckpumpe* supergun, which potentially was the most destructive of the *Vergeltungswaffe* to be built. The V-3 was a huge cannon able to fire 308-pound shells at ranges of over 100 miles for sustained periods of time. As might be imagined, Allied leaders were deeply concerned over the potential of the *Vergeltungswaffe* to disrupt Operation Overlord. They had good reason to be concerned. In 1991, the handful of SCUD missiles fired by Iraq against Israel, Saudi Arabia, and other nations in the Persian Gulf nearly destroyed the Allied Coalition. Also, in an incident that was never reported in detail, one SCUD very nearly destroyed a port facility packed with munitions and fuel, as well as amphibious, hospital, and cargo vessels fully loaded with supplies and personnel! It is easy to imagine what might have happened if the *Vergeltung-*

swaffe had been used in a focused campaign against Allied invasion ports in England.

Such dangers were clear to Allied leaders all the way up to Prime Minister Winston Churchill. Always a proponent of what he called "the Wizard War," Churchill pushed the Allied military leadership hard to counter the *Vergeltungswaffe*. In the case of the above ground launchers, air attacks were mounted any time that one of the V-1 or V-2 units was located. The Allies even mounted a major airborne/armored thrust, Operation Market Garden, into Holland in September 1944 to overrun the *Vergeltungswaffe* launch sites located there. In addition, the RAF bombed the development facilities at Peenemunde on the Baltic Sea to slow down the *Vergeltungswaffe* effort. However, as Operation Overlord began to be mounted in June 1944, there were some *Vergeltungswaffe* facilities in France that were not going to be destroyed with conventional air raids.

Like something out of an Alistair McLean novel, the Germans began in 1943 to construct vast underground *Blockhaus* facilities to house V-2 and V-3 launchers and superguns. Protected by reinforced concrete, armored blast doors, and natural bedrock, these amazing bunkers were among the largest ever built, and were designed to be almost impervious to conventional bombing and even commando raids. Given the obvious potential of weapons being fired from these sites, Allied leaders initiated a series of "crash" programs to destroy the underground V-2 and V-3 facilities.

Perhaps the most outlandish and visionary came from the fertile mind of the Commanding General of the U.S. 8th Air Force, the legendary James H. "Jimmy" Doolittle. Best known for leading the daring bombing raid on Tokyo in April 1942, Doolittle had moved rapidly up the ladder of command to take the helm of the "Mighty Eight" in 1944. But few people knew then or now Doolittle's innumerable contributions to the development of weapons and sensors, some of which led to the modern reconnaissance satellites we take for granted today. Doolittle's idea was to take "war weary" B-17 bombers, load them with 10 tons of either high explosive or napalm, and then use a then state-of-the-art remote control system with an early television camera system to fly the whole affair into the *Vergeltungswaffe Blockhaus* sites in France. Within days of the first V-1's falling onto London in June 1944, Doolittle formed a small development unit in England to make the "war wearies" into viable weapons of war. This became Project Aphrodite.

Aphrodite was America's first real attempt to develop and deploy a usable PGM system in combat. Unfortunately, it never really worked out very well. Aphrodite required a volunteer pilot and flight engineer to launch the drone bomber, and get it flying stable and safely on its way towards the target. Then, once the "mother" aircraft flying alongside had taken over remote control of the "baby" drone, the two crewmen would bail out using their parachutes to descend back to safety. However, the actual process never quite worked out so simply. Problems with the television and remote control systems made the big "war wearies" difficult to handle under the best of circumstances. Even more dangerous though was the payload of explosives or napalm, which proved to be quite "twitchy" to handle. These were the largest explosive and incendiary payloads ever taken into the air at that time, and each of the drones was a "rat's nest" of control cables and electrical lines. Just one spark could set off the entire explosive load vaporizing the two-man crew and a significant chunk of their base in England. Nevertheless, the men of Project Aphrodite pushed forward as more the *Vergeltungswaffe* weapons continued to fall on London.

Eventually the program evolved into a multi-service affair, adding Navy pilots and patrol bomber to the attempt to destroy the *Vergeltungswaffe Blockhaus*. It was this turn that was to give Aphrodite (now called Anvil) its infamous reputation. One of the volunteer naval aviators was a young patrol bomber pilot from Massachusetts, who had already completed his tour of duty. Lieutenant Joseph Kennedy, Jr. was the son of the former Ambassador to the Court of St. James, and the older brother of future President John F. Kennedy. Lieutenant Kennedy and his flight engineer, Lieutenant Bud Willy, were killed on August 12, 1944, when their PB4Y-1 exploded over southern England before they could bail out. Apparently a problem in the arming circuitry had caused the premature detonation, which knocked windows out of house for miles around.

A number of actual missions were run against targets in France, none actually getting a killing hit. The problems lay primarily in the control system, which were several decades away from the technology which could have made the concept work. The final missions against targets in Germany were run in early 1945, after which the program was quietly disestablished. The *Vergeltungswaffe Blockhaus* were eventually destroyed not by PGMs, but by precisely aimed unguided bombs with penetration warheads. The RAF's elite 617 Squadron (the famous "Dambusters"), managed to destroy most of the sites with 12,000-pound "Tallboy" bombs, leaving little more than smoking holes in the ground where the massive *Vergeltungswaffe Blockhaus* had once been. Ironically, the *Vergeltungswaffe* were never used against the invasion ports on the southeastern coast of England. Hitler never saw the value of the *Vergeltungswaffe* against military targets, preferring instead to use them as terror weapons against the civilian population of London. Only later in the war, when the war was already lost, did the Germans use their *Vergeltungswaffe* against military targets in the port of Antwerp.

But for the notoriety of being the instrument of Joe Kennedy, Jr.'s death, Project Aphrodite might have been nothing more than a long-forgotten footnote in aviation history. That is, except for the war in Southeast Asia begun by his brother, President John F. Kennedy. By the mid-1960s, the need to strike point targets in Vietnam like bridges made the need for an operational PGM imperative, given the restrictive rules of engagement enforced upon American aircrews. The need to minimize collateral damage while striking at targets that sometimes were located in civilian neighborhoods made the need for PGMs imperative. So the Navy and Air Force began to develop new PGMs, based around laser beams and automated versions of the same television guidance system used on Project Aphrodite.

About the time that author Jack Olsen published *Aphrodite: Desperate Mission* in 1970, the 8th Tactical Fighter Wing in Thailand was regularly flying missions with the new PGMs. The vital need to strike with precision, seen with such vision by Jimmy Doolittle in 1944, had come full circle as the new Paveway laser guided bombs, and their television guided cousins, began to deliver pin-point hits against enemy targets in Southeast Asia. Versions of the same weapons continued to be used in Iraq and in the Global War on Terror three decades later.

As I wrote earlier, *Aphrodite: Desperate Mission* is a "little" book, which tells the story of a gallant and tragic failure. While the men of Project Aphrodite may have failed to achieve their goals in World War II, their effort showed the way forward towards the modern PGMs still used today. As you read *Aphrodite: Desperate Mission*, think about the men who tried to bend the vacuum-tube technology of 1944 to their will as they desperately tried to blunt the threat of Hitler's weapons of mass destruction. And if you get some sense of the kind of men who would take on a desperate and intimately unsuccessful job and still keep trying, then *Aphrodite: Desperate Mission* will have once again taught its vital lesson to a new generation of readers.

John D. Gresham
Fairfax, Virginia
May 2004

A NOTE

I was the commanding officer of the U.S. Army Air Corps substation at Fersfield, England, at the time of the events described in this book. Apart from a tendency to treat me with more attention than I deserve, the author tells the story of Aphrodite exactly as it happened. Reading these pages, I can hear and see (and almost feel that I can touch) the stalwart men who enlivened those most unusual months of my life, and once again I find myself mourning those who died. They were good men, trying to do a difficult job that had to be done. They made mistakes, like all of us, and they tried to atone for them, like some of us, under conditions that would have led many a brave man to go over the hill in terror. I would face dragons with any one of those men. In fact, I have. God rest their souls, and grant them the peace for which they laid down their lives.

Roy W. Forrest
(Former Lieutenant Colonel,
United States Army Air Corps,
commanding Project Aphrodite, Fersfield,
England, 1944)

PREFACE

ONE DAY in the early 1960's a Navy captain called on Earl P. Olsen of the Systems Integration Laboratory at the Navy Missile Center, Point Mugu, California. "Earl," he said, "President Kennedy's flying here for a visit, and I'm gonna get the two of you together for a long talk."

"Why?" Olsen asked.

"So you can talk over old times about his big brother Joe! Weren't you on that secret mission with Joe in World War II?"

The usually relaxed Olsen became excited. "For God's sake, Captain," he said, "don't do that! I don't want to talk to the President about that mission."

"Why not?"

"I don't want to have to tell him the truth."

1. Double Azon

The moment might come very quickly for us to use a weapon with which we ourselves cannot be attacked.
—Adolf Hitler, September 19, 1939, at Danzig

There are a number of German weapons . . . which must be considered seriously. They include: bacterial warfare; new gases; flame weapons; gliding bombs; aerial torpedoes and pilotless aircraft; long-range guns and rockets; new torpedoes, mines and submarines; death rays, engine-stopping rays and magnetic mines.
—Dr. R. V. Jones, British scientist and defense adviser, November 11, 1939

The speeches of the German leaders contain mysterious allusions to new methods and new weapons which will presently be tried against us. It would, of course, be natural for the enemy to spread such rumors in order to encourage his own people. But there is probably more in it than that.—Winston Churchill, to the House of Commons, September 21, 1943

I ought to let you know that during the last six months evidence has continued to accumulate from many sources that the Germans are preparing an attack on England, particularly London, by means of very long-range rockets which may conceivably weigh 60 tons and carry an explosive charge of 10 to 20 tons.
—Churchill, to Franklin D. Roosevelt, October 25, 1943

*The Führer and I have marked off the most rewarding
targets on a map of London. Twice as many people are
jammed into London as Berlin. For three and one-half
years they have had no air-raid sirens. Imagine the terrific
awakening that is coming! Our weapons are absolutely
unprecedented. There is no defense, no warning at all.
Bang! It hurtles down into the city, all unexpected! I
cannot imagine a more devastating attack on their morale. . . .*—Joseph Goebbels, January 5, 1944, to his press
  secretary

*There is no doubt that the Germans are preparing on
the French shore new means of attack on this country,
either by pilotless aircraft or possibly rockets, or both,
on a considerable scale.*—Churchill, to Commons, February 22, 1944

*The remaining German rocket site, at Wizernes, caused
some anxiety, as it was not obviously aligned on any city
in Europe. One interpreter caused a high degree of alarm
early in the year [1944] when he discovered that one facet
of the workings was within a half a degree of the accurate
Great Circle bearing on New York.*—David Irving, *The
  Mare's Nest* (Little, Brown, 1964)

*There is little of humorous nature in the statement so
often heard that the Germans intended to bombard New
York from launching sites in Europe, as two missiles, the
A-9 and A-10, were under development for use against
the United States in the early months of 1946. This contemplated use was scientifically possible and undoubtedly
would have been realized had time permitted.*—Postwar
Study, U.S. Navy Technical Mission on Guided Missiles

BELIEF EXISTS HERE AFTER CAREFUL EXAMINATION OF
KNOWN DATA THAT THE LARGE ROCKET SITES ARE PRACTI-
CALLY INVULNERABLE TO NORMAL BOMBING ATTACKS.

STRONG INDICATIONS THAT SITES MUST BE NEUTRALIZED
IMMEDIATELY. . . .
—Message from Lieutenant General Carl Spaatz, com-
mander U.S. Strategic Air Forces in Europe, to General
H. H. Arnold, commander U.S. Army Air Corps, June
20, 1944

ONE spring day in 1944 the telephone buzzed in the small
office where Major Henry James Rand was directing his
latest personal campaign against the Nazi war machine.
Rand picked up the phone and said hello in his usual gruff
manner, signifying that he was a busy man with no time for extended palaver. The voice was female, and it asked Rand to
"Hold on, General Doolittle is calling." Rand waited impatiently for several minutes, and by the time he heard Doolittle's
voice he was annoyed.

"What the hell do you want?" he snapped into the mouth-
piece.

It did not bother him that the caller, James H. Doolittle,
was a lieutenant general, five ranks and several solar systems
above himself. It did not bother him that James H. Doolittle
was commander of the Eighth Air Force, under whose aegis
Rand was conducting his latest anti-Nazi experiments, and it
did not bother him that Jimmy Doolittle, like almost all short
men, could be as acerbic and feisty as Rand himself.

"Speak up, Jimmy," Rand said, "I'm very busy today."

The two Jims, Rand and Doolittle, had known each other for
years, ever since Rand had been secretary of the National Aeronautics Association and Doolittle had been the hottest air
racer on earth. Now Doolittle was saying that Rand had better,
by God, pay attention, that the whole damned war might depend on him, and no more fooling around with his head in the
clouds either. Rand perked up and listened closely. He knew
the Nazis even better than Jimmy Doolittle. He had lived with
them, had gone into Czechoslovakia as an observer with the
German Army, and had learned to detest everything about Hit-

ler's military machine. Now he wondered what Doolittle could be talking about; the German Army was on the run; the June 6 landing in Europe had been a success, and it was just a matter of time before the Allies would sweep across France and into Germany. How could the war depend on anything Jim Rand could do?

"Jim," Doolittle said, "you've been shooting off your mouth about being able to guide a bomb right into a hole. The Germans have a lot of big concrete bunkers in the side of cliffs and hills, in the Pas-de-Calais, twenty-five or thirty miles across the Channel, and they're gonna use 'em to destroy London. We've got to knock 'em out, and our bombers aren't getting the job done. We're losing five percent of our planes on missions against these sites. They've got four hundred guns around each one. I want you to figure out how to fly a plane into these things and blow them up. And I want you to do it fast. If you don't do it fast, London is done for, and maybe New York, too."

Rand knew that flying bombs had been falling on London for a few days, but intelligence had reported that they were being launched from portable gear on the French coast. There had also been talk about heavy German rockets, but no such rockets had fallen, at least so far as Rand was aware.

"What are they gonna shoot out of these sites?" Rand asked.

"None of your damned business!" Doolittle said. "You just worry about blowing them up. Now what do you need?"

Rand said that he needed priorities, instant and sweeping. Doolittle said that they would be typed up within the hour. Rand said that he needed flexibility and mobility; Doolittle said that two airplanes with pilots would be put at his immediate disposal, "and if you want to pilot a plane yourself, we can arrange that, too."

"The Air Corps won't let me fly," Rand said. "I'm colorblind."

"You just made a miraculous recovery," Doolittle said. "What else do you need?"

Rand rattled off a long list of electronic equipment.

"You'll get it," Doolittle said.

Not long after the conversation, a C-54 cargo plane arrived from the United States with a bellyful of gear consigned to Major H. J. Rand. Two small aircraft landed at Rand's headquarters at Horsham St. Faith, and two pilots reported that they were at his disposal. A card arrived from Supreme Headquarters. It informed the reader that Major H. J. Rand was not to be interfered with in the performance of his duty by the military police or any other military organization, that he was engaged in a special mission, that he could commandeer any service or civilian transport, interrogate anyone, see any document, and demand any assistance he required, "by order of General Eisenhower." Printed orders arrived, too. They gave Rand and his operation the highest priorities in the theater. Rand looked at all the papers and realized that the Nazis must be on the verge of a major weapons breakthrough, one that the General Staff was taking most seriously. He wondered what it could be. For a year now intelligence had been hinting that the Germans were working on some terrifying concepts. Rand knew that experiments with heavy water had been conducted by the Germans at a base in Norway and that such experiments could be the key to unlocking the devastating forces in the atom. There were also reports of rockets with warheads up to 20 tons, enough to level dozens of city blocks at a single blow. Intelligence agents sent reports by the dozens about Nazi experiments with poison gas, and information in such quantity could not be discounted. Rand knew that the Allies had made their own plans for reprisal and that hundreds of canisters of mustard gas were stored at a secret place in England for instant retaliation. And beyond all the official and quasi-official information about German secret weapons, he had seen some of the news articles that kept popping up in neutral capitals like Bern and Stockholm. A recent one had hinted that the Germans would soon bombard London with flasks of bacilli that would turn the city into a giant deathbed. The Germans were said to be readying devices that would freeze the English Channel and litter it with giant icebergs, paralyzing Allied shipping. There were articles about a sleek German rocket with a new type of warhead so powerful that it would kill everything within 20 miles and other reports of a gas so concentrated that a few gallons of it dropped from high-altitude German bombers could paralyze London within hours.

With his strong scientific background, Rand was in a better position than most to determine where the truth ended and the propaganda began, but in truth there was nothing about the Nazis' technological ingenuity that would have surprised him. In 1938 he had gone to Berlin to research a subject that fascinated him—cancer and its cure. As the precocious son of James H. Rand, Jr., president of Remington Rand, doors were opened to him that were closed to others, and soon he found himself performing special missions for the United States military attaché in the German capital. He had attended the universities of Vienna and Berlin, he spoke fluent German and passable French, and his easy familiarity with the twin worlds of science and aviation brought him into close contact with Ernst Udet, World War I ace and influential German general. Soon the two men were sharing a small *pied-à-terre* in Berlin. One day Rand said to his German friend, "Ernst, I understand you're making television cameras in one of your war plants. Why?"

Udet flared up. "I'm not going to tell you that," he snapped. "I could have you put in jail right now for asking such a question! Stick to your cancer research!"

Rand reported to the U.S. Embassy that the Germans were making television cameras and that several military uses were possible. TV could be used to send back reconnaissance pictures over enemy territory, and it could be used in the noses of missiles for guidance. His reports were filed and, so far as he could determine, forgotten.

Rand got out of Berlin just ahead of the Japanese attack on Pearl Harbor and went into military intelligence as a second lieutenant, working undercover in places like Switzerland, occupied France, and Portugal. Then he was posted to the White House map room, where he engaged in frequent conversations with Franklin D. Roosevelt, who liked to wheel into the room and study the day's progress on the war fronts. But desk duty soon palled on Rand, and he wangled a transfer to Army antisubmarine patrol, where he operated as an observer in an all-weather night fighter. Within a few months he ws transferred to a top-secret intelligence assignment in North Africa. Using tied-up Remington Rand funds, he bought a nightclub and apartment house in Algiers as a cover and chuckled to himself when a newspaper headlined DRAFT DODGER-PLAY BOY RAND BUYS NIGHTCLUB. As a first lieutenant, he was gathering intelligence all the time.

When his cover was blown after a year, Rand climbed back into uniform, this time as a captain. One day he found himself in the Mediterranean, standing on the bridge of a Liberty ship watching a German bombing raid, and he noticed that one of the bombs was emitting smoke. "That's a guided missile!" Rand said excitedly to his nearest companion, but no one seemed interested. More and more of the smoke-trailing bombs came down, and Rand noticed that they seemed to flatten out their glide paths and move almost imperceptibly from side to side as they whistled toward the target. Later he learned that he had been watching Fritz-X, a German bomb that could be controlled by radio in both azimuth (side-to-side direction) and range. Rand could not get to Washington fast enough. There he suggested that the Allies copy the Fritz-X, but with one essential improvement: an expendable television camera in the nose of each bomb, so that the controller in the mother aircraft could look into a television screen and see exactly where the

bomb was headed and make the necessary corrections. Rand
knew the idea was feasible, practical, and even economical; as a
teen-ager, he had built a 300-line TV receiver in his father's garage in Connecticut, long before most Americans had even
heard of the strange new process.

The American imitation of the Fritz-X underwent many
changes and modifications before it saw action. Television was
in its infancy, too primitive and too expensive, and one of the
first items discarded was Rand's plan to equip each bomb with
a nose camera. The first bombs to be put into production were
called razon (for range and azimuth only), but American ordnance experts were unable to solve the problems of range; the
bombs would respond to azimuth control sent to their tail flip-
pers by radio from the mother aircraft, but range control was
erratic, and soon the effort was reduced to azon (azimuth only)
bombs, suitable for targets, like long bridges and railroad
tracks, where range errors were not critical. Because of his pi-
oneering work with the bombs, Rand was sent to England as
the technical chief of a small Air Corps task force working with
the azon program. By now the bombs had been equipped with
million-candlepower flares in their tails, so that the controllers
could see them all the way down, and Rand and his crack unit
of four-engine bombers scored a few random successes with the
new weapon, including the blowing up of railroad tracks going
through the Brenner Pass connecting Italy to Austria and the
destruction of several strategic bridges on the Continent. The
project had been gaining momentum at Horsham St. Faith
airfield in eastern England when Rand answered the telephone
call from Jimmy Doolittle. Rand dropped the azon program,
ordered three of his azon "mother" crews to follow him, and
took off for Burtonwood, an Army Air Corps station with facilities for modifying and repairing aircraft. There he swore the
men to secrecy and outlined his plan. "We're going to take old,
used-up B-17's and rip their insides out and replace those in-

sides with high explosives," he said. "We're going to equip
those B-17's with azon and fly them into enemy targets by radio
control."

"What enemy targets?" a pilot asked.

"I wish I knew for sure," Rand said. He explained that the
targets were top priority, that bombers had been hitting them
for months without success, and that radical new methods were
required. He said that the robot planes would be modified so
that they could be controlled in both azimuth and range. One
complete azon control system would work on azimuth, and another on range. The system would be called double azon and
would be operated visually from a mother aircraft. In effect,
the robot planes would be nothing more than giant razon
bombs, the largest single explosive missiles ever devised by man.

For several days, Rand and his hastily impressed maintenance crews waited at Burtonwood for the necessary equipment. When it arrived, late in June, 1944, he quickly made
himself the most detested man on the base. Like many another
incipient genius, Rand was not always the most personable of
men, for all his obvious talents. He was a short, fat, dumpy man
with watery blue eyes and thick lips and a loud contempt for
military protocol, including the uniform, which he wore as
though it had been thrown on him in darkness by a drunken
batman. "Let's get to work, and let's make it fast!" Rand would
snap at the crews of technicians working on the first double
azon bomber, and the crews would look down at the hen-shaped
little man wreathed in clouds of smelly cigar smoke and utter
under their breaths the classic two words of personal military
mutiny. The unperturbed Rand would order them to work
harder, and then run off to another part of the operation and
make himself personally detestable to a new group of men. At
the end of twenty hours of bludgeoning by Rand, the technicians were ready to fall atop their soldering irons, but the
blustering major said, "Take a ten-minute break and get back

to work!" At the end of twenty-five hours, the technicians were creeping into hidden parts of the old and battered B-17 for cat-naps, and even the indefatigable Rand was holding his eyelids open with his fingertips.

"Why don't you take a nap, sir?" one of the junior officers suggested.

Rand laid a blanket under the wing and said, "Wake me in an hour!" He was deep in a dream when he felt a foot dig into his shoulder. He sat up and saw a general standing over him. "What the hell's going on here?" the general demanded.

Rand was seldom respectful of rank, and least of all when he was bone-weary. "What the hell do *you* think's going on?" he said through a yawn. "Look for yourself."

"I've looked around, and I've talked to a few people," the general said, "and let me tell you something, Major. You're on the verge of a court-martial for the way you're handling these men!"

Rand rubbed his eyes. "Then you'd better court-martial Jimmy Doolittle, too," he said. "He's working me just as hard as I'm working these men."

"You'll get a medal out of this, Rand," the general said, "and when you're up there getting your medal, these men will be for-gotten."

Rand lit up a cigar and blew a cloud in the direction of the general's star. "Are we fighting a war or aren't we?" he asked evenly.

"Yes, we're fighting a war, but we have no intention of de-stroying the morale of the Army Air Corps just for your convenience!"

Rand pulled out his special card and his priorities and watched as the general perused them. "Now," said Rand, "do we do it my way or do I call General Doolittle?"

The general stalked off in a rage. Rand turned and saw his technicians assembled in various states of pop-eyed conscious-ness around the aircraft. "All right now, goddamn it," he said.

"Let's get on the ball!" Five hours later, after thirty consecutive hours of work, the first drone was ready for testing.

The preliminary tests, that evening, were satisfactory, but they established only that the stripped and war-weary B-17 could fly straight and level, take off and land, and not fall apart in midair despite the removal of about four tons of innards, some of them structural. Two days later, at 7:30 P.M., the first crucial tests were performed. These were to answer a simple question: Could the same remote-control system that steered the comparatively lightweight azon bombs be used to steer a four-engine aircraft with a wingspan of 104 feet and a loaded weight of some 65,000 pounds? No one was sure, except perhaps the cocky Rand. He took off in the mother control ship and ordered the pilot to climb to 20,000 feet, the preselected control altitude. Thirty minutes later, when the mother ship passed over the field where the piloted robot was supposed to be circling at 2,000 feet awaiting control, neither the robot nor the field was visible through the thickening clouds. The men of the secret project were getting their first taste of the problem that was to plague them through almost twelve months: the fickle English weather, with highs and lows bumping across the narrow island in rapid alternation and weather forecasting reduced to guesswork and probabilities.

The two aircraft were in radio contact, and Rand kept telling the pilots in the robot to stand by while the mother ship worked its way down through the soup. The robot was not spotted until Rand's B-17 had descended to 6,000 feet, but from then on the testing exceeded all expectations. Rand guided the rickety old B-17 drone around a course for two hours, diving on pseudo targets and making the drone's nose dip over certain landmarks to show the precision of his control. Only one problem arose: The mother ship, in higher, thinner air, tended to overrun the robot by as much as 60 miles per hour. All pilots agreed that this problem could be solved by the use of wing flaps, cowl flaps, propeller pitch, essing, and even an occasional 360-degree turn. "The manner of control is good," veteran test pilot Cass Hough wrote in the daily report. "Given decent visibility, it is entirely possible for a trained controller to 'plant' the low ship on a target." It was late June, 1944. Buzz bombs had been falling off and on for two weeks, killing thousands, and military intelligence had reported that huge rockets were set to open fire any moment from gigantic concrete bunkers across the channel in France, in areas thus far unscathed by the Allied landings to the west. If London were not to be leveled, the bunkers had to be blown out of the earth.

APHRODITE IS THE CODE NAME WHICH THIS HEADQUARTERS WILL USE TO REFER TO THE OVERALL PROJECT OF ATTACKING TARGETS BY SPECIAL TECHNIQUES. OUR FIRST FLIGHT TEST WITH MODIFIED AZON UNITS IN WAR WEARY AIRPLANE DEMONSTRATED THE PRACTICABILITY OF THIS MAKESHIFT AND WE ARE GOING AHEAD IMMEDIATELY WITH FOUR MORE WAR WEARIES. . . .
—Message from Lieutenant General Carl Spaatz, commander United States Strategic Air Forces in Europe, to General H. H. Arnold, commander United States Army Air Corps, June 23, 1944

A few days after the first tests of Major Rand's double azon-controlled B-17, the telephone rang in the office of a long, lean Air Corps major general named Earle Partridge. Eighth Air Force Headquarters was on the line, Colonel W. E. Todd speaking, and he would like to outline to the general an experimental program for knocking out the massive concrete bunkers that lay so ominously just across the Channel. Todd said that headquarters had devised a system whereby pilots would take off war-weary B-17's loaded with high explosives, adjust the radio-control equipment, and then bail out over England, leaving the unmanned aircraft to be dived into the bunkers by radio control. Did Partridge's Third Bombardment Division want the job of turning this highly experimental system into an operational reality? "No, we don't," Partridge said in his customary no-nonsense manner, "and for very good reason. We're fully operational. We're flying day after day against the enemy. We're going hard, day in, day out, and this takes a great deal of management and supervision. I don't want to divert any time from the job. So let me out."

Colonel Todd said he would pass the message along. "The boss won't like this, General, I can tell you that," Todd said.

"If I know General Doolittle," Partridge said, "he'll understand my position completely."

Three days later orders came in from Jimmy Doolittle's Eighth Air Force Headquarters at High Wycombe. The Third Bombardment Division, Major General Earle Partridge commanding, was to run the mission called Aphrodite.

> *So I'd go around to these different air bases all over England and I'd get these pilots to one side and I'd say, "How'd you like a job flying an airplane on a special mission?" They'd laugh. I'd say, "How'd you like a caterpillar on your cap for bailing out?" They'd laugh harder. So I'd say, "How many missions you got to go yet?" Then I'd say, "Well, how'd you like to get credit for five missions just for doing one job?" They'd say, "Parachuting?" and I'd say, "Yes." Then we'd go off for a walk someplace, just him and I. I'd be like a salesman. He'd say, "What kind of a mission are you talking about?" I'd say, "It involves a bailout and a little hazard." He'd say, "Where?" "Over friendly territory," I'd say. "Now do you volunteer or don't you?" He'd say, "Well, would you do it if you were in my shoes?" "Sure," I'd say. "I'd rather do that than fly five missions over Germany." Then he'd say, "Okay, put me on."—Aphrodite recruiter*

Some jump pilots were recruited in other ways. A pilot named Fain Pool, a sturdily built Oklahoman with a thick shock of coal-black hair, was sitting around the rec hall of the 385th

Bomb Group at Great Ashfield, near the village of Elmswell, when he was summoned before the commanding officer, a young West Pointer. Four other pilots were already in the room when Pool arrived. "Gentlemen," the CO said, "everything that I am about to say is top secret. It is not to be discussed with anyone outside this room—not even among yourselves. Don't ask me any questions—I can tell you all I know in a few sentences. You've been selected because you're the best pilots we have. You're being asked to volunteer for a hazardous mission, an extremely important mission. It involves flying a four-engine aircraft, and it involves a bailout. You'll be sent on temporary duty to another outfit; you'll leave your regular crew behind. They don't want crews, just pilots. But you won't be allowed to tell your crew anything except that you'll be going on detached service for a few weeks. That's the whole proposition. Now don't feel bad if you don't want to volunteer. Most of you have finished your tours, or almost finished them. You've got a hell of a lot behind you and not much ahead of you before you go home. I understand that."

"Sir," one of the other pilots said. "Can you tell us any more about the mission?"

"I can only tell you what headquarters told me," the colonel said. "But if you want a little speculation on my part, I'd guess that they want you to bail out of some aircraft, possibly over occupied territory—Belgium, France, Holland—and maybe contact the underground. Where the four-engine aircraft part comes in, I don't know."

"How long can we think about it?" a pilot asked.

"About two minutes," the colonel said. "I want your decision before you leave this room."

"Colonel," a first lieutenant said, "I'm too near the end of my tour." Another said he appreciated being selected as one of the best pilots in the group, but he already had his orders to return to America. A third said bluntly, "No soap, sir. I'll read about it in the papers," and a fourth declined on the ground that he enjoyed flying but hated parachuting. That left Fain Pool. His situation was slightly different. He had just flown his fourteenth mission; he still had sixteen to go to complete his tour and become eligible for rotation home. He had bombed Berlin several times, Hanover, Bremen, other difficult targets, and he had begun to develop a faith in his own indestructibility. He had gone on three forty-eight-hour passes since flying his first mission, and each time a substitute crew had used his aircraft and been "hacked"—shot down. Among his fellows, Pool was known as the best formation pilot in the group. "You look out the hatch to the place where Pool is supposed to be," said a lead pilot from Pool's squadron, "and there he is, hanging on with three engines and a raggedy prop, but hanging on somehow." Hanging on was what formation bombing was all about, with the airplanes in a tight interweave of cross-protection from their own .50-caliber machine guns and the straggler an easy mark for Messerschmitt 109's and Focke-Wulf 190's, German fighters that waited high in the sun to pounce on the weak and the damaged. Pool prided himself on never becoming a straggler, and the kidding about his advanced age (he was twenty-six and had already been married for five years), quickly eased when the younger pilots recognized his skill.

But Fain Pool had another quality that was highly useful to his superiors. He was eager. Apart from any feelings of indestructibility, he had developed a strong, personal abhorrence of Adolf Hitler. A few weekends after the start of his tour, he had spent a pass in London and watched death and pain descend on the city from Geman V-1's, the flying bombs that had been falling indiscriminately for several weeks. One of his own crew members suffered a slashed arm from flying glass, and Pool and his crewmates saw people lying in the street in puddles of their own blood. War was war, but Pool could not see the justification for this haphazard method of killing old ladies and children with push-button bombs that came without warning in the night.

"I'll go," Pool was saying now. "I'll go, sir."

"No doubts in your mind?" the baby-faced colonel asked.

"No doubts, Colonel," Fain Pool answered. About ten hours later he and his barracks bags were unloaded at a Royal Air Force depot called Honington and jeeped to a corner of the field where a small detachment of Army Air Corps had been set up. Pool stepped into a Nissen hut to find several other pilots unpacking their gear. One of them looked up, stuck out his hand, and said, "Hey, fellows, another nut's arrived!"

Everybody laughed, including Pool, and after introductions had been made, the five or six pilots in the room began speculating on the future. One of them seemed to have the whole mission figured out. "We're gonna bail out and meet a member of the French Maquis," the young barracks lawyer was saying. "He's gonna lead us to an airfield where there's a German four-engine aircraft, maybe a Dornier or something like that. We're all four-engine pilots, right? And if we're lucky enough to be able to beat the security on the German air base, then we have to make a dash for this aircraft, see, and if we're lucky enough to get into the aircraft, then we've got to figure out where the battery switch is. And once we find it, we've got to hope that it isn't booby-trapped. So then we've got to rev it up real fast, get it off the ground before they shoot us, and get back to England with the whole German Air Force on our ass. And then our troubles are over, right?"

"Right!" somebody said.

"Wrong!" the other pilot said. "Then we've got to figure out how to get through the British flak. And then we've got to figure out how to land the damned thing. So you can see our chances aren't too good."

Another pilot said that he had heard the Germans were in production on a rocket that could reach New York and that he suspected the mission was somehow related to this new threat. "How the hell's it gonna reach New York when they've just barely learned how to reach London?" a pilot asked.

"Simple," the voice answered in the darkness. "It goes straight up above the pull of gravity, and then it stays up there while the earth spins under it, and then it drops like a rock on Broadway and Forty-Second Street. *Pow!*"

Pool went to sleep with his head spinning with ideas and conjectures. He dreamed that he parachuted into France and was surrounded by a dozen armed peasants, and when he pointed to his American uniform and wings, the peasants answered in a guttural tongue that sounded like German. For the rest of the night he slept lightly.

Some came into the program with flags flying, like Fain Pool. Some came in because they were bored with what they were doing, and any risk was better than the risk of boredom. Some came in by inadvertence and, once in, were unable to quit. Frank "Sam" or "Old Sam" Houston, a slightly built young man from Montana, was like that. The laconic Houston had always wanted to be an airline pilot and he had seen the Army Air Corps as the logical stepping-stone. The Army Air Corps had not reciprocated the feeling. When Sam Houston applied for pilot training in Missoula, Montana, he was told that he had a deviated septum and could not qualify. Houston left the examining offices and checked into the nearest hospital for corrective surgery. When he returned to the Air Corps medics a week later, he was told that his night vision was below par. For two weeks he drank carrot juice by the bucketfuls. At last the Air Corps accepted him, but his widowed mother refused to sign the necessary papers. Houston said, "Mother, I love you, but if you don't sign for me, so help me I'm going into the infantry." His mother signed.

Two years later, in the summer of 1944, First Lieutenant Frank Houston had completed a tour of duty in England and won the Distinguished Flying Cross and various other medals. His flight record included seven raids on Berlin, the toughest target in Europe, and missions to Augsburg, Frankfurt, Brunswick, and other German cities, plus "intruder" missions to drop OSS operatives and arm the Maquis. At the end of his thirty missions, Old Sam was so pleased with the war that he went before a special board and pleaded to be allowed to fly thirty more missions. Houston was a man with a highly developed sense of comradeship, and it annoyed him that certain newer members of his crew were now flying with other pilots. In a word, he missed his old buddies. The review board denied his petition for thirty more missions but told him he could remain in the theater if he could find another job. Houston begged his commanding officer for an assignment, and the colonel told him there was nothing available, but if he was so determined to stay away from the United States, he could keep himself busy around the hangar, slow-timing bombers that needed engine break-in and performing various other drudgeries. This kept Houston on the same premises as his buddies in the 730th Squadron of the 452d Bomb Group, stationed near Norwich by the little town of Attleborough. Almost every morning Houston would watch his old friends roll out to the end of the runway and take off on bombing raids, but he was reasonably happy. At least most of them came back at night.

Then one night none came home. "I knew it!" Houston stormed at the operations officer. "Goddamn it, Captain, I knew it! I told you! I warned you! Didn't I tell you that if you didn't let me fly with them there'd be trouble?" The captain told him to be at ease—Army talk for "shut up!" "Well, where the hell are they?" Houston said. The captain walked off.

Every hangar was empty. Every B-17 was gone. The beds in the crew's quarters were unruffled. There was no one in the mess except the cooks and an elderly master sergeant of the ground crew. Houston thought he would go out of his head if he did not learn something about his buddies. All he knew was that the Air Corps had scheduled a heavy raid on a target near Berlin, and the fighters and their fighter cover were to continue into Russia and land. That was the way the raid was briefed, and the planes had taken off and disappeared. Houston was beside himself. He had begged to be allowed to fly the mission, and he had had a sixth sense that there would be trouble without him.

All morning long he hung around the empty hangar talking to old Master Sergeant McGuire, who was busy, as usual, regaling his captive audience with hoary stories about World War I. At lunchtime Houston walked across the silent flight strip to pick up the intelligence officer for lunch, and when he entered the little office, he noticed that it was empty. As was his custom, Houston began shuffling through all available papers for a hint of what was going on in the military world around him, and all at once he found out where his buddies were. A top secret report told how more than 100 bombers and about 150 fighters had completed their bombing runs and landed at a remote airport in Russia. There they had been bedded down in neat rows for the night, just in time for a withering strafing and bombing attack by the Luftwaffe. The Russian gun crews had fought back with 20-mm artillery, more suitable for shooting crows, and the American pilots had emptied their service revolvers at the screaming German planes, but when all the smoke had cleared sometime after midnight, few intact aircraft remained of the hundreds that had flown the mission, and carloads of American airmen were stranded, without transportation, in the Soviet Union. As he read the report, Frank Houston could not hold back a smile and then a laugh. He was not happy that the American airplanes had been destroyed, but he was greatly relieved that the crews were safe. "Hot damn!" he was saying, just as the intelligence officer stepped into the shack.

"For Christ's sake, Houston, you're not supposed to be reading that stuff!" he said, and snatched the report from the pilot's hand.

"Why not?" Houston said.

"Don't act stupid! You know why not. It's top secret."

"Well, if it's so secret, then it's supposed to be in your safe, not lying on your desk," Houston said. "It's your fault. You're supposed to be here guarding this stuff, and the first time you have to go take a leak, you just walk off and leave it here. You ought to be court-martialed, letting somebody like me read stuff like this!"

"Good God," the chagrined intelligence officer said, "you won't tell anybody, will you?"

Houston said he could be trusted. "Well, let's make sure," the intelligence officer said. "Hold up your right hand." A bemused Houston held up his right hand and swore never to divulge the contents of the messages he had just read. Then the two officers stuffed the papers in the safe and strolled over to the empty officers' mess. They had hardly finished eating when the Tannoy PA system boomed the news that Lieutenant Frank Houston was wanted at the colonel's office.

Houston had spent many long hours in the company of Colonel Thetus Odom, commanding officer of the squadron, and although he thought highly of the colonel and his method of command, Houston could not remember ever winning an argument with him. He had begged Colonel Odom to let him fly another tour and been turned down. He had all but prostrated himself asking for permission to go on the shuttle raid to Russia and been turned down again. Now what was the colonel going to turn down?

The meeting lasted about two minutes. "Houston," the colonel snapped, "General Partridge over at the Third Bomb Division just called, and he's got a secret mission on. You meet the qualifications. Yes or no?"

Houston was so bored and jittery that he would have volunteered for almost anything, and anyway a whole galaxy of interesting ideas was flashing through his brain. He saw how obvious it all was. There were hundreds of fliers stranded in Russia without visible means of locomotion. Somebody had to go and get them. "I volunteer!" Houston said. Odom told him to pack and be ready to leave practically instantly.

Houston was ecstatic at the prospect of more flying time and a reconciliation with his buddies. Already he was planning his landing in Russia. He would throw the empty B-17 into a chandelle, level out, and "paint" it onto the runway as though it were a P-38 winning the Bendix race. Then he would slip out of the navigator's hatch like Douglas Fairbanks and swagger over to the side of the apron where all his buddies would be standing goggle-eyed. "Well, well," he would say, giving his scarf a brisk toss around his neck, "so you guys go out on a mission and Old Sam's gotta come and bring you home. Can't do a thing without Old Sam, can you, boys? Well, have no fear! Old Sam is here." Then he would load his B-17 with his buddies, and they would head back to England via the grand route around the war fronts, stopping off at Istanbul and Teheran and Casablanca to lie on the beach for a few days. Frank "Sam" Houston went to sleep on the pleasant thought.

The next morning a jeep called for the young pilot, and he got in for the drive to the jumping-off place. But after a few hours of bumping across the English countryside, watching drops of precipitation fall from his nose, Houston realized that the jeep was headed west, away from the various logical ports of exit for his grand tour of the Continent. "Hey," he said to the enlisted man at the wheel, "where the hell are we going?"

"My orders are to take you to Honington, near Newark," the driver said.

"Honington?" Houston said. "Isn't that the big British depot where they repair airplanes and do experimental work and that?"

"Yes, sir."

Houston was puzzled. He became unnerved when the jeep driver took him through the gates at Honington and drove him for what seemed like hours to a small collection of dreary Nissen huts and outbuildings in the farthest corner of the aerodrome, and there Frank Houston looked into the eyes of an officer who had been known far and wide as the most useless character back at Attleborough. For weeks now this officer had been mysteriously absent from the bomb group, but no one had missed him. The officer was "old Army," and although he professed to have become a gung ho bomber pilot, he had somehow managed to abort more missions than anyone else in the squadron. This tendency to turn back before reaching the target was known to the pilots as "getting shit in the neck" and finally resulted in the officer's grounding. As a ground officer, he specialized in pulling rank on junior officers, even to the point of trying to separate them from their girlfriends when the squadron was on pass. Frank Houston detested the man, and now he was being told that the officer was one of the more important members of a secret project. "My God," Houston said under his breath. "What have I done?"

Less than an hour later a small group of multiengine pilots was sitting in a ready room listening to the officer explain the mission. "Essentially this is what you will do," Frank Houston heard the man say in his usual pompous manner. "You will take off a B-17 carrying twenty thousand pounds of high explosives and nothing else, no co-pilot, no radio operator, no engineer, no gunners, nothing except you and twenty thousand pounds of nitrostarch. After you reach about a thousand feet, you will put the aircraft into a gentle glide and bail out. You will be picked up and returned to your original squadron. Are there any questions?"

There were dozens of questions, but the officer refused to answer them on the grounds of security. "I've told you all you need to know," he said curtly after a few minutes. "Dismissed!"

When the others had left, Houston lagged behind and said to the officer, "Sir, I don't know about this. This isn't exactly what I had in mind."

"Now you listen," the man said. "You volunteered, and you heard a lot of classified information, and now you're in to stay! Do you understand that?"

"Yes, sir," Houston said, "but, sir, I only volunteered to go pick up my buddies in Russia."

"You what?"

"To pick up my buddies in Russia."

The officer snorted and gave Houston to understand that he was excused, but Houston followed as they walked toward the orderly room. "Sir," he said, "I'm not sure I want to sit on twenty thousand pounds of explosive and bail out at one thousand feet." The officer increased his pace.

"Sir," Houston blurted, "is it possible to get a transfer?" The officer reached the door and stepped inside.

"Sir, there's been a terrible mistake," Houston said, but the door slammed in his face. "Shit in the neck!" Houston said through the closed door, and stomped off to commiserate with the other pilots. There were six or eight of them altogether, and none seemed to be overjoyed by the latest intelligence about the mission. Their very misery made Houston feel better. He was a man who believed in camaraderie above all else, even if the common denominator of the camaraderie was despair.

Someone said, "Look, we're in this now and we've all got to make one jump, so we might as well accept it."

"I'll do it, but I'll be damned if I'll like it," someone else said.

"Nobody asked you to like it," said a voice from the corner. "They only asked you to do it, and you volunteered. You guys joined the Air Corps to fly, didn't you?"

Old Sam Houston seized the opening. "Yeah," he said, "I joined the Air Corps to fly, but in a plane."

Somebody said that it would be at least two months before the project would be operational, and so there was no point in beginning a worry schedule so early.

"I'll be too busy to worry," Houston said. "I've got two months to do something I haven't been able to do in twenty-three years."

"What's that?"

"Grow wings," Houston said, and nobody laughed.

The day after his Third Bomb Division drew the Aphrodite assignment, Major General Earle Partridge called in one of his staff captains. "Bender," he said, "can you tell me where a B-17 will hit the ground if you give it full down elevator at an indicated speed of one hundred eighty and an altitude of three hundred feet?"

"Excuse me, sir?" Captain Carroll J. "Joe" Bender said. Partridge repeated the question.

"No, sir," Bender said. "I can't tell you that, sir."

"Would the wings come off?" the general asked. "Would the plane break up?"

"I don't think so, sir, but I'm not sure, sir," Bender said.

Partridge was not known as a martinet or a screamer, but the personality of this soft-spoken blond-haired officer of forty-four was such that his aides ran, not walked, when he so much as hinted that he would like something done. So when Partridge said, "Well, go and find out these things, Bender, and report back to me," the burly captain was already halfway to the door, off and running.

"Wait!" the general called. "One more thing. You're not to tell anybody what you're after or why you're after it. This is top secret. Is that clear?"

"Yes, sir," Captain Bender said, and vanished down the corridor of Elveden Hall, the English manor house near Thetford where Partridge maintained his headquarters.

The general pondered his choice for the preliminary assignment. The twenty-nine-year-old Bender was not formally disciplined in any sciences, including aeronautical engineering, but he was uncommonly intelligent, and he knew everything there was to know about the B-17, the Flying Fortress, Boeing Aircraft's sterling contribution to the fighting of World War II. Bender had completed a bloody tour of duty, using up fifteen bombers to complete twenty-seven missions, watching crew members die, wiping away oil from shattered lines, diving full bore to find oxygen before he blacked out. To tell the truth, Bender was slightly "nervous in the service," although he had been pulled off flight duty before reaching the true state of flak-happiness, and now he was regaining his aplomb and his assurance bit by bit in his ground work at headquarters, lecturing to bomber crews and doing odd jobs. This new assignment would help him, and it would help the Aphrodite project. Although the key scientists of the project had been testing and planning for more than a month now, certain questions remained, and no general officer with the methodical, orderly mind of Earle Partridge was going to send pilots into the air until there were some answers. He knew that the radio-control system had been tested and worked, but he was not sure exactly what that meant. Did it work every time? Did it work once in a while? Did it work often enough to carry out a combat mission of the highest priority? He also knew that volunteer pilots were available, but were volunteers ever unavailable? There were always men who would volunteer for anything. In some ways, these heroes were like babies, blindly trusting in the abilities of their surrogate fathers, the generals and colonels who did the planning. This faith had to go both ways in the eyes of men like Earle Partridge. The planners had to do everything humanly possible to make the missions safe. When everything humanly possible had been done, then one ordered the pilots into the air with a clear conscience.

Partridge figured that everything humanly possible had not yet been done in this Aphrodite business. He knew enough about the priority targets—four mysterious concrete bunkers across the English Channel in France—to realize that nothing less than direct hits by the explosive-laden bombers would do the job. The bunkers were 300 and 400 feet across, some shaped like domes, some rectangular or trapezoidal, and all of them big enough to accommodate a couple of football fields simultaneously. For almost a year now, planes of the American and British air forces had been plastering the gray-white targets with bombs of all kinds, including armor-piercing bombs and 12,000-pound British "tallboys," the biggest bombs on earth, and still there were signs of ground activity around the bunkers. Every new intelligence photograph showed where adjoining railroad tracks had been relaid, new cement had been poured, forms erected, outbuildings thrown up. Plainly, the Germans did not intend to quit the sites until they were pulverized, and Aphrodite had been set up to accommodate them. But a high degree of accuracy would be required along with the great amount of explosives in each stripped B-17. Partridge knew that one of the sites was mostly underground and that each afternoon at a certain hour the methodical Germans opened a steel door leading into the workings. The other three targets were aboveground, but large expanses of their surfaces were covered with impenetrable 20- and 30-foot thicknesses of concrete. The small areas of vulnerability had to be hit precisely. But at the present state of the radio-control art, could any such accuracy be achieved? How did the radio controller know what the loaded B-17 would do when he gave it a down signal? Would it go into what used to be called a nose dive and slam to earth at a 180-degree angle? Would it go into a flatter path and glide a mile or two before hitting the ground? Would it do tricks, such as picking up airspeed and buoyancy and leveling out, even climbing a little, before resuming its descent, and thus reach the target by a series of imprecise swoops? And assuming it would make a nice, neat dive toward the target, would the wings stay on? Would the flying four-engine bomb hold together under the tremendous torsions and tensions?

Questions tumbled through the general's head. As always he thought of safety factors. Would a B-17 loaded with 20,000 pounds of high-explosive nitrostarch or jellied gasoline (napalm) be stable on takeoff? How should the load be arranged, armed, fused? Where should the jump pilots exit, and how?

What kind of chute should they use? Most previous military parachuting had been done at speeds of less than 100 miles per hour. The Aphrodite parachutists would be asked to leave a plane going nearly twice that fast, thus bringing up problems that had barely been studied. Certainly, men had bailed out of planes going at high speed, and most of them had lived, but it was a dangerous process at best.

Finally, there were problems of tactics. Should the robots be brought over the targets at high altitude and sent into their dives before coming into range of enemy aircraft guns, or should they be brought in at medium altitude, twisting and turning in evasive courses? *Could* they be twisted and turned sharply by radio control? Perhaps it would be better to send them across the Channel at wave-top level, below the German radar, but would it be safe to radio-control an explosive-laden bomber on the deck?

No one knew the answers. Partridge assumed that scientists were working on the problems right now. Meanwhile, he would send off a few wise heads like Carroll Bender to see what they could see. All haste was required; the War Department was applying daily pressure, asking for full reports, demanding to know how soon Aphrodite would be operational, letting it be known that the Old Man, General Arnold, "Hap" to his friends, was personally taking an interest in the project. Partridge still regarded his regular bombing raids against the German military machine as the overriding priority of his Third Bombardment Division, but he would give Project Aphrodite every second he could spare.

Captain Carroll "Joe" Bender adjusted his powerful build into the undersized wood-backed seat in the second-class compartment of the train to London, and thought about the inauspicious start he had made on his personal assignment from the general. He wondered if he would be court-martialed. No, that was impossible. General Partridge did not conduct vendettas.

There were other P-47's available, and the general would never miss the personal plane that Bender had crashed in his rush to begin his assignment. Anyway, there had been no malicious intent. Bender had only wanted to make a quick trip to another air base, and the general's personal P-47 Thunderbolt was all that was available, and the ground chief had said, "Go ahead, take it, everybody else does. The general won't even know it's gone." Bender, the consummate multiengine pilot, had hauled the little "jug" into the air without trouble, but suddenly the engine quit, and Bender was enveloped in smoke. Somehow he steered the burning fighter back to a flat spot and dumped it, wiping out the bottom of the fuselage and tearing off the wings. The ground chief saw the wreckage and told Bender, "Goddamn! If I were you, I'd get lost for a couple of days."

Now Bender was on the train to London, getting lost in his assignment. From London he went to the nearby American air base at Bovingdon, where he had a personal friend, a colonel, who was a genius in mathematics. The two men put their heads together for two days, with Bender throwing the practical figures at the colonel and the colonel whirling them around theoretically. They walked out to the flight line and measured the angle of a B-17's elevators when they were on full down. They measured the chord of the B-17's wing, computed tangents and cosecants, and all but memorized the statistics in the technical manuals prepared by Boeing. At least a dozen times the colonel asked Bender why he needed all this information, and at least a dozen times Bender refused to answer. When he figured he had picked his friend's mind clean of all applicable information, he said good-bye and headed for the Boeing office in London. He wanted stress figures, polar moments of inertia, ultimate yield factors on various parts of the airplane. If he could get the figures and correlate them with the mathematical information provided by the colonel at Bovingdon, he could begin to answer General Partridge's questions. Maybe. Or maybe he would have to do some test flying first, to confirm the paper work. Bender had absolutely no fear about testing a B-17 under any conditions. He firmly doubted that there were any forces on earth, short of enemy firepower, that could break up a Flying Fortress. He had seen pilotless B-17's fall off into power dives and suddenly go into steep climbs, then fall off again and climb again, and repeat the pattern five or six times before leveling off and flying out of sight. He had seen B-17's land with the entire empennage shot off on one side, and he had seen B-17's land with holes the size of cartwheels punched out of their wings. Every now and then one of the gallant ships, its pilots dead in their seats, its crew gone or dead, would appear over England and circle an air base before running out of fuel and diving reluctantly to earth. It was Captain Joe Bender's opinion that the Flying Fortress was the most stable warplane ever built. It was his opinion that there were *no* natural stresses or torsions that could snap the sturdy bomber. But General Partridge had not asked for Captain Joe Bender's opinion. He had asked for facts.

Bender entered the Boeing office in London to get the facts. Particularly, he needed the yield figures for the circular bulkhead behind the wing, the part that would be subjected to the greatest strain in a power dive under full load.

Bender talked to a Boeing representative, a feather merchant, and the company man walked to the files and removed the document bearing the necessary figures. "But first you won't mind while I make a call?" the man said, and disappeared into a side office. A few minutes later he returned and said, "I'm sorry, Captain, but it's against company policy for me to release such information without a thorough check, and that would take several days."

Bender fussed and fumed and argued, but the Boeing representative said he had no choice in the matter, policy was policy, and anyway he had to go to lunch. When the man had left, Bender turned to the lone secretary in the office and observed to himself that she was one of the dreariest specimens of woman-

APHRODITE: DESPERATE MISSION 44

kind in the entire Western Hemisphere. He swallowed hard and said, "Excuse me, ma'am, but I was wondering if you would do me the honor of joining me for lunch?" The words tasted like a mouthful of dry peanut butter, but Bender had to say them. He had struck out with the man; perhaps he could do better with the woman.

It annoyed Bender that this beast in female clothing, this mustached, corpulent, flat-chested, stubby-legged specimen of alleged womankind should have the nerve to act coy about his luncheon invitation, but she did. It took five minutes of sweet talk for Bender to extract an acceptance, and then the woman asked him to excuse her while she adjourned to the powder room. "Why, certainly," Bender said with a deep bow, and the second the door closed behind the secretary he dashed to the files, riffled through the reams of statistical information, and pulled out the sheet he had been denied. The door opened just as he had completed stuffing it into his pants pocket. "Shall we be off?" he said, and they went to lunch.

On the way back to Elveden Hall by another slow train, Bender studied the figures and compared them to those worked up by his friend, the colonel at Bovingdon. Everything seemed to check. The answer to General Partridge's questions—"Would the wings come off? Would the plane break up?"—seemed to be No. But there was only one way to be certain.

Back at Third Bomb Division Headquarters, Bender looked around for a B-17 to test. There was only one available. It was shiny, brand-new, and in perfect condition, and it bore on the sides the inscription *The Silver Queen*. Bender recognized the stripped-down Flying Fortress as a headquarters aircraft that was one of General Partridge's favorites. He gulped and told the crew chief that he wanted to borrow the Silver Queen for a few hours.

"By yourself, sir?" the chief asked.

"By myself," Bender said.

"But that's impossible," the crew sergeant said. "You'll need a crew."

"No, I won't, Sergeant," Bender said. "Get the plane ready for me. I'll be ready to take off in an hour."

"But, sir—"

"No buts!" Bender snapped. "That's an order!"

For three days Bender put *The Silver Queen* through his own personal torture tests. He power-dived it, rolled it, looped it, and climbed it until he thought the wings must surely come off under the G forces. Reports came in to Third Bomb Headquarters that a maniac was doing insane stunts in a B-17; where should they send the body when the plane crashed? When Bender had satisfied himself about the aircraft's structural dependability, he turned to the other part of General Partridge's assignment: Where will a B-17 hit the ground if it is given full down elevator at indicated 180 and altitude 300 feet?

Bender took *The Silver Queen* in search of flat cirrus clouds. He measured their altitude and then climbed 300 feet above the cloud level and kicked full down elevator, managing the aircraft with one hand and a stopwatch with the other, each time starting at a precise 180-mph indicated airspeed. Then he would turn the aircraft to another heading and repeat the operation. When he had eight or ten sets of figures, he would return to the ground and consult with a Boeing feather merchant who was permanently assigned to the headquarters, and little by little a pattern began to emerge. To increase the accuracy of his figures, Bender measured off certain reference points on the ground, and he inserted a wooden stopblock in front of the control column, so that he could be sure that he was giving the aircraft exactly the same amount of down elevator each time he kicked the column forward. At last the flight tests were over. Behind blackout curtains, Bender and the technical representative from Boeing sat up till midnight working over their final figures, and the next day Bender called on General Partridge.

"Captain Bender reporting, sir," he said, and Partridge looked up from his usual towering stack of paper work and said, "Yes, Bender?"

Bender remembered the general's admonition about the secrecy of the operation. A WAAF was in the room, and Bender cast a sideways look in her direction.

"Don't worry about her, Captain," General Partridge said. "She wouldn't be in this room if she weren't cleared."

Bender said, "Yes, sir. Sir, a loaded B-17 flying at three hundred feet altitude and one hundred eighty indicated will hit the ground approximately nine hundred and seventy-five feet after application of full down control. An empty B-17 will hit the ground at approximately one thousand and eighty-eight feet under the same conditions."

Partridge asked Bender to repeat, and Bender spoke more slowly as the general jotted the figures down. "Will that be all, sir?" Bender asked.

"How long did it take you to figure this out?" the general said.

"Nine days, sir."

"And how many planes did you wreck?"

"Just one, sir," Bender said. He did not volunteer details.

"Couldn't have been a P-47, could it?" Partridge said, his face immobile and unrevealing.

"Yes, sir," Bender said. "It could have been, sir."

Partridge stood up, reached across his desk and shook Bender's hand. "Well, Captain," he said, "it was worth it."

AGAINST LAUNCHING POINTS OF GERMAN PILOTLESS AIR-CRAFT SPAATZ IS CONSIDERING SENDING WAR WEARY B-17 WITHOUT CREW AND LOADED WITH UP TO 25,000 POUNDS OF NITRO STARCH. THIS SUGGESTS AN EFFECTIVE METHOD OF DISPOSING OF OUR GREAT AND GROWING NUMBERS OF WAR WEARY AIRCRAFT OF ALL TYPES IN ALL THEATRES. FOR EXAMPLE: IN EUROPE CREWLESS AIRCRAFT HEAVILY LADEN WITH VERY HIGH EXPLOSIVES MIGHT BE GUIDED BY

TELEVISION PRINCIPLE AND COULD POSSIBLY BE STEERED INTO ANY REMAINING OBJECTIVES IN THE THEATRE; WHILE IN THE FAR EAST SUCH AIRCRAFT, OPERATING TO MAXIMUM RANGE NOT REPEAT NOT RADIUS, COULD POSSIBLY BE GUIDED ACROSS VAST STRETCHES OF WATER AND THEN BE STEERED BY HEAT OR MAGNETIC TARGET SEEKING DEVICES INTO CITIES OR SHIPS. BEFORE PUTTING OUR SCIENTIFIC RESOURCES TO WORK ON THIS PROJECT, HAVE YOUR IMAGINATIVE ENGINEERS TAKE A READING ON THE SUBJECT AND RADIO ME YOUR PRELIMINARY VIEWS.
—General H. H. Arnold to various Army Air Corps generals, July 1, 1944

THE INITIATIVE AND IMAGINATION SHOWN IN YOUR PLANS TO FLY CREWLESS AIRCRAFT WITH HEAVY LOADS OF HIGH EXPLOSIVES INTO NOBALL [ROCKET] TARGETS IS A SOURCE OF GENUINE PLEASURE! MORE POWER TO YOU.—Arnold to Spaatz, same date

The total weight of bombs so far dropped by us on flying bomb and rocket targets in France and Germany, including Peenemünde, has now reached about 50,000 tons, and the number of reconnaissance flights totals many thousands. . . . The Germans for their part have sacrificed a great deal of manufacturing strength which would have increased their fighter and bomber forces working with their hard-pressed armies on every front. It has yet to be decided who has suffered and who will suffer the most in the process. There has in fact been in progress for a year past an unseen battle into which great resources have been poured by both sides. This invisible battle has now flashed into the open, and we shall be able, and indeed obliged, to watch its progress at fairly close quarters. . . .

We must neither underrate nor exaggerate. In all, up to six o'clock this morning, about 2750 flying bombs have been discharged from the launching-stations along the French coast . . . a very high proportion of the casualties, somewhere around 10,000, not always severe or

mortal, has fallen upon London, which presents to the enemy a target 18 miles wide by over 20 miles deep. It is therefore the unique target of the world for the use of a weapon of such proved inaccuracy. The flying bomb is a weapon literally and essentially indiscriminate in its nature, purpose and effect. The introduction by the Germans of such a weapon obviously raises some grave questions, upon which I do not propose to trench today.

—Churchill, to Commons, July 6, 1944

In an effort to eliminate the threat of the enemy's large rockets and their effect upon England, the Aphrodite project has been set into motion by this headquarters . . . the task of knocking out the rocket sites must be accomplished at once. . . . It is now contemplated to use at least sixty-five (65) robot aircraft. . . . Approximately twenty-one (21) of the sixty-five (65) aircraft (1/4 of the total) will be loaded with jellied gasoline. Approximately forty-four (44) aircraft (3/4 of total) will be loaded with nitro-strach.

—Command of Lieutenant General Spaatz, July 8, 1944

The crash training course for Aphrodite jump pilots, mother ship pilots, and controllers was going full blast at the big British depot called Honington, and Frank Houston, the reluctant jump pilot, was slowly learning to accept the fact that he was going to make a parachute jump from an airplane crammed with explosives. "Okay, okay, okay!" Houston said to one of his fellow volunteers. "I'll do it, I'll do it! But did I volunteer to laugh about it? Did I volunteer to jump from the plane waving the flag and singing 'My Country 'Tis of Thee'? Get off my ass! I'll fly the mission just like you."

One day Houston was ordered to hop over to his home base at Attleborough and pick up a part, and when he landed, the old pangs returned with double intensity. There were his buddies, the ones he had volunteered to haul home from Russia. "Jesus Christ!" Houston said to himself. "They're home safe, and now *I'm* in the soup!" When his friends smacked him on the back and asked him what he was doing, Houston gulped and said, "Oh, er, uh, nothing much."

"What's that mean, Sam?" asked his old bombardier.

"Oh, er, uh, nothing much," the flustered pilot answered. "Just fooling around."

Back at Honington that night, Houston resumed his attempts to come to grips with the English food, the English warm beer, the English beds, the English weather, and the English decorum. The sky was like a giant gray sponge gripped by a huge, nervous hand. It was June, and back home in Montana the pasqueflowers and Indian paintbrush were in bloom, but here at Honington it might as well have been winter. Wilfred Ferguson "Pappy" Tooman, the hottest mother pilot of them all, never tired of kidding Houston and the others about their chill discomfort. "Listen, fellows," Tooman would say. "I heard today that you can sunbathe in England at least once every year. When? *Just now, while I was talking!* You just missed it!" Then he would roar a big old Oklahoma laugh and continue shivering under his flight jacket.

The mess was run by the British, and three times a day the men of the Aphrodite project had to walk a half mile from their quarters in a remote corner of the field to the main mess hall, where they were treated to five or six courses, all of which tasted like cheese. "Goddamn it," Houston said to Fain Pool. "How do they do it? How do they make every single course taste like cheese? The bread tastes like cheese; the meat tastes like cheese; the tea tastes like cheese."

"Yeh," said Pool, reaching for a slab of pale, gelatinous stuff. "Everything tastes like cheese except this. It tastes like—"

"I know what it tastes like," Houston interrupted. "Don't remind me."

One night some of the jump pilots were invited to the British officers club, where they huddled around pitchers of warm beer and bemoaned their fate. "Hey, miss," one of them said to a waitress. "Why in hell don't you English keep ice?"

"Keep ice?" the Wren enlisted woman said. "You *cawn't* keep it, 'Leftenant,' it melts!"

When the woman walked out of earshot, Frank Houston said, "I *know* there'll always be an England, but the sixty-four-dollar question is why."

As usual, the talk turned to the mission, but the senior men in the group quickly turned that conversation off. Too many British airmen were circulating around the table, and even though Aphrodite was based at an English air depot, it remained a secret strictly unto itself. Not that any of the pilots knew much about it anyway. But they had been told to keep quiet under penalty of being broken in grade all the way down to Pfc.

Soon the group was embroiled in the oldest argument in the Army Air Corps: Which was the better bomber, Consolidated's B-24 Liberator, with the gracefully tapered Davis wings and the frankly blunt fuselage, or Boeing's B-17 Flying Fortress, with its superstructure like a Japanese battleship and its broad, functional wings? There were five full mother ship crews on the base by now, two of them trained on B-24's, two on B-17's, and one on both aircraft, and there were ten jump pilots, all of them from B-17 squadrons, and each comment on behalf of the Liberators was drowned in a sea of derision from the others. "Goddamn banana boats!" Houston shouted. "They look like banana boats, they act like banana boats, and after the war they'll be banana boats!"

Indeed, "banana boat" was the most common description of the B-24's by non B-24 crewmen. No one knew where the appellation came from, except that the Liberator had tricycle landing gear and relatively soft springing, and when one taxied along the apron, it tended to wobble and lurch like a small boat at anchor in a light blow. But the B-24, banana boat or not, had certain advantages over the older Flying Fortress. The high aspect wing was more efficient. The top speed was slightly greater, and the range and bombload higher. In the Pacific theater, where such advantages were important, the B-24 was clearly the superior aircraft. Here in the European theater, where durability and structural strength counted for more, most pilots favored the B-17. "Jimmy Doolittle likes the B-17," one of the pilots was shouting. "I heard him say it myself."

"Sure you did," said a B-24 pilot, "and you heard Hap Arnold say the same thing, the last time you went bowling together."

The first pilot continued undismayed. "Jimmy Doolittle stood right in our O club and he said, 'An airplane to be safe has to be able to fly twice its landing speed.' "

"The 17 can," said Fain Pool, "and the 24 can't. That settles *that!*"

But it settled nothing. The argument went on for an hour or so, until there was a knock on the door. "Excuse me, sirs," a young English airman said. "Please, I've been told that some of you gentlemen fly banana boats. Could I have a banana? I have a five-year-old daughter, and she's never seen one."

"Get your ass out of here, Limey!" a B-24 pilot called from the corner of the darkened hut.

"You'll have to excuse him," said one of the others. "He flies B-24's, and he's having his period." The young Englishman walked away, looked back over his shoulder, and then increased his pace until he disappeared into the sodden Lincolnshire night.

A sort of assembly line had been set up at three air bases in England, but nobody knew that it was an assembly line except General Earle Partridge and Major Henry James Rand and the few other masterminds of the Aphrodite project. Elderly B-17's consigned for return to the United States or the scrap heap were taxied out to the flight line and flown to the depot at Hon-

ington, where crews of enlisted men would swarm aboard and
take out everything that was not bolted down and some parts
that were. One crew would specialize in removing the radio
equipment, and then the plane would pass to a crew that specialized in the deft excision of bomb racks, and meanwhile,
another crew would be hacking away at gun turrets and ordnance. The co-pilot's seat came out, the navigator's table, the
bins for machine-gun ammunition, the engineer's tools—everything removable except the pilot's seat. No one crew knew what
the others were doing or why. At the end of the line, the plane's
papers would vanish, and then the plane itself would disappear,
bound for Burtonwood, where more Army Air Corps crews
quickly installed 4 by 4 beams to shore up the bomb bay and a
few electronic furbishes, such as an automatic radio altimeter
that worked with the autopilot to hold the plane at any preset
altitude. Then the unlisted, uninventoried B-17's were flown to
their penultimate port of call: Woodbridge, a vast RAF base
near the southeast coast of England. There they were loaded
with box after box of nitrostarch, and a few of them with a new
weapon of war called jellied gasoline. Back at the Air Corps experimental station at Eglin Field, Florida, war scientists had
discovered that rats would die within two minutes if they were
trapped in bunkers and covered with burning gasoline. From
this research information, Eglin extrapolated a plan for attacking the personnel working belowground in the mysterious
German bunkers, the so-called large sites across the Channel.
"It is believed that if a cover of flame is placed over the Large
Site entrances and is maintained for a period of ten (10) minutes that most, if not all, personnel in the site would die of
suffocation," Eglin's commanding general reported. Aphrodite
planners decided to ram nitrostarch-laden B-17's into each large
site, then follow up with a suffocating dose of napalm, carried
in another Aphrodite robot.

Even while the loading of the first ten drones was going forward at Woodbridge, techniques were being devised at Honing-

ton for the attacks. At first it was decided that the mother and robot task forces should cross the Channel at very high altitude, beyond the effective range of German antiaircraft batteries, and then dive to a low altitude for a run on the target. But early tests with sand-loaded robots showed that the B-17 was too stable an aircraft to allow itself to be dived pell mell for 30,000 feet. The natural tendency of the plane as it fell faster and faster was to level off, and the C-1 servomotors controlling the robot plane were not strong enough to overcome this tendency. A test pilot and co-pilot shoving at the control column with all their strength could hardly keep the B-17 in the power dive, thanks to the inherent stability built into the plane by its manufacturers.

It was decided to go to the other extreme, to guide the robot into the target at a very low altitude and dump it suddenly, "short and sweet and to the point," as Major Rand put it. The radio altimeter (nicknamed Ace, for "automatic control equipment") would hold the robot at 300 feet all the way across the Channel, and the mother ship high above would send steering signals to the autopilot and finally give the radio impulse that would overpower the Ace and send 20,000 pounds of explosives plummeting into the bunker. The system was primitive, but early testing convinced the planners that it would work. Weather remained the main problem. Banks of clouds would suddenly come between mother and robot. Television cameras mounted in the noses of the robots and transmitting to screens in the mothers would have helped solve the problem of maintaining contact, but Rand was told that there was no time for such sophisticated electronics. Control had to be maintained visually, and in England this presented major problems. The tops of the robot wings were painted a high-visibility yellow, and smoke pots were installed in wing-tip tanks so that the flight of the plane could be picked up.

Early test pilots found themselves in an experimentalist's paradise. An intrepid major named Ralph Hayes drew the assignment of testing the first smoke-equipped robot. He flew the B-17 over an American air base to the north and toggled the smoke on, and down below him he saw a scene of pandemonium. Fire-fighting equipment was scrambling, airmen ran toward the nearest bunkers, and taxiing aircraft pulled off the line and headed full speed for remote hardstands in the far corners of the field. Hayes looked out and saw smoke pouring gloriously from his wing tips, and he enjoyed the effect so much that he turned and made another low pass over the field, causing still more confusion below as the ground crews prepared for the crash of the bomber. Then he turned off the smoke and roared away toward Honington. The same Hayes made the first flight tests of a fully loaded robot, and his tests had the undivided attention of the ten jump pilots who ultimately would have to perform the same task, with nitrostarch and napalm instead of the sand that filled Hayes' B-17 from nose to tail. "It'll break right in half," Frank Houston said as the loaded bomber taxied down the runway.

"Well, if it's gonna break right in half," said Fain Pool, "this is the time for it, not when we're sitting on top of all that nitrostarch."

But Hayes experienced no crucial problems with the loaded robot. Along with the other bomber pilots in the Aphrodite project, he was accustomed to handling aircraft laden to capacity with bombs. The only difference was that the bombs were compactly located in the bomb bay, whereas the Aphrodite loads were distributed evenly. Hayes noticed that the B-17 handled slightly heavily, but not enough to endanger the mission. He bumped a few times on takeoff, finally pulled the bomber off with flaps, and then "walked" the rudder to keep from stalling. He felt that the merest application of aileron would have dumped the loaded aircraft into the runway, but he knew that any skilled pilot would stay away from the aileron control instinctively, "walking" the rudder instead in an anti-stall maneuver. The landing was hairy and imprecise; the tail would not come up, and on one particular jolt Hayes was certain that he was going to wash out the landing gear. But the sturdy Flying Fortress held together, and Hayes did not even bother to report the hazardous landing, since no one else would ever be landing a fully loaded Aphrodite drone anyway.

When the earliest bugs were ironed out, the ten jump pilots were unleashed and escorted to the robots for their first training flights. "My God!" said Fain Pool when he climbed into the cabin of the drone. "My God!" he said again and again. "Where's the co-pilot's seat? Where's the radio? Where's the navigator's table? Where's everything?" The bomber looked naked, and it gave Pool an eerie feeling. There was a rack of electrical equipment bolted just below the pilot's line of vision, but Pool recognized nothing except a few autopilot switches. He was told to take the plane off, get the feel of it, and then return to the field for further instruction.

Like the other jump pilots, Pool was a master pilot, accustomed to all the routine behavior patterns of the B-17 and a few that were not so routine, but he would never forget this first flight in the robot airplane as long as he lived. Even the taxiing was strange. Usually the pilot would pour on the power to get the heavy airplane rolling, then reduce power in an attempt to keep the plane moving at the approximate speed of a man walking, and the whole process was a tedious one. But the robot aircraft began moving the instant the chocks were removed and Pool released the brake. Since primary training, he had not flown an aircraft that rolled so easily on the ground, and he had to throttle back to keep the ship from overrunning the ground crew.

The takeoff confused Pool even more. Halfway down the runway he realized that the B-17 was riding extremely smoothly, and then he realized he was already airborne. He waited for the slight sinking feeling that accompanied the first attempts to put a B-17 into a climbing attitude, but there was no sinking whatever. The four engines bit into the air and hauled the aircraft up at a steep angle that once again reminded Pool of his days in single-engine trainers. He had only been in the air for a few minutes when he realized that he was having the time of his life. After months of fighting the controls of bomb-laden B-17's, trying to stay in formation with engines out and flaps down and speed barely off a cold stall, he was able to whip the big airplane around in tight turns, haul back on the stick and climb at impossible angles, and dive and pirouette in the air like a member of a flying circus.

The other pilots were experiencing the same airy feelings. Frank Houston took off his empty B-17 and caught up to a group of heavy-laden B-24 Liberators, forming for a mission into Germany. Houston rolled around the edges of the struggling formation, dipped and darted among the confused pilots, and finally shoved the throttles forward and disappeared over the horizon with the agility of a P-51 Mustang. "Hot damn!" he said aloud. "That's a lot of banana boat drivers that'll never drink again!"

When all the jump pilots had taken their turns at the controls of the feather-light bombers, the men were assembled for a preliminary briefing. "I'm sorry that we've been able to tell you so little," a headquarters officer told them, "and I'm sorry that we'll have to keep it that way for a while."

"Sir," said Fain Pool, "I want to ask one question. When the war's over, can I take one of these planes home with me?"

The officer said, "When you find out what's going to happen to these planes, Lieutenant, you'll understand why *nobody's* going to take one home." He went on to explain that the robots were going to be filled with explosives and radio-controlled into high-priority targets on the Continent. He was sorry that he could not tell them *what* high-priority targets; he would only say that some day they would all realize that they had helped to steer the course of the war at an extremely decisive period, and that they would certainly be decorated by the American Army and almost certainly by the British as well. "So much for the morale building," the officer said. "Now here's how it's all going to be done." He outlined the latest operational plan. Each plane would take off with a crew of two. A jump pilot would get the loaded aircraft into the air and start heading it around a rectangular course over eastern England at an altitude of 1,800 feet. While he was doing this, the other member of the crew, an enlisted electronics expert, would "tune" the autopilot to the high degree of response and precision required for an accurate run on the target. When the autopilot was fully set up, the pilot would radio a code word to the mother ship high above, and the mother ship would prepare to take control. The autopilot expert would clamber to the navigator's escape hatch in the front of the airplane, just behind the No. 2 engine, and bail out. The pilot would put the aircraft in a gentle dive, jerk our fourteen cables that would arm the munitions load (an action equivalent to cocking a revolver), and bail out himself. The robot would automatically level off at Ace altitude, and then the mother ship would take it across the Channel and into the target.

"Whew!" Fain Pool said. "As simple as that, eh?"

"So simple," said the officer, "that we don't see how it can fail."

Within a few days the first mission was ready to go, but the English weather intervened. On those rare days when the sky was blue over England, the meteorological officer would report that it was still socked in over the Channel or the target. Everyone agreed that the first Aphrodite mission should have the benefit of perfect weather all the way, but perfect weather is a rarity in Europe in July. During the early part of the month, while crews stood by their aircraft anxiously, the cloud cover persisted. On the single day when the weather was CAVU (ceiling and visibility unlimited) over both takeoff point and target, the mission had to be scrubbed because a girl-crazy navigator from one of the mother crews had sneaked off to London and failed to return by daybreak. The navigator drew a punishment detail—censoring the project's mail for a period of thirty days—and all personnel were restricted to the base indefinitely. Meanwhile, the clouds and the fog rolled in thicker than ever.

Through the waiting and testing, Major H. J. Rand and his own personal cloud cover of cigar smoke seemed to be everyplace at once, shouting, arguing, cajoling, ordering, whining, and wheedling. "He seemed like an obsessed person," one of the jump pilots said later. "He had no normal feelings of fatigue or pity or anything else. All he wanted to do was get the job done, and whenever anybody would gripe about the schedule, he'd say, 'We're fighting a war, aren't we?' What the hell could you answer to that?"

One day Rand unrattled a long stream of obscenities at First Lieutenant John "Jack" Lansing, a former cavalry officer and football player who did much of the airborne chauffeuring of the squat little major on his wheelings and dealings around the countryside. "Now goddamn it, Major, you've got to cut that out," Lansing said. "You're really hurting my feelings."

Rand took a deep breath and unloaded another string of invective. Lansing walked up to Rand, stared through the cloud of cigar smoke, and said evenly, "One of these days, Major, I'm gonna punch you right in the mouth."

Rand put a finger on Lansing's pilot's wings. "Go ahead and try it," he said, "if you want to walk for the rest of your life!"

Lansing shoved Rand, and Rand shoved Lansing, and then someone stepped in between, and an hour later the incident was forgotten by both parties. "You learn to get used to it," Lansing explained to another pilot. "He means well, he really does. He thinks he's fighting World War Two all by himself."

One day Rand was standing in the mother ship between Lansing and his co-pilot while they maneuvered at 20,000 feet for a better look at a training robot far below. "Put the nose down!" Rand ordered. Lansing dipped the nose a few degrees.

"Goddamn it," Rand said. "I said put the nose down! Quit playing around. If you can't get the nose down on this airplane, then I'll find a pilot who can!" Lansing kicked the control column of the B-24 and applied full throttle, and the plane leaned into a power dive. All 210 pounds of Rand went sailing through the air, over the top of both pilots and facedown on the control panel, and the co-pilot had to wrench Rand clear of the instruments. His nose was gushing blood, his ear was cut, and he was spouting a long list of unintelligibilities from his split lips.

"What did you say?" Lansing said.

"I said, goddamn it, now you're getting the idea!" Rand sputtered.

A few days later Rand and Lansing were forced down at a strange airfield by a faulty engine, and Rand said, "Goddamn it, I've got to get to Bovingdon right away." He ordered Lansing to commandeer a British single-engine aircraft sitting on the apron nearby.

"Without permission?" Lansing said.

"We haven't got the time," Rand said. "Can you fly that thing?"

"If I can start it, I can fly it," Lansing said, and the two men jumped in and began looking for a battery switch. "Here!" Lansing said, and a few minutes later they were airborne, while signal flares were being shot in their direction from the control tower.

"Shag ass for Bovingdon," Rand said, "we'll straighten this out later."

At Bovingdon, Lansing taxied into a swarm of British military police and irate RAF officers with quivering mustaches. When the propeller stopped spinning, Rand said, "I'll see you later, I've got to get right into London." He jumped out, threaded his way through the crowd of greeters, and stuck his special pass from General Eisenhower under all interested noses. Lansing, minus a special pass from SHAEF or even the simplest authorization for the use of the English plane, spent three hours explaining what had happened and finally extricated himself by the simple device of slipping away, like a common criminal. One word about the Aphrodite project would have sufficed, but Lansing had a highly developed sense of responsibility, and he knew that nothing could be said off the base about the secret project.

Back at Honington, he collared Rand, busy as usual running from plane to plane and office to office. "How'd you get out of that one?" Rand said, blowing cigar smoke in Lansing's face.

"I talked for three hours and finally ducked out," Lansing said. "Now listen here, Major!"

Rand poked a stubby finger into Lansing's wings again. "Good experience," he said, "good experience," and whirled away. Lansing took a few steps after him and then stopped. "What's the use?" he asked himself. Later he explained to a friend: "No matter what he does, he intrigues me. Something about this crazy little fat man defies the probabilities. By the looks of him, he should be in the Quartermaster Corps, right? He should be doling out underwear and service caps, but that little mind of his is always whirling around."

Lansing feared the worst one day when he learned that Winston Churchill and an aide were on the base, asking for a guided tour of the project that was designed to save London and England and maybe even New York City. "They'd just better keep Rand away from him," Lansing said. "The higher the rank, the less respect he has." All went well for a while, as various American generals and marshals of the RAF showed Churchill around the secret project. At last Churchill came into range of two explosive items: a robot loaded with nine tons of nitrostarch and Major Henry James Rand. Without ado, Churchill began to clamber through the open navigator's hatch of the drone, and as he managed to get both knees inside the airplane, Rand came running over, shouting, "He's wearing golf shoes! He's wearing golf shoes!" The others saw that Rand was right, and the Prime Minister of England was about to take his first step into a plane that was laced with wires and cables that could very easily be shorted and blown by a single puncture.

Rand reached the plane and grabbed Churchill by the first available handhold: the trousers covering the Prime Minister's ample posterior. "Mr. Prime Minister," Rand shouted, "you can't get in that airplane with those spikes!"

"Oh, I can't, can't I?" Churchill said in the mellifluous voice that had moved legions. The onlookers waited for the inevitable explosion, but instead Churchill said politely, "Very well, then, just show me where to put my foot and I'll climb out." Rand assisted Churchill to the ground, drew the Prime Minister's thanks and his handshake, and went about his business. No one who missed the scene could believe it. "You mean he actually called him 'Mr. Prime Minister'?" Jack Lansing said incredulously. "He didn't call him 'Hey, Fats'?"

After Churchill left, the weather improved in England, but remained bad over the target, and the order of the day, as promulgated by the intense Major Rand, was practice, practice, and more practice. The jump pilots would take off the drones and then sit back while the mother crews controlled them for hours. Rand ordered tests of the automatic radio altimeter, Ace, to see how low it would function, and several pilots came back with tree leaves in their nacelles to prove that the Ace would work at a very low altitude indeed. One fearless jump pilot named Glen Barnes, testing the Ace, stripped the entire leading edge off his left wing. As a result of that flight, the Ace altimeters were ordered set at 300 feet and no lower, and it was decided that the missions would be flown at that same altitude. Mother crews and baby crews were told that they could practice at 300 feet with complete safety over most of England, but they were warned not to spend too much time over Elveden Hall or High Wycombe or other places where the top brass lived, and they were also told to steer away from cities like Peterborough, where huge open-hearth furnaces and steam condensers and power lines jutted into the sky. They were also ordered to haul clear of British military installations and to avoid buzzing shipping in the North Sea and the Channel. Pilot Foster Falkenstine ignored this last instruction one day and flew low over a flotilla of the Royal Navy, receiving several near hits with flak for his pains. British naval gunners did not stand on ceremony; if an aircraft was not supposed to be in their vicinity at a certain time, they fired on it, whatever its silhouette. They had been burned too many times by German crews flying captured Allied aircraft, laying their bombs on ships, and hustling back across the Channel before they could be shot down.

Aphrodite pilots did not file flight plans; they just climbed into their airplanes and took off, and the standard method of navigation was to fly low over railroad stations and read the placards. Sometimes they dived on castles, perfecting their technique, and sometimes they would zoom down low and blow over sailboats on The Wash. Occasionally a general like Partridge or Doolittle would arrive to check on progress, and usually he would demand a ride in a mother ship or robot as a practical test. One day when Doolittle was in a mother ship at nearly 20,000 feet, he turned to pilot Foster Falkenstine and said, "Let's get down closer to the robot." Each time Falkenstine would descend several thousand feet and level off, and the general would say, "Get down more."

"I didn't realize for a long time," Falkenstine told his buddies later. "He wanted to get *under* the robot. He wanted to look *up* at it!"

Pappy Tooman, oldest and most skillful of the mother pilots, was shaken to his Oklahoma-style boot tops when he hauled Doolittle aloft for an on-the-spot inspection of control techniques. Tooman was very much aware that Doolittle was partial to fighters like the P-47 Thunderbolt and the P-51 Mustang, reminders of his days as a racing pilot, and did not enjoy traveling in the slow, clumsy bombers, especially the B-24, which he did not deem airworthy. "Captain, how much time do you have in this thing?" Doolittle said before the takeoff.

"Too much, sir," Tooman said jovially.

"How much is that?" Doolittle snapped. "Thirty minutes?"

The takeoff, into a crosswind, was difficult, and Tooman wound up hopping the B-24 off the runway with flaps. The landing was smoother. After he climbed out, Doolittle turned to the acknowledged virtuoso of the mother ship art and said, "I've got to hand it to you, Captain, you learn fast. The takeoff was stinking rotten, but your landing was only poor."

By July 10, 1944, seven B-17's were fully loaded with nitrostarch and ready to go against the still unscathed rocket-launching bunkers in Germany. An eighth would have been ready, but it was scheduled to carry jell gas, and no one had been able to figure out what kind of container to use. The discussion was reminiscent of the old chemistry-class riddle: If you invented the universal solvent, what would you keep it in? No pilot could be asked to take off a drone loosely packed with jerricans of jellied gasoline, and experiments were going forward to increase the size of the regular tanks and the bomb bay tanks to carry enough incendiary jelly to produce the suffocating effects so carefully worked out at Eglin Field. Meanwhile, the British had promised to supply the needed explosives, and there was talk about a new formula called Torpex (copied from an explosive of the Germans) that would enable the drones to destroy every building, protrusion, and human within a mile and a half of the impact point, or so the cloistered Aphrodite pilots were led to believe. Thus there was consternation among the pilots when the whole operation was moved to the fogbound jumping-off point called Woodbridge, seven miles inland from the North Sea, and the resident British officers insisted that the loaded Aphrodite bombers be lined up wing tip to wing tip in a far corner of the field and the Aphrodite personnel be quartered nearby.

"Damn it to hell!" Frank Houston said in the middle of a red dog game in the least leaky of the Nissen huts assigned to the Americans. "In one breath they tell us they're glad to have us, and in the other they tell us to get our asses over to the corner of the field so nobody'll be hurt but us if anything goes off."

"What else can they do?" asked a jovial jump pilot named Joe Andrecheck. "What's the point of putting the babies where they can blow up the whole base?"

"They should be dispersed," Fain Pool said. "Maybe they'll blow up everything within a mile and a half, and maybe they won't, but what's the harm in putting one loaded ship at every corner of the base, maybe taxi some into the woods so at least they wouldn't detonate each other if something happened? Woodbridge is big enough to disperse them all."

"Absolutely," Houston said, and most of the other pilots agreed.

Whatever the feelings about the lined-up robots, there was unanimity among the pilots that Woodbridge was the most depressing military base in the European theater of operations. Its very purpose was depressing. With its runways two miles long and a quarter mile wide and its proximity to the coastline, Woodbridge had been built as a last-resort landing place for disabled aircraft. Whenever a bomber straggled back from a mission with its wheels shot off or its bombs stuck in the bomb bay or both pilots dead and a crew member fighting the controls, it was directed to Woodbridge. The runways were so spacious that neat, precise landings were unnecessary, and the British quartered on the base their slickest crews of fire fighters and medical teams and wrecking teams to rush to the aid of stricken aircraft. The field was equipped with FIDO lights, long rows of gasoline-fired high-pressure jets that could burn a hole through thick fog, and when the FIDOs issued their flaming hiss late at night, everyone tumbled out of his bed to watch as some poor lost pilot tried to poke his broken airplane down through the man-made hole in the soup to safety. Now and then one made it.

"Sweet Jesus," said a jump pilot named John Sollars as he picked at his British-style cold lunch one day. "It's a barrel of fun around here, isn't it?" That day an all-plywood British Mosquito had arrived in a ball of flame and reduced itself and its two-man crew to a pair of smoldering engines. There was a reforestation project all around the sprawling base, and a B-17 pilot had landed short and deforested about 600 feet of medium-sized conifers, somehow surviving the two-engine wheelless landing himself. An American P-51 had tried to come in on one wheel, ripping out the air scoop, flipping the little fighter plane, and decapitating the pilot. Only a few nights before, in a nearby incident, the Aphrodite pilots had watched as British fighters shot down the last three members of an American bomber formation of B-24's, fully lighted, returning late from a mission. In the Battle of Britain, every Englishman had been seared to the soul by the horrors that fell from the sky, and they were still shooting first and asking questions afterward, and if there was a single pilot in the Aphrodite project who had not been fired on by British antiaircraft gunners at least once, he was keeping quiet about it. If one's automatic radio-signaled IFF (identification friend or foe) was not functioning perfectly and one's voice signals did not conform precisely to the code of the day, one could be expected to be worked over by the British ack-ack or the British fighters. More than once an exasperated American pilot had swooped low to fire a few bursts into English antiaircraft batteries, and everybody knew the story of the command pilot who had ordered his lead bombardier to save one bomb and on the return to England toggled it smack on top of a trigger-happy flak crew. "It is far more blessed to give than to receive," the colonel said on the intercom, and flew back to his base with a clear conscience.

"It's just the English way of doing things," the tolerant Frank Houston tried to explain one night. "We weren't around for the Battle of Britain, so we can't understand how they feel. They learned to do things by the numbers for their own protection, and they're still doing things by the numbers."

One day Houston was crouched under the wing tip of an observation B-17, while sheets of rain spattered all around him, when a heavyset form appeared in the foggy drizzle. Houston recognized Staff Sergeant Willard Smith, the autopilot expert who was assigned to fly with him if they ever got a loaded Aphrodite robot off the ground. Smith, normally a philosophical and placid type, was boiling with rage. He told Houston that he had been sitting in the robot assigned to them, preflighting the aircraft, a process which consisted of revving up the engines, checking to see that the various instrument readings were correct, and trying out controls to make sure they were working free and easy. Daily prefight checks were routine for all bomber aircraft, but with the flabby-muscled old wrecks of the Aphrodite program, they were an absolute necessity. A mission might be called on a few hours' notice, and each aircraft had to be ready to go. There were risks enough without adding the risks of negligence.

"So I had just started two engines," Willard Smith was telling Houston, "when this English officer with pips all over his shoulder tore-ass into the plane and started screaming at me. 'What in the bloody hell do you think you're doing?' Stuff like that. I told him I was preflighting the plane. He said, 'By God, Sergeant, it's bloody stupid that we have to put up with these loaded planes of yours lying about waiting to blow us all up.' I yessired him to death, and when he left, I finished the job. Plane checks out, Lieutenant. But just when I finished, he came back and told me to report to his CO for punishment. What do I do now?"

"Well," said the bemused Houston, "you could go play cribbage, or maybe there's a red dog game going on down at hut four. Or you could take a nice walk in this lovely rain."

"But he ordered me to report for punishment!"

"Sergeant," Houston said, patting his enlisted friend on the shoulder, "there's a lot you don't understand about the British. They like to fuss and fume, but that's usually the end of it. Now you go play poker. That's an order!"

"And if they court-martial me?"

"Tell them I ordered you to ignore them, and I'll back you up."

The sturdy form of Willard Smith disappeared in the distance. Frank Houston shook his head. The British defied his understanding. What was the purpose of Aphrodite? To save the British civilians. Was there a military necessity to save the British civilians? Of course not. The only pure military necessity was to bomb out the German oil refineries and steel mills and ball-bearing factories and railheads and power plants, and just as surely as Adolf Hitler was a lunatic, the war would thus be brought to a successful conclusion. But was there a humane necessity to save London? Of course there was, and the Americans had created Aphrodite to meet this need. Now, in return, they were ordered to the farthest corner of this British aerodrome, placed in the most dangerous proximity to the loaded robots, and harassed and hindered when they tried to carry out their routine maintenance tasks.

Houston was all the more puzzled a few days later when various mother ship crews returned from intense briefing sessions at Spaatzhouse, the nickname for the headquarters of the U.S. Strategic Air Force in Europe. Robot crews were not briefed extensively; their role was simple (if vital), and there was evidently no need for them to learn details about targets and headings and military imperatives. But the mother crews came back bursting with information. They had been briefed by high-ranking British officers, and they had been told in the plainest terms that their mission was to save London. "They told us about all kinds of crazy things," one of the mother pilots reported. "They had big tables covered with papier-mâché mock-ups of the targets across the Channel, and they showed us how they were designed to launch these monster rockets dead at London. The targets are great big roofs of concrete—three hundred and four hundred feet across and twenty or thirty feet thick—more cement than Boulder Dam! They told us that we had the most important mission in the European theater, the number one priority, and by order of General Eisenhower himself. They said the Germans were going to blow London right off the map any day now; they were going to send over rockets that would make these V-1 buzz bombs look like toys, twenty-five hundred rockets a night. And not only that: Another British officer took over and he said that they had absolutely reliable intelligence that the Germans are building rockets for New York. They have one that's going to make three skips across the atmosphere and come down in Manhattan. They have another one that is piloted, and the pilot is supposed to bail out off Long Island and be picked up by a submarine on station."

"So we're going to save everybody's ass," Frank Houston said. "Then how come we don't have fried chicken and fresh eggs once in a while? Did they tell you that?"

"They couldn't have treated us nicer," the mother pilot went on. "They told us that Churchill was watching every move we made, and they had all kinds of British decorations for us, starting with the British Distinguished Flying Cross. And one of the American generals said we'd all get the American DFC, too."

"I'd rather have fried chicken and fresh eggs," Houston said, and went off to play red dog. He had lost $13 in the morning session, and before he set out to save London and New York and win World War II, he wanted to get back to even.

Late that night the red dog game was still going on, and Houston had gained back a few dollars of his missing $13. Suddenly one of the pilots said, "Ssshhh!" Everyone stopped and listened. The pilot said, "Hear that?" At first the noise was barely perceptible, and the other pilots marveled at their comrade's acuteness of hearing. But then the droning noise became unmistakable. It lacked smoothness; it sounded as much like a normal multiengine aircraft as a donkey engine sounded like a finely tuned inboard engine. There were few aircraft in the theater that made such a noise; one was the German JU-88, which could be used as a night fighter, as an intruder aircraft gathering intelligence, or even as a light bomber. There did not seem to be a Luftwaffe mechanic alive who could synchronize the two engines of the Junkers airplane—hence the odd, paddle-beating sound.

When they first recognized the distinctive racket, the pilots had distrusted their ears. No one had spelled out an official policy, but it was understood that the Germans would not attack Woodbridge intentionally, any more than they would intentionally bomb a hospital ship or a church. The Germans were said to have several rescue-and-salvage bases of their own a few miles inside the French coastline, and the Allies had marked them off limits to bombers. At least that was the rumor.

But now the clattering whine of the Nazis' finest night fighter was screaming over the fogbound aerodrome, and all at once the card table was knocked over, chairs overturned, and a dozen or so pilots had disappeared under beds and cupboards. One ran inside the fireplace and now was trying to get his breath in a cloud of noxious gas from burning peat and coke. Only Frank Houston remained at the table. He was just as frightened as the others, but more attuned to reality. With a quarter million pounds of nitrostarch loaded just outside the window, a bed or a fireplace afforded no protection. "Hey, you guys," Houston hollered, "I'm losing eleven fifty—you can't quit winners!"

The drone of the Junkers seemed to be disappearing into the foggy night, and a few faces began peeping out from under shelter. But then the noise increased, coming from another direction. Once again the faces vanished like chipmunks in a woodpile. Frank Houston was debating whether to take cover when suddenly there was a hissing sound and the whole world seemed to light up. He waited for the explosion, but the sibilance merely grew louder and the lights brighter.

"The FIDO lights!" he shouted. "The Limeys have turned on the FIDO lights."

"Jesus Christ," a muffled voice cried out. "Can't they tell that's a German plane?"

Houston dashed for the fireplace. "Move over!" he said to the gasping bombardier. "They're showing the pilot where to bomb."

Minutes passed. The sound of the enemy plane disappeared into the distance for the second time and then returned from still another direction. The FIDO lights flamed brighter and louder, and the smell of burning gas filled the air. The pilot seemed to be quartering the field. It occurred to Houston that there must have been a security leak, that the German must be seeking the loaded drones so that he could wipe out the whole Aphrodite project. "What a blast!" Houston said to himself. "Good-bye, Woodbridge! Good-bye, county of Suffolk! Good-bye, eastern England! We'll all go together, me and all the Limey farmers and all those dumb bastards in the control tower that turned on the FIDOs to give the Kraut a better target."

On the fourth pass the German seemed to be flying with reduced power, and erratic spurts of noise began to come from the engines. Houston recognized them as the snaps and pops of high-powered engines being throttled back. He ran to the window and parted the blackout curtains in time to see a twin-engine aircraft flash by, wheels down, just above the runway. The plane was silver except for a large black Maltese cross on the sides. Houston watched as it touched wheels in the harsh orange glare of the FIDO lights and disappeared down the runway.

"He landed!" Houston shouted, and the other pilots rushed

from their hiding places. Pool, Andrecheck, and Houston threw on fatigues and shoes and dashed into the sodden night in the direction of the plane's landing, but when they had run several hundred yards, they were confronted by a British MP with drawn pistol. "That's all, sirs," the Englishman said. "From this point on the field is quarantined."

"What the hell was that German plane doing here?" Houston said, but the sentry had moved away to confront a group of Aphrodite enlisted men rushing to the scene of the action.

The pilots went back to their huts, and the next morning the air base was filled with rumors. One had it that the German pilot had lost his bearings in the fog and landed by mistake, and the Englishman driving the guide jeep had led the taxiing JU-88 into a cul-de-sac behind a Lancaster, so that the German could not rev up his engines and make a getaway when he discovered his atrocious error. According to this version of the incident, British sentries had rushed up to the side of the enemy plane, smashed the canopy with a wrench, and brought the pilot and radarman out at gunpoint. There was another rumor to the effect that the pilot was defecting intentionally, and the proof of his intent was supposed to lie in the fact that he was wearing a freshly pressed powder-blue Luftwaffe uniform with highly polished boots, hardly the outfit for mucking around in the fog on a nighttime intruder mission. Still a third rumor had it that the German had been under orders to fake a defection, so that he could land at Woodbridge, get a good look at the mysterious Aphrodite project, and quickly radio back a fix to the German bombers standing by across the Channel.

No one connected with Aphrodite knew exactly what to believe, and as usual, the British were not sharing everything they knew. Major Henry James Rand came puffing back to the Aphrodite area late in the morning and told an aide, "I can't get it straight from British Intelligence—they're still questioning the pilot—but I'll tell you one thing: We'd better get the hell out of here—and fast. I had a look at that JU-88 close up, and if there's one item of advanced electronics that isn't on that plane, I don't know what it is. It looks like a porcupine with all those high-frequency antennas sticking out. It's got equipment for homing right on our bomber frequencies! That son of a bitch has got *everything,* and there's no telling what he radioed back to Germany. Our security is shot, and we've got to pull up and get out!"

Shortly after noon the tedious and dangerous job of unloading and defusing ten drones began in what quixotically turned out to be a bright, hot day. Toward late afternoon the drones that remained loaded sank into the asphalt up to their hubs, and a British maintenance officer put in a complaint that the Americans were ruining the air base. "You'll pay for this damage!" the irate lieutenant shouted at the unloading crews, and a young American ordnance officer told the Britisher to "stick it up your Limey ass!" When the Britisher shook a riding crop at the young officer, the American told him to take the riding crop and do the same. On that note the Englishman stomped away, his boots sucking at the asphalt, making a dignified exit impossible. After that, the unloading continued undisturbed. It continued, in fact, for three days, until the last ounce of nitrostarch was repacked in its original boxes and the ten aircraft flown away. The new home office of Aphrodite was to be an unused RAF airbase called Fersfield, 30 miles northwest of Woodbridge and surrounded by British and American air bases of every description. Fersfield had never been put into operation because its logical landing patterns would have conflicted with the existing landing patterns of the adjoining bases.

"So now we're going there to conflict with the other landing patterns in planes full of nitrostarch?" mother pilot Pappy Tooman moaned in the middle of the moving operation. "What kind of sense is that?"

"Don't worry about it, Pappy," Fain Pool said. "When you

understand this move, you'll understand the whole history of warfare."

"Yeah," said Frank Houston, "and warm beer and grouchy leftenants, too."

Tooman smiled in spite of himself. These men, not himself and his crew, would be piloting the flying bombs. He would be 20,000 feet above, controlling, watching the show. With B-24's and B-17's and Lancasters and Halifaxes and Mosquitos and weather planes and fighters and hails of V-1 flying bombs and barrage balloons and Aphrodite drones swirling around beneath him, he knew it would be a good one.

At Fersfield, after nearly a month of answering to voices on the telephone, scientific types like Rand, and various project officers who shuttled in and out of the program, the men of Aphrodite were drawn under the command of a single officer. The new CO was a thirty-one-year-old lieutenant colonel, Roy Forrest, a distant relative of General Nathan Bedford Forrest ("Git thar fustest with the mostest"). A squadron commander with a B-17 bomb group, Forrest was tall and skinny and saturnine, his looks falling between those of Errol Flynn and John Carradine. He had been well blooded in the European theater. For more than a year he had flown as a lead pilot directing squadrons and wings and groups over the industrial targets of Germany. He had led the entire air force on its third raid on Berlin and more than once found himself out in front of 1,000 bombers at a time. He was known in the air for his colorful language on the radio ("Goddamn it, Featherington, get your hairy ass back in formation or I'll kick your balls!") and on the ground for his love of gambling, personal comfort, and dogs. The air crewmen around him were always adopting animals, and each time a plane would be shot down, several pets would be homeless. Forrest built a kennel for them, and assigned one of his aides, a Yugoslav GI from the isle of Hvar in Dalmatia, to feed them and brush them and worm them and see that they received their share of love and attention. Forrest also sent some of his enlisted men out on a series of "midnight requisitions" and built himself the finest all-weather toilet in England, with hot and cold running water, tub, shower, lavatory, and an improvised bidet. When it was finished, he hired a muralist to paint rustic scenes and nudes on the walls and called in his crews and said, "There you are, gentlemen. Be my guest. This is not a latrine; this is a *men's room*. No more riding the bicycle a half a mile to take a crap. No more washing your face in cold water." From then on, everybody in Forrest's corner of the field used the toilet for personal hygiene in the daytime and dice games at night, and soon Forrest was flying with a $6,000 money belt strapped to his stomach in place of the $40 or $50 in "funny money" issued by intelligence before each raid. "If I get hacked," he had explained, "I want to have a bankroll to begin the new game in the POW camp."

Despite his generous sharing of the toilet and his energetic participation in the friendly crap games, Roy Forrest was not universally liked and admired at his old 388th Bomb Group. A brilliant, eccentric, individualistic person, he seemed to some to be the prototype loudmouth Texan, arrogant, vain, and tasteless. His main personality defect was, in fact, his searing truthfulness, combined with a blunt manner that led to many misunderstandings. If he were the hero of a story, he would tell it flat out. If he were the goat, he would also tell the story. Some were not accustomed to such frankness. One of his favorite expressions was "That's no mystery to me," which he applied to engines, planes, tactics, strategies, plumbing, and almost everything that he came across. But the simple fact was that in the relatively circumscribed lives and activities of a squadron of fuzzy-cheeked B-17 crews, very little *was* a mystery to the six-foot-four-inch lieutenant colonel with the brown hair and the green eyes and the sallow complexion. He was seven or eight years older than most of his comrades, he had won his wings a year before Pearl Harbor, he had tinkered with engines and machines ever since childhood (his father was a Ford dealer in the little town of Jacksonville, Texas), and he had even gone to the University of Texas. The Lone Star flag flew over his squadron office, and sometimes during the night it would be torn down or inverted, but Forrest would say, "That don't get me excited, boys. Nothing that is motivated by jealousy gets me excited." He was given to other sayings, such as "Disappointment is the greatest brood pond for anger," and "What is security? Faith! How do you get it? You *emit* it!" He would pronounce these conclusions pompously, produce a wide, disarming smile, then tilt back his chair, throw his cowboy boots up on his desk and begin to play his tonette, a small flutelike instrument, the name of which he pronounced "toinette," as though it were abbreviated from "Antoinette." In the middle of each performance, he would say something like "Boys, you are being entertained by a concert toinetteist. Please hold your applause until the final number, and do not throw vegetables at the soloist, as there is a war on, I am told."

Project Aphrodite tightened up with the appearance of the new CO from Texas, despite his wide reputation as a character. There was another side to the playful Roy Forrest, and his close friends were well aware of it. Forrest was utterly, unalteringly, and unremittingly serious about winning the war. He had arrived in the European theater early, and he had flown on DP (deep penetration) raids into Germany against a holocaust of enemy fighters and ack-ack. Of the nine full crews that had gone overseas with him early in 1942, there was one left. With and without fighter escort, but mostly without, he had flown day after day into the bloody skies over cities like Hamburg and Berlin and Munich and Stuttgart. After fifteen missions, he could count only two times when he had brought back an undamaged aircraft. He had returned with engines shot out, fires on board, tires shredded, landing gear out, hydraulic system and oil lines spraying hot fluid all over the cockpit. For Forrest and the other crews on those early bomb-

...us against Germany, it was routine to clean the inside of the returned aircraft with hoses, both to wash away the random fluids of the plane's circulatory system and to wash away the blood and pieces of human being.

Forrest had lost track of the buddies and crewmates shot out from under him. He preferred not to think about them, to shoot craps and play his "toinette" instead. He was one of the few pilots of his era of the war with a complete and perfect combat complex, a state of mind that he explained as "half a feeling that I couldn't get hit and half a feeling that I didn't give a shit if I was." Pilots with a true combat complex had experienced so much and had grown accustomed to so much that their fear of death was almost nonexistent, and to them the theater of war was no more or less than an assembly line was to an auto worker or an office to a certified public accountant: a place to work. And despite his eccentricities and his playfulness, Roy Forrest wanted desperately to work, to win the war, to get back home. In Texas, he had a year-old daughter he had never seen. He had been in the European theater a long time; he was not in the least afraid, but he had had enough.

At Fersfield, where the project was bedding down for its first nights at a home of its own, Forrest saw immediately that Aphrodite was being strangled in red tape. Major Henry James Rand was able to slash his way through the technicalities, but he was only one person, and everyone else seemed to be doing things by the book. "The whole thing's so goddamned supersecret," Forrest told his former commanding officer, Bill David, in a telephone conversation, "that they can't get anything done. If they want a goat turd, first the goat has to be put through a six-week security check! It's ridiculous!" The old midnight requisitioner went to work. For a time, robot B-17's were flying all over East Anglia, picking up parts and pieces that Forrest had uncleared by personal telephone call to various commanding officers, most of whom had flown with him at one time or another. Every now and then he would run into someone still doing business the

old way, and Forrest would scream into the telephone, "Goddamn it, this war ain't gonna be won by the numbers. I want
that part this afternoon, and I'm coming over personally to get
it! Now do you read me?"

Missions were still being scheduled and scrubbed almost
daily, and crew morale was falling. The meteorological officers
had to take the brunt of the ill feelings; routinely they would
predict CAVU weather for the next day and then wake up in a
thundershower, or advise Forrest to schedule a mission only to
find that the target sites were shrouded in fog. Forrest fought
and argued and screamed at the meteorologists, and when they
had begun to steer clear of him and file their predictions by
messenger, he took out his wrath on the weather-plane pilots.
"What do you mean you can't make a weather check at five
hundred feet?" he said to a reconnaissance pilot one day. "My
men fly at three hundred feet routinely. How'd you get shit in
the neck in a weather plane?"

The pilot explained that the weather recon missions had always been flown at higher altitudes. "That's because you've
always dealt with high-altitude bombing raids!" Forrest exploded. "Now you're dealing with something else! You get your
ass over that target at five hundred feet and tell me what the
weather is!"

When the telephone rang thirty minutes later and a colonel
of the weather unit began to tell Forrest off for issuing outlandish instructions, the blunt Texan slammed down the phone,
stalked out to the flight line and took off in his personal P-38
for a weather run over the target. "Forget it," he said when he
came back an hour later. "At low altitude the winds are impossible. You couldn't control a box kite over there, let alone a
drone." Thereafter, Forrest made many of Aphrodite's weather
runs over the English Channel, and day after day he would
come back and report that the weather was below minimum.
Because of its complex radio guidance system, the Aphrodite
project still required perfect weather, and imperfect weather

was general over Europe. Television would have eased the visibility problem, but there was hardly any reliable TV equipment to be had.

Stymied in their plans to knock out the German rocket bunkers quickly, the pilots tried to adjust to their austere new surroundings. There was little to do; every crew was restricted to the new air base indefinitely. The British were still around. Since the base was nominally the RAF's, a stiff-upper-lipped lieutenant named Baker remained on the station as a sort of landlord, and the cooks and maintenance personnel were all English. At first there were certain problems with the cuisine. Four British kitchen policemen had been on the premises when Aphrodite suddenly dropped out of the sky and landed on the abandoned base, and they were hard pressed to keep up with the demands of the Americans. The food was routinely flat and insipid, but everyone could see that the cooks were overworked, and some of the pilots tried to work out ways to help. One pilot had a friend in the Ferry Command, and a few exchanges of letters resulted in the delivery of a live turkey fresh from a farm in New Jersey. The cooks boiled it.

The runways had been constructed in the classical overlapping triangle, like a billiards rack, and in between the asphalt strips a local farmer raised wheat and other grains. The farmhouse was just outside the gate, and every now and then a half-wit would come to the fence near the farmhouse and exchange eggs with the airmen for cigarettes and shillings. The pilots thought he was a farmer. For a few weeks the men enjoyed an egg or two apiece for breakfast. One morning the half-wit failed to arrive, and the next day the pilots asked him where he had been. "Oh, I couldn't steal eggs on Tuesday evening," he said blandly. "The sheriff was out riding!" That ended the eggs for breakfast.

The malnutrition problem went on. A pilot came back from a low-altitude training mission with a chicken in his nacelle, and two enlisted men had a roaring fistfight over it, finally tearing the chicken in two bloody pieces and running toward the mess hall with it. One night the farmer stalked through the gates of the base with his special pass and went into the pilot's quarters carrying a dripping and unmistakably deceased pair of chickens. "Yer bloody black dog did this," he said, "and I want satisfaction."

Everyone knew who the bloody black dog was. Captain Loyd "Humpy" Humphries, one of Forrest's aides, had brought the half cocker, half spaniel to Fersfield from the 388th Bomb Group at Knettishall, a few miles away, and now the dog, Missy, was serving Aphrodite as mascot. Humphries was a gentle soul who loved animals, and he had had the dog for a year, but the instant he saw the farmer standing there in his bloodstained overalls, he knew what had to be done. Back on the farm in Arizona, Humphries had seen a few dogs corrupted to the taste of chickens, and the only way to cure a dog like that was to tie a chicken around its neck and let it rot out. But who had the time —or the chickens or the patience—to try something like that on an air base already congested with humans and airplanes? "All right," Humphries said to the farmer, "how much?"

"A quid apiece," the farmer said.

Humphries did a quick computation. A quid was a pound and a pound was $4.05, so he owed the farmer $8.10 for two emaciated, scrawny chickens. The argument went on for five minutes, and the farmer would not budge, so Humphries paid off and took Missy out behind the hangar and shot her with his service .45. Tears were streaming down his face when he finished laying the dog away, and then he saw the surly old farmer strolling down the military road toward the gate carrying the two chickens. The squatly built Humphries rushed to the farmer and said, "Where the hell do you think you're going with my chickens?"

"*Your* chickens?" the farmer said.

"Gimme the chickens or gimme the money!" Humphries stammered through his tears, and the farmer handed over the birds and scurried away.

Not long after, the food problem was solved in two quick strokes. The pilots began taking up a collection among themselves, and they found that the payment of this lagniappe to the harassed cooks worked wonders in helping them learn the American cuisine. Then Roy Forrest made a few phone calls and convinced a colonel in the Quartermaster Corps that the men of Aphrodite were engaged in hazardous duty and therefore were entitled to double rations. From then on, the eating was good. Soon after, the men were put on triple PX rations, which meant practically unlimited supplies of such rarities as cigarettes and cigars and candy, and there were no more complaints about sustenance.

But Fersfield remained something less than a paradise in East Anglia. The Nissen huts where the fliers were quartered were cold and dank, heated only by a single stove in the middle. "Where the hell's the central heating?" Pappy Tooman had called out when they had first arrived.

"The only central heating in England," said RAF Lieutenant Baker, who fancied himself a humorist, "is a Scot standing in front of an open fire with his kilt up!"

Tooman and the others did not see the joke, and they did not particularly like RAF Lieutenant Baker anyway, but the constant squabbling with Fersfield's only representative of His Majesty's Government did nothing to alleviate the chill that permeated every nook of the Nissen huts when the fogs and drizzles of the North Sea came rolling over the base. The only available fuel was a sort of coke-and-peat mixture that was totally misunderstood by the Americans. They expected it to flame up and burn like coal or wood, but it was only intended to glow and release its warmth slowly like the charcoal in a barbecue fire. The ration was one pound of coke per man per night, or roughly about one-tenth of what was required to heat

the Nissen huts by American standards. The pilots tried everything to get some warmth out of the stuff. They soaked it in aviation gasoline before burning it, but the resulting fumes were
more taxing than the cold. They squirted oxygen from their
high-altitude bottles on the coke, but it would only flare
momentarily. Some of the men tore up an old ammunition box
for fuel, and the next day Colonel Forrest was presented with a
bill for 25 pounds from the irate Lieutenant Baker. Forrest
calmly referred the matter to Third Bomb Division Headquarters, which was footing the bills, and forgot about it.

The final living problem was the rats—long, solidly built, be-
whiskered and white-fanged rats that ran about the huts like
freeholders. Twelve men lived in each Nissen, so tightly packed
together that the shelves for their footlockers were cantilevered
over their beds, and every night the rats would gallop up and
down the shelves like horses. Now and then one would tumble
off and land on a pilot's head, and the poor man would jump
up and head for the exit, screaming. Forrest recruited enough
cats to provide one for each Nissen, but they did not make the
slightest impact on the problem. Several men had lost their
tempers and pegged shots at the rats, but each new hole in the
tin side of the huts let in more frigid English air, and the other
pilots laid down a rule against firearms.

The officers' club, normally a place where one could repair to
soak away the troubles of the day, was of small consolation to
the men at Project Aphrodite, Fersfield, Norfolk, England. At
first, there was no ice, and the only palatable drink to the
American taste was a mixture of gin and fruit juice that could
be purchased for a quarter and chugalugged rapidly as though
one were swigging citrate of magnesia. For a while, the situation improved; the club steward, an Englishman, began arriv-
ing nightly with small barrels of crushed ice, and for an hour or
two, before the supply ran out, the pilots could drink in the
style to which they were accustomed. But one night Loyd
Humphries was sitting back to sip an ice-filled bourbon and

water when he noticed a fleck of light coming from the bottom of the glass. He reached in and extracted a fish scale. "Hey, steward," he said, "where the hell did you get this ice?"

"Same place I get it every morning, sir," the Englishman said. "At the fish market!" The men went back to warm drinks and constantly complained.

Not even the chaplain could find it in his heart to criticize the personnel of Aphrodite for their heavy drinking. The chaplain was stationed at an adjacent B-24 base; he was functioning strictly in an ex officio capacity at Fersfield, but he proved to be a man of liberal persuasion, and the pilots were happy to see him settle into an almost nightly routine of visiting the tiny officers' club and cheering up the men. One night a B-24 crashed and burned in the woods just outside the fence at Fersfield, and the chaplain raced into the wreckage to give the last rites to smoking bits of spar and fairing and engines. An hour later he returned, stinking of fire and human flesh, and asked for a double gin and fruit juice, which he swallowed in one gulp. "These are long nights, gentlemen," he said to the assembled pilots. "Long nights."

All were agreed. Every crew was confined strictly to the base, under penalty of court-martial. In the month or so since the first few drones had been fully loaded and the first few crews readied for missions against the enemy, there had been exactly one day when the weather had been CAVU at the base, across the Channel, *and* over the targets—the day a frolicsome navigator had overslept in a tart's bed in London and wiped out the whole mission. Roy Forrest was not having a repetition of that incident. "You fellers can drink your heads off and play cribbage to a fare-thee-well right here on the base," Forrest said, "but nobody is setting foot outside till we get our targets. Is that clear?" It was all too depressingly clear to the air crews.

One evening the door to the officers' club burst open, and a short man in a long raincoat came vibrating into the room, spraying water all around. At Tooman's strident "Ten-hut!"

the crews snapped to; the little man in the raincoat carried three stars on top of his green flying fatigues.

"As you were, gentlemen, as you were," his loud voice rang out, and everybody in the officers' club recognized the world's first-ranking hot pilot, Lieutenant General James H. Doolittle, commanding the Eighth Air Force. "Just dropped in to see how you boys were making out," he said.

To pilots like Fain Pool and Frank Houston, Doolittle's three stars meant nothing; he was still Jimmy Doolittle, the hero of their childhood memories. They could see him in his midget low-wing racer, skidding around the pylons at air shows, setting speed records, winning everything available, including the prestigious Bendix and Thompson trophy races. Then he had capped off a long distinguished career as a pilot by leading the B-25 raid on Tokyo, landing safely in China after handing the Japanese a personal taste of the future. "Yes, sir, General, sir," Fain Pool stammered as Doolittle ordered a drink and plopped down in a chair between Pool and Houston. "Yes, sir, General, sir, it's certainly an honor to have you with us, sir."

"Honor, my ass," Doolittle snapped. "Once in a while I like to have a drink with some real pilots!"

As the evening went on, formalities and neckties and belts loosened, and the dismal status of the Aphrodite program was discussed and bemoaned. Only one pilot took the familiarization process a step too far. "General," he said, "who was your pilot on the Tokyo raid?"

Doolittle reddened. "What did you say?" he said.

"I was just wondering, sir, who was your pilot on the Tokyo raid?"

Doolittle dashed his glass to the cement floor. "Who was my pilot? Why, goddamn it, *I* was my pilot!" Not long after, Doolittle shook hands all around, donned his damp slicker, climbed into his personal P-47 Thunderbolt, and roared off the runway into the sheets of rain. He came back over the field a few minutes later, buzzed the little officers' club and disappeared straight up into the gloom, climbing on his prop. "My good-ness," Pappy Tooman said to the pilot who had committed the social gaffe of the evening, "he certainly do fly nice for a old codger, don't he?"

A captured German, aged 18, had told our interrogators that V-2 is the rocket we have been expecting. The chemical-filled rocket on explosion will destroy by burning an area of (presumably) 25 square kilometers. The V-2s are to be fired at English ports, so our supplies will be destroyed and traffic to the continent disrupted. The prisoner said that V-2 is Germany's last hope of preventing defeat.—Captain Harry C. Butcher, naval aide to General Eisenhower, July 8, 1944*

Work of an unexplained nature, including railway sidings, turntables, buildings and concrete erections, is proceeding in northwest France. At most of these places, construction is going ahead at a considerable pace, particularly in the case of Watten, where great activity is developing.—British intelligence report, July 19, 1944

An organizer in the southwest (of France) reports 17 July the following characteristics of the V-3:

1.	*Wing span*	*36 metres*
2.	*Length*	*28 "*
3.	*Height*	*3 "*
4.	*Weight*	*20 tons*
5.	*Range*	*10,000 kms.*
6.	*Speed*	*700 kms. per hour*
7.	*Altitude*	*stratospheric*
8.	*Charge*	*10 tons high explosive*

---

* Harry C. Butcher, *My Three Years with Eisenhower*, New York (Simon & Shuster, 1946), p. 35.

It has a crew of one who is sacrificed, but it is understood he will have a parachute supplied. The bomb explodes on impact.

This information came from an engineer working in TOULOUSE. States he has a chance of sabotaging the prototypes. The organizer has sent 2 of his best men to TOULOUSE to do this, and hopes to be able to get the plans.—Message to British Air Ministry from acting chief of staff, U.S. military intelligence, July 20, 1944

TOP SECRET. PERFORMANCE OF THE LARGE GERMAN ROCKET IN TEST SHOOTING IN POLAND IS GOOD ENOUGH TO JUSTIFY ITS IMMEDIATE USE AGAINST LARGE OBJECTIVES IN ENGLAND. INTELLIGENCE SOURCES INDICATE THE MOVEMENT OF OBJECTS THAT MIGHT BE THESE PROJECTILES TO THE LAUNCHING REGIONS IN FRANCE. ASIDE FROM THE GRAVE THREAT TO LONDON, THIS WEAPON DIRECTLY THREATENS OUR WAR EFFORT, SINCE IT MAY BE USED TO DESTROY COMMUNICATIONS AND PORT FACILITIES ON BOTH SIDES OF THE CHANNEL. . . .—Spaatz to Arnold, July 22, 1944

A million people should be evacuated from London as quickly as possible.—Proposal by British Home Secretary Herbert Morrison to the British War Cabinet, July 27, 1944

Based on the best information available to this headquarters, it is considered entirely within the realm of possibility that the Germans may soon employ long range rockets in desultory bombing attacks against this country, particularly the London area. It is recommended that all personnel and activities whose operation in this area are not vitally essential be moved to some other location as expeditiously as possible.—Message from Brigadier General Pleas B. Rogers, commander Communications Zone, U.S. Army, European theater of operations, to Spaatz, July 28, 1944

Roy Forrest was not a person who became aggravated easily, but one night early in August he confided to his friend Loyd

Humphries, "I swear and be damned, Humpy, if we have to abort one more of these missions, I'm gonna check myself into a flakhouse for a few weeks."

No one had to tell Forrest what the jump crews were going through. He could see it in their eyes and their mannerisms, and he had his own vivid memories of steeling himself to fly a tough mission and having it scrubbed on the runway three or four times in a row. Lieutenant Frank Houston and his auto-pilot expert, Staff Sergeant Willard Smith, had revved up their drone B-17 six times for the mission, Fain Pool and Staff Sergeant Philip Enterline six times, Lieutenant Joe Andrecheck and Sergeant Raymond Healy five times, and the others three or four times each. Somehow Houston and Andrecheck and Pool had managed to hang onto their good humor, but a few of the others had become visibly tense. Jump pilot Lieutenant John Fisher was flying "nervous," shooting ragged landings and behaving erratically. Jump pilot John Sollars had come into the group as a friendly, outgoing sort of a person, like Andrecheck, and now he was getting into arguments and snapping back at his former friends. Jump pilot Cornelius Engel, who had always had a reputation for devastating honesty, was being more devastatingly honest than ever. Forrest had to take it from both ends. The pilots of Aphrodite, with whom he identified easily, were reaching the ragged edge and complaining about everything, and Forrest knew that there was such a thing as sending a man to the well too often. And the brass hats at headquarters, whom Forrest considered necessary evils, were on the phone at least twice a day demanding to know why no missions had been flown.

"How long are you gonna take this horseshit from the pilots?" an aide asked Forrest one day.

Forrest shrugged. "Well, how long you gonna take it from the brass?" the aide asked.

"That, my friend, is another matter," Forrest said. "If those guys don't get off my ass very quickly, I'm gonna tell them where to stuff the Aphrodite program and go home and see my new baby."

Forrest knew that deep in their minds, the desk pilots at Third Bomb Division Headquarters and Eighth Air Force Headquarters and Strategic Air Forces Headquarters and Supreme Allied Headquarters all knew that the Aphrodite delay was due to the weather, but he also knew that certain psychological laws prevailed in the military. If a commanding officer was associated with lack of progress for a long enough time, he became stigmatized, no matter what the reasons for the lack of progress. Roy Forrest had had a very successful and valorous war, and he was getting as bored as the men under his command with this perpetual waiting and peering at the sky for the perfect weather required for the complex Aphrodite mission. He had been highly involved in the fighting when the Allies had been losing the war and again when they had begun to pull even. But now that they were winning decisively, he was sitting on the sidelines. Tinian and Guam were about to fall, B-29 Superfortresses were leveling Japan's manufacturing industries, Allied armored troops were pushing into Avranches and Brest and threatening the entire German rocket coast, and Forrest's old buddies at the 388th were visiting daily punishment on the Germans and encountering only light flak in return. Forrest wanted a piece of the action, but instead he found himself mired at Fersfield. To make matters worse, a haughty detachment of Navy radio-control specialists had arrived almost simultaneously with a similar detachment from the Army Air Corps, to the complete and total amazement of the commanding officer, who had been led to believe that nothing was known about Aphrodite outside England.

Neither of the new groups got along with the other, and both abhorred the ragtag double azon crews working under Major Rand. Soon Forrest found himself having to iron out internecine squabbles and play peacemaker like a Cub Scout den mother. The task did not come naturally to him. At first, he found it hard to understand what all the shouting was about. "I'll put it to you straight and simple," said a captain of the new Army radio-control group in the officers' club one night. "We've been working on the remote radio control of aircraft at Wright Field for five or six years. We know exactly what we're doing. We've put on some spectacular exhibitions for the top brass and the Secretary of War. So what happens the first time there's a chance to put radio control to good use in a combat situation? You go out and get yourself a half-ass system of bomb guidance, a system that hasn't even been working well in bombs, and before we know what you're up to, you're using it to steer around B-17 drones full of explosives. We know exactly how to handle a problem like that, and your guys here don't have the slightest idea! If this wasn't the Army, I'd say that everybody had gone nuts!"

The Navy attitude was similar. Navy experience with robot airplanes was even longer and more extensive than the Army's. One night a Navy radio controller told Forrest, "You show me the crossroads you want me to hit with a robot plane, and I'll not only hit the crossroads but I'll hit whatever *corner* of the crossroads you specify. And I'll do it ten times out of ten. And I've been doing it for three years!" Forrest liked the pride and confidence of these new additions to the Aphrodite project, but he knew that the program was solidly committed to the relatively new double azon system of guidance for the time being. The Army and Navy specialists would have to wait their turn, despite their superior experience, and anyway the point was moot so long as the rains continued to fall.

One day Forrest was sitting in his tiny office reading about the latest Allied successes and biting his nails and listening to the nerve-racking spatter on the corrugated roof, when the telephone rang and he recognized the voice of an unpleasant shrimp of a colonel from headquarters. "Goddamn it, Forrest," the grating voice was saying almost before the Texan could say hello, "what the hell are you guys doing over there? Don't you know there's a war on?"

Forrest exploded. He had never liked this particular colonel in the first place. "Sir," he snapped into the telephone, "do you know how to piss up a rainspout?" Without waiting for an answer, he plunged ahead. "Well, when you learn how to piss up a rainspout, come over here and show us how to turn off the weather. Then we'll be glad to fly those missions." He slammed down the phone and stomped out to the flight line.

Ten B-17's, fully loaded with nitrostarch and jell gas, were distributed about on hardstands, some of them so far away as to be mere outlines in the rain. A cluster of mother ships, B-17 Flying Fortresses and B-24 Liberators, loomed black and squat in silhouette outside the hangars. Inside the officers' club, four or five jump pilots were playing their incessant game of red dog. Pappy Tooman was beating another member of his crew into financial submission with a deck of cards and a cribbage board. A bombardier was cleaning his dress pinks with aviation gasoline, strictly forbidden by both British and American regulations, but Forrest understood and said nothing.

He wandered over to the shops, where the cigar-chomping Major James Rand and his electronic experts were trying to win the war with soldering irons and galvanometers. "Here's the answer to our problem, Colonel," said Rand. "Do you realize what we could do if we could just equip these drones with television?"

Forrest realized, but he said, "No."

"We can lick the weather!" Rand said. "If we can get visibility for the drone on the deck, it doesn't make any difference what kind of weather the mother ship's in. With a television camera mounted in the nose of the baby and the receiver in the mother, we can fly against *any* target! The controller just watches his screen, and he can see every place the drone goes."

"What's holding us back?" Forrest asked.

"Come here," Rand said. He led Forrest to the corner of the shop, where technicians fiddled with a box with a screen about seven inches square. Now and then some vague ripplings would appear on the green phosphorescent face of the box. "That's it?" Forrest said.

"That's television," Rand said, "being transmitted from a half mile away. Isn't that some picture?" The pattern had come on bright and vivid, but before Forrest could comment, it had flickered off again.

"How many drones can you equip with television in a week or so?" Forrest asked.

"The way parts are coming in, and the way parts are burning out, I wouldn't count on more than one," Rand said. "We're doing the best we can."

"I know you are, Major," Forrest said, clapping the weary-looking bespectacled inventor on the back. "We all are. Everybody doesn't think so, but we are."

Back outside, Forrest checked the tie-down ropes on one of the wet and gleaming mother ships. There was a sentry on each aircraft, but they all knew the lanky Texan on sight, and as each one jerked his rifle into the salute position, Forrest would say, "Be at ease, soldier, your Army days are over."

Some of the guards would laugh sheepishly, but Forrest was halfway serious. Here at Fersfield he was satisfying an obsession that had been with him since his early days in the aviation cadets. He had always wanted to run his own army, and now he was doing it. "In my army," he had once told Loyd Humphries when they were back at the 388th, "the first guy that salutes I'm gonna put him up against a wall and shoot him." At Fersfield, Forrest compromised by permitting saluting but discouraging it whenever possible. There was only one Army tradition he could not seem to upset. Bombing missions, even supersophisticated bombing missions with radio control and television and automatic radio altimeters, could not fly in pea-soup weather.

Back at his office, Forrest picked up a message from Eighth

Air Force Headquarters. It said that four Aphrodite drones would be launched at enemy targets the next day, August 4. "Ha, ha," Forrest said to the ops officer. "Another mission's laid on."

The ops captain looked up and yawned. "What are they going to do about the weather?"

"I don't know," Forrest said. "Maybe some little colonel has learned how to piss up a rainspout."

That night a big poker game cut across all social lines. It was as though everyone knew that so long as a dangerous mission lay somewhere ahead of them, money or the lack of it and social customs or the lack of them had no final meaning. Officers played; enlisted men sat in, British cooks played for a while, and even the commanding officer won a few pots. Staff Sergeant Willard Smith was kibitzing the game in the mess hall, and as usual his attention was half on the reality in front of him and half on the philosophical and psychological questions that continually obsessed him. There was one in every outfit: a thinker. Willard Smith, with his innocent-looking round face and his stubby arms and soft, husky voice, appeared to be an unlikely candidate, but in his footlocker were odd items like a slide rule and a typewriter and some of the works of Nietzsche, Schopenhauer, and Plato. All that had kept this highly intelligent individual from becoming an officer himself were poor vision and the Army's chronic inability to tell a bright soldier from a loud soldier.

Smith departed from his kibitzing post when he saw a paratrooper officer enter the room. He had wanted to have a private discussion with the officer for several days, ever since certain disturbing thoughts had entered his mind and he had checked some of them out on his slide rule only to find that the figures made the thoughts even more disturbing. "Excuse me, Lieutenant," Smith said. "Do you have any idea how fast C-47's are going when paratroopers jump out?"

"Maybe eighty-five or ninety," the young paratrooper said. "Why?"

"No disrespect, Lieutenant," Smith said, "but I can't figure how your career in the paratroops prepared you to teach us how to do what we're gonna have to do."

"What do you mean?"

"If I figure correctly, we'll be bailing out at something between one hundred and seventy and two hundred miles an hour, and not out of the broad side of a C-47 either, but out of a little tiny navigator's hatch just behind one of the engines."

The lieutenant made placating noises, but Smith went on. "Now terminal velocity's about one hundred and twenty or one hundred and thirty miles an hour, right? And it takes about ten seconds to slow down to terminal velocity, right?"

The paratrooper said, "More or less."

"But we'll never have a chance to slow down!" Smith said. "We'll be jumping from too low an altitude. Can you imagine the jolt when the chute opens?"

"Sergeant, since you've already figured it out for yourself, I'll tell you something frankly," the paratroop officer said. "They say you guys are all gonna be in for the DFC. Well, anybody who knows anything about parachuting can tell you you'll earn it. You want to know about the jolt? Well, imagine yourself running down a road full speed, and here comes a Mack truck straight at you doing forty miles an hour, and *you jump into the radiator.* That's how it's gonna feel."

Smith thanked the officer for his honesty and wandered off to another part of the big room where his pilot, Frank "Sam" Houston, and several other jump pilots were engaged in deep conversation. "Let me tell you what I just found out from the paratrooper," Smith told Houston.

"Don't tell me," Houston whispered. "Let me stay ignorant."

"He said we might bounce a few times on landing."

"Now, damn it, Sergeant," Houston said jovially, "sit down here and have a drink and knock off that bad talk!"

Smith sat and listened as the jump pilots—Houston and Pool and Andrecheck and several others—talked and drank and talked some more. Fragments stuck in his memory.

"Hey, what do you think of those kamikazes?"

"Crazy. Raving lunatics."

"Anybody would fly a plane into a target—"

There was a silence. Everybody looked at everybody else, and suddenly the whole group broke into a laugh. "We're not that different from the kamikazes, are we?" Frank Houston said, and somebody else said, "Who the hell are *we* to call *them* nuts?"

Later somebody said, "Suppose you get out there in the robot and the mother ship can't get control. You try and you try, and she can't establish any control over you at all. What do you do?"

"I'd fly the son of a bitch into the target myself," said a pilot who was feeling no pain.

"You'd kamikaze it in?" someone else said.

"I certainly would," the contented pilot said, "but only if I was drunk, like now."

Everybody laughed again, and Willard Smith took his leave and headed back to the enlisted men's quarters under a crystalline sky full of stars. As he walked, he felt a certain relief that the jump pilots seemed to lack the pathological dedication of the Japanese kamikaze pilots. Willard Smith, the resident thinker of the Aphrodite project, did not consider such dedication a healthy attitude, and it would have made him nervous to have thrown in his lot with men who confused patriotism with mental illness. "A man's first instinct is to survive," Smith told himself as he walked in the cool night, "and when he defeats that first basic instinct of survival, then there has to be a screw loose somewhere." What was it Freud had said on the subject? Smith could not remember. He would look it up in the morning.

When he reached the enlisted men's huts far down at the other end of the air base from the mess hall, he glanced at the bulletin board. A mission was scheduled to take off the next afternoon, and the four jump crews were listed as Lieutenant Fain Pool and Staff Sergeant Philip Enterline, Lieutenant John Fisher and Technical Sergeant Elmer Most, Lieutenant Joseph Andrecheck and Sergeant Raymond Healy, and Lieutenant Cornelius Engel and Technical Sergeant Clifford Parsons. The first standby crew would be Frank Houston and Staff Sergeant Willard Smith. The pensive autopilot expert walked to the blackout curtain and took another peek at the sky. It was still clear. He went to bed with the feeling that the weather would hold this time, and he was just as happy that he and Houston would remain in the wings for the mission. He wanted some more time to think about Mack trucks and the science of physics and certain relationships between the two. Tomorrow four pilots and four sergeants would make the first practical test of the paratrooper's dire prediction; Staff Sergeant Willard Smith was very pleased to be included out.

At dawn on August 4, Roy Forrest's private army shook itself into wakefulness and peered into a sunrise totally uncontaminated by the slightest refractive distortion from cloud or fog or haze. The day was like the night, flawless, and certain of the more cynical crew members began to admit that there was a slight possibility the project was going to get off the ground at last. As though to dispel any semblance of doubt, Generals Doolittle and Partridge arrived in their personal fighter planes just after breakfast. They wanted to sit in on the briefings, which would last almost all morning. Four mother ship crews had to be briefed, and for purposes of security each briefing was separate from the others. Target names were encoded, and the navigational maps that were issued to each mother ship crew bore place-names that were different from the names on the maps of the others.

By now the crews needed no further physical briefings on the targets. Mock-ups of each rocket site lay on Ping-pong tables

wherever one turned, and each mother crew had all but memorized the movies shot from reconnaissance aircraft making low-
level passes at the sites. Over and over the crews had studied the
recognition points around the countryside, analyzed the areas
of greatest vulnerability in the patches of concrete bunker,
memorized altitudes and headings and the exact location of flak
corridors—anything that could affect the flight of the drone.
The crew attacking Mimoyecques would have the most taxing
job. The Germans had built most of the site underground, and
only once each day did the great steel doors of the main building swing open. During that brief thirty-minute period, the
men of Project Aphrodite planned to stuff a planeload of explosives down its gullet. The attack had to come from precisely the
west-northwest, and if it deviated by so little as 10 feet, the
whole load of nitrostarch would explode harmlessly against the
earth.

There was nothing especially inspiring about the briefings;
all the crews had been through them before. The only difference on the morning of August 4 was an attitude of assurance
by the senior officers, as though the science of weather forecasting had suddenly reached maturity and could be depended on
with certitude. As the morning wore on and the sun rose higher
and higher, the sky remained unmarred by even the slightest
blemish of cloud. Crews bustled in and out of the briefing
room, on the first level of the control tower, and the pace of the
preflighting activity increased in every corner of the field,
where the fully loaded drones were hidden under camouflage
nets. Major Henry James Rand, who was to control drones into
targets at Wizernes and Siracourt, paid a visit to his mother
ship along with pilot Foster Falkenstine, and when the two
men climbed into the bombardier's bubble in the front of the
B-17, Falkenstine rapped on the bulkhead and said, "Major, we
don't have any armor plate. That tinny sound you hear is all
that's between you and the enemy flak."

"I'll be damned," Rand said, and scurried away to call a gen-

eral at a nearby headquarters base and bawl him out for not
providing the most rudimentary protection for his men.

"He chewed out that general as though he was some flunky
in a shop," Falkenstine told his crew later in the morning. "He
actually told him to blow it out his barracks bag! That's how
come they rushed that armor plate over here so quick."

Other aspects of the mission were better planned, under
the direction of Partridge and Doolittle. A diversionary force of
250 RAF bombers was to bomb targets north of Paris just before the 3 P.M. zero hour for Aphrodite, sixteen P-38's were to
fly cover for the mother ships, and there were to be observation
B-17's and navigational B-17's and covers of fighter planes for
each. Four P-38 photo ships were to take movie and still pictures, two Mosquitoes would photograph the critical exits of
each jumper from his drone, and two squadrons of Spitfires
were to hover above the air armada like protective umbrellas.
Out over the Channel, other Spitfires were on patrol, and
launches of the Royal Navy were on station, to pick up jumpers
who might overshoot the coastline. Flak batteries had been
alerted to the mission, but since the British antiaircraft artillery
was notoriously trigger-happy, jump pilots were briefed to get
out of their planes at the first sign of friendly fire. Mother pilots
were instructed to take any arrant drones out to the North Sea
and dump them, and if no control could be established, they
were to call in the fighters to shoot the drones down. The ultimate irony would have been for one of the robots to refuse to
accept control and turn around and crash on England. In their
worst nightmares, the Aphrodite planners saw a robot de-
stroying Ipswich or Norwich or even flying the 100-odd miles to
London. The possibility was remote, but real, and every possible precaution had to be taken against it.

First Lieutenant Fain Pool walked across the tarmac with his
autopilot expert, twenty-three-year-old Staff Sergeant Philip En-

terline of Kittanning, Pennsylvania. "Well, here we go again, eh?" Pool said. " 'Hurry up and wait.' "

"Yeah," Pool said. "Say, what'd you have for breakfast?"

"Everything except eggs Benedict," Enterline answered.

"So'd we," Pool said, and laughed grimly. "The condemned men ate a hearty meal."

A jeep took the No. 1 drone crew to a far corner of the field, where several mechanics were making last-minute checks. Pool and Enterline walked around the loaded robot several times, preflighting it. Everything seemed to be in order. The only hitch came when Enterline donned his seat-pack parachute. "Damned thing's too big," he said. "I can't figure it out. I've been trying it on and adjusting it every day for a month, and it's always fit me perfectly."

"Maybe somebody else switched with you by mistake," Pool said. Enterline remembered that his bunkmate was Technical Sergeant Elmer Most, who was well over six feet tall and also scheduled to fly today.

"That must be it," Enterline said. Pool helped him to cinch up the straps until the seat-pack chute approximated a fit. There remained chest packs to be donned, but that was almost a final step, just before dropping through the navigator's hatch into the slipstream.

"Everything's in order, sir," a crew chief reported. "We'll be leaving you now." Pool and Enterline noticed that the ground crewmen wasted no time in hopping into their jeep and driving away toward the shop area. "They don't want to be around when we give her the juice," Pool said.

"Neither do we," Enterline said.

"Hey, look at that!" Pool said. A bank of low clouds was beginning to materialize on the western horizon.

"Damn!" Enterline said. "We'll be scrubbed again, sure as hell."

"I don't believe it," Pool said. "C'mon, let's go."

Several days had gone by since the two fliers had been inside their aircraft, and now they noticed that certain changes had been made. The boxed nitrostarch was piled all the way to the top of every bulkhead, giving the aircraft an unnaturally high center of gravity. "I don't like that," Enterline said.

"Well, I'll tell you something I've learned, Sergeant," Pool said in his most serious manner. "They've got the finest technicians and scientists in the world behind this project, and it's the number one priority in the theater, and I just can't believe that they haven't thought of everything. If that nitrostarch is piled high, it's for a reason."

The explosives filled every available inch of the big B-17. The entrance door on the side had been bolted shut and boxes of nitrostarch bound to the longerons. The radio room was a solid fused mass of boxes, and half the pilot's compartment was loaded as well. The two crewmen found themselves operating in an abnormally cramped area. They had had to wriggle up into the aircraft through the navigator's escape hatch in the belly, a hole that measured only about 2 by 2½ feet, ease their way past boxes of nitrostarch heaped up in the forward compartment, and finally haul themselves into a cabin from which the co-pilot's seat had been removed to make room for still more explosives. Every place they looked they were surrounded by nitrostarch, and when they moved about, they had to be careful. Wires were everywhere; some of them would carry electricity, but others were primacord, the explosive material designed to blow up simultaneously along its entire length and thus cause all nine tons of nitrostarch aboard to go off at once.

When the two men had finished preflighting the controls and found them in order, Pool threw the switches and listened for the familiar whine of the inverters, normally located under the seats. To his surprise, he smelled ozone and saw that the inverter across the way had been exposed by the removal of the co-pilot's seat. Now it was showering sparks on a nearby box of nitrostarch wrapped in primacord. "Sergeant!" Pool shouted. "How stable is that stuff?"

"I haven't the slightest idea," Enterline said. "But remember what you said: They've thought of everything."

"Well, I don't like that goddamn box so close to the inverter," Pool said. "If one of those sparks takes hold—"

"Don't think about it," Enterline said. "We've got enough to do."

Through the windshield, both men could see that they were now totally alone. The ground crew's jeep was a dot near the hangars, almost a mile away. Here and there along the taxiway, ant-sized knots of personnel could be seen, but as Pool eased the 32 tons of B-17 into taxiing motion, he noticed that the groups dispersed, and now and then a head would pop up from behind one of the slit trenches that had been dug along the way for air-raid protection.

"They certainly show a lot of faith in our scientists," Enterline said. "There isn't a human being in sight for at least a mile. Well, let's get up to the flight line. I don't want to open the chocolate till the last minute."

Opening the chocolate had been the only pleasant part of the earlier scrubbings. At the briefings, each jump crewman was handed an escape kit, and each escape kit contained a chocolate bar. Waiting at the end of the runway, the men would gobble up their chocolate bars and then feign innocence when the mission was scrubbed and the chocolate discovered missing.

"You won't be opening any chocolate bars today," Pool said, as he worked to keep the outboard props turning just fast enough to maintain the speed of a man talking. "I've got a feeling."

"I've got a feeling, too," Enterline said. "We're gonna get another rain check." Pool pushed the throttles slightly forward, and a thunk-thunk noise began to emanate from the undercarriage, and the stacked boxes of explosives started quivering.

"What's that?" Enterline said from his kneeling position alongside the pilot.

"She's been sitting on that hardstand fully loaded, and the tires have flat spots," Pool said calmly as he throttled back once again. Now the plane was rolling more smoothly except for an occasional hole in the taxiway, and soon the mammoth flying bomb had reached a point just off the end of the runway. Pool slammed the power to the No. 4 engine and turned the aircraft into the wind and locked the parking brakes for the final engine checks. He ran up each engine in turn and then throttled each back to 1,000 rpm, and when all the checks were completed, there was nothing to do but wait for the exact takeoff time. "Now listen, Phil," Pool said, "you've got only one thing to do on takeoff, but it's important."

"Yeah, I know," Enterline said. "When we reach sixty, give us a quarter flaps. Right?"

"Right," Pool said, "and just in case you should forget, let me take this opportunity to say good-bye. We'll never get off without flaps, so it's up to you."

"I'm not worried," Enterline said. "Besides, it's just about time to abort. I can taste that chocolate already."

But the order to abort the mission still did not come, and the two comrades were hit at the same time with the chilling realization that they were about to fly the largest airborne load of explosives ever assembled by man. "Do you get that same feeling?" Enterline said, and held out his sweaty hands for Pool to see.

"Yeah," Pool said. "We're going." His voice trembled slightly, and to cover his embarrassment, he looked at his watch. It was 1:40 P.M., British double standard time. Takeoff was scheduled for 1:45, and Lieutenant John Fisher and Technical Sergeant Elmer Most were to follow in the second drone five minutes later. The seconds ticked away. Suddenly a high, screaming noise blasted right through the sounds of the idling engines, and the last few visible ground personnel dashed for the sidelines and dived into slit trenches.

"My God," Enterline said, "what was that?"

"The air-raid siren," Pool said. "It was for us." He asked the tower for a time check, and with the same precision that had characterized his career as a formation pilot, he began a countdown to takeoff. Exactly on zero, he shoved all four throttles forward, and the aging, war-weary No. 342 jerked into motion. Enterline gripped the sides of Pool's seat to keep from being thrown, but now the plane was rolling smoothly and evenly, slowly gathering momentum, headed for the far end of the runway. Almost imperceptibly the old B-17 gained speed, but Pool felt his heart start to pound as he realized that this first of all takeoffs in the Aphrodite was not going as planned. At the point on the runway where Pool had lifted many unloaded Aphrodite drones into the air, the weary plane was still rolling tail down. At the point where he had expected to become airborne, the tail wheel had barely lifted, and now they were rushing toward the scrub woods ahead. "Goddamn!" Pool said in mingled rage and fright and frustration. When he could distinctly make out the rows of vegetables growing at the end of the runway, he jerked back sharply on the control column. The robot airplane shuddered once, parted itself from the runway, mushed a few feet downward and then began a slow, ungainly ascent that barely took it above the young pines in the surrounding forest.

"Thank God!" Pool said when he realized they were free of the earth. He turned and saw Enterline clutching at his handholds, his knuckles white and his face drenched in beads of sweat. "We're okay," Pool said, smacking his temporary co-pilot on the arm. "We're airborne!"

Enterline seemed to take in a great quantity of air and then expelled it all at once in a massive statement of relief. "Lieutenant," he said, "I'm sorry I put you through that."

"Put me through what?" Pool asked.

"I forgot to lower the flaps," Enterline said. He waited for the explosion. He deserved it. He had one task to remember, and he had forgotten it, and he had almost killed them both.

But Pool did not explode. "We're up now," the quiet Oklahoman said. "Anyway, it's just as much my fault. I'm supposed to remind you."

"What a couple of sad sacks!" Enterline said.

"Yeah," said Pool, "but we're alive."

The two admitted sad sacks set about their varied duties. Merely to keep the unbalanced B-17 flying straight and level was a task that the Air Corps would have normally assigned to two experienced pilots. Now Pool was busy accomplishing the task single-handedly, and to his surprise he found few problems. He had the presence of mind not to attempt any sharp turns, and when he came to each of his checkpoints—Orford Ness, Southwold, Eye—he skidded the plane around in flat rudder turns that did not cause the wings to bank sharply. The chances were good that the plane could handle a steep bank—Pool had flown equally heavily loaded B-17's, although with the load concentrated in the bomb bay—but he was playing it safe. He knew that a stall or a spin in this robot aircraft would be irreversible.

As soon as he established total control over the cruising B-17, he flipped a switch and told Pappy Tooman in the mother ship, 19,000 feet above, that he was beginning his checks. He was at 2,000 feet now; the drill called for Enterline to check the radio altimeter called Ace and the autopilot. Enterline set the automatic altitude device at 1,800 and asked Pool to put the plane into a glide. The old B-17 dropped quickly to 1,800 feet and kept right on dropping. "What's the matter?" Pool shouted.

"I don't know," Enterline said. "The Ace is supposed to get a bounce-back signal from the earth and read the altitude and hold us there, but I don't think we're getting the bounce back. Let's try a little lower."

At 1,600 and 1,400 feet, the Ace altimeter still would not hold the aircraft, and Pool had to drop all the way down to 1,200 before the device would feed an up signal to the elevators and cause the plane to level off. "Okay," Enterline said. "She's working. Now I'll set it for three hundred feet." That was the predetermined altitude at which the old airplane would fly across the Channel on radio control, after the two crewmen had parachuted to safety. "Better hurry up," Pool said. "We're halfway around the checking course already." But Enterline, confronting the knobs and dials of the autopilot in the crawl space underneath, was having more trouble. Three gyroscopes controlled the aircraft on three axes—roll, pitch, and azimuth —and each axis had its own pair of warning lights. Ordinarily the pilot put the plane on a precisely straight-and-level course, the lights went out to confirm the level flight, and each axis was "set up" precisely on the center point. Pool was flying his customary exact course, and Enterline had set up the roll and azimuth axes without trouble, but no matter what he did, the "up" warning light on the pitch axis remained on. Often this signaled nothing more ominous than a defective warning system, but Enterline could take no chances. If the light remained on and the autopilot were clutched in, it might put the aircraft in an immediate climb. The plane would stall quickly and spiral into the ground with its heavy load. "What's going on?" Pool called down.

"I can't get rid of the up light," Enterline shouted.

"Well, we haven't got much more time," Pool called. "We've passed Southwold and Eye, and we're almost over Stowmarket. After that it's Woodbridge, and we jump there!"

"I know it," the harassed Enterline said. "But I just can't get rid of this damned light."

At exactly two minutes after three, seventy-seven minutes after take off, the drone with its troubled crew passed over the town of Stowmarket. Seven minutes ahead lay Woodbridge, where Pool and Enterline were to jump, and a few minutes beyond that the southeast coast of England. "We're almost out of time," Pool shouted.

Enterline fidgeted with the potentiometers on the pitch axis, but the warning light would not even flicker. He toyed with the idea of assuming that the light was lying and clutching it in anyway, but if the autopilot were receiving a genuine "up" impulse, as the light indicated, the result would be catastrophic.

"I just can't balance the circuit!" Enterline shouted.

"Woodbridge is dead ahead," Pool called down. "Get ready to jump!"

Enterline took a final look at the irritatingly steady light on the autopilot, shrugged his shoulders, and began to struggle into his chest pack. He knew that the mother ship had no chance whatever of controlling the drone into a target without pitch control, but he had done everything he could. He remembered certain similar incidents in training, and almost always it had turned out to be a burned-out tube or a short circuit or some minor malfunction. But there was no time now for a complete check of the autopilot, and there was no way to take the war-weary bomber back to earth. The mother ship crew had strict orders to carry out the mission or dump the old B-17 in the channel. No one at Fersfield wanted to lay eyes on No. 342 again. Enterline wondered what would happen at the target. The Ace altimeter seemed to be working, and it would hold the aircraft at a steady 300 feet, but the mother ship would not be able to make the drone descend or dump. The mission, therefore, was predestined to fail.

"Get ready to jump!" Pool was shouting again. "You'll be landing right near Woodbridge, and we've still got fifteen hundred feet, you lucky bastard!"

"They'll never be able to dive this thing!" Enterline called from the hatchway.

"Get out of here!" Pool hollered. "I can see the coast!"

Enterline took off his glasses and put them in the breast

pocket of his jump suit. He connected the snap of his seat pack to the static line, balanced himself over the narrow, open navigator's hatch, and shoved himself outward into space.

As he left the aircraft, his head bumped lightly against the hatch, but he remained conscious as a blast of air grabbed at his body. Through myopic eyes he saw the earth and the sky and the earth and the sky in rapid alternation, and then there was a sharp jerk and he thought his legs were going to be sliced in two across the thighs. He looked up and saw a white parachute flapping over his head, and he could feel the G forces of deceleration shoving the blood down toward his feet. He could tell that he was in a wide pendulous swing, covering hundreds of feet at a time, and he grabbed at the risers to spill air and cut down on the motion, but his parachute training had been limited, and he did not know how to control the swing. He stopped pulling at the risers; his fingertips were bloody and sore, and he realized that he must have instinctively grabbed at the sharp metal lip of the nagivator's hatch as he plummeted through. With fumbling fingers, he reached in his pocket and put on his glasses.

Now the ground was coming up quickly. At about 500 feet he saw a woman bicycling on a country road. He shouted, "Hey, look!" The woman turned her head and pedaled faster. About 100 yards away on the other side of a road, a platoon of workers hacked away at a field, and Enterline knew that they had all been taught to report German parachuters and even take them prisoner. Quickly the farmworkers passed out of his sight as he began another giant upswing, and just as he reached the top of the rise, he heard twigs breaking and realized he was falling through a tree. He covered his eyes and pressed his paratrooper's boots together and waited for the impact, and a split second later he slipped to the ground as gently as a soap bubble. His first impulse was to emit a mighty shout of joy. For him, Project Aphrodite was over. The high-speed parachute jump was a snap. But then he realized that his life had been

APHRODITE: DESPERATE MISSION   106

saved by sheer luck. His landing in the small tree had coincided exactly with the apex of the up cycle of his swing. If he had hit the ground at the maximum point of the down cycle, his body would have been broken in half.

The thought sobered the young staff sergeant. He slashed himself free from the risers of the chute that now hung limp and lifeless in the tree above him, and he set off toward the place where he thought he had seen the road. He walked for about 100 yards and stopped. Seven or eight young women in the drab apparel of the Women's Land Army were marching at him, pitchforks and hoes at the ready. "Hey!" Enterline called across the field. "I just jumped out of an airplane!" The women raised their implements and kept on coming.

Back in No. 342, Fain Pool's hour had arrived. He was supposed to put the airplane in a shallow dive and turn it over to the mother ship, then arm the firing system and bail out. Theoretically, the aircraft would continue in its shallow dive until it reached 300 feet, where the automatic radio altimeter would take hold, and Tooman and his crew in the mother ship would utilize the primitive double azon controls to steer the plane to the target and dive it in. Pool was aware that Enterline had been having a difficult time with the autopilot, but he had his own jobs to do, and he was not positive what had gone wrong. Now he had several ticklish assignments to carry out before he could bail out himself, and he went briskly to work. He flicked the servo switch to "on" and turned the autopilot to "remote." He looked at the barometric altimeter; it showed 1,200 feet. He was supposed to be at 1,800 for these crucial operations, but with the coast of England coming up sharply, there was no time to regain the altitude lost in setting up the defective Ace altimeter. The plane was flying level and showing 34 inches of manifold pressure. The indicated airspeed was 175, but Pool knew it would increase in the glide before he could make his way out the escape hatch. He called Tooman in the mother ship and reported in voice code that he was getting out. "Watch that first step!" Tooman replied. "It's a son of a bitch!" Pool throttled the engines back to 32 inches, pulled off his headphones and throat microphone, put the aircraft into a gentle, downward angle, and set a safety clock on the control panel for "10 minutes." Then he climbed out of the pilot's seat and dropped into the well leading down to the nose and the navigator's hatch. Wherever he looked as he crawled through the well, there were explosives, primacord, and electrical wire, and he carefully avoided bumping into anything. Just alongside the navigator's escape hatch, he grabbed a lanyard connected to fourteen cables going back to the fuses of the various clumps of nitrostarch in the aircraft. When he pulled the cables out, each grouping of explosives would be armed, ready to explode on any high-G impact. Pool tugged at the lanyard, but nothing happened. He yanked again, but the cables held. Then he braced his boots against the bulkhead and pulled with every ounce of his strength, and the cables came loose and deposited him, sprawling, on the catwalk. He scrambled to his knees; he could tell that the plane was gaining speed and losing altitude, and he had to work fast if he were to get out safely.

Now that the load was armed manually, it had to be armed electrically. Rand and the other scientists had designed the system with built-in redundance. One system would detonate the load if the other failed. Pool checked a pair of short-circuit warning lights, saw that they were off, and plugged in the jacks that would cause the electrical fuses to arm as soon as the safety clock went off on the control panel. Sitting in the crawlway next to the exit hole, he wriggled into his safety chest pack, tightened all straps, clipped the back pack to the static line, and swung his feet out into the slipstream. He could hear the No. 2 propeller whirling away a few feet from his legs, and he decided to thrust himself out of the hole sharply to avoid the slashing steel. He gripped the sides of the exit with his hands and lifted his body directly over open space and propelled himself down-

ward with all his strength. His forehead ticked against something as he went out of the airplane, but he felt no discomfort
until a second or so later when the chute opened and his legs
flashed with pain and then went dead all over. Pool looked
down, saw to his surprise that his legs were intact, and also saw
that he was only 500 or so feet above the ground. Despite the
parachute, he could tell that he was in rapid motion, both forward and downward. He knew that he was supposed to deceler-
ate sharply, but now he saw that he was tracking perfectly on a
row of high-tension cables that seemed to be coming up at him
at 1,000 miles an hour. Frantically he hauled on the risers, first
on one side and then on the other, but he continued in a perfect course from one tower to the next. Now everything was
happening too fast, and he resigned himself to his fate. "Well,
here we go," he said as the ground and the wires came up. He
was mumbling, "Our Father who art in heaven . . ." when he
slammed into the ground, picked himself up quickly, and fell
back down.

He was in a ditch in a plowed field, near a patch of trees.
The high-tension wires stretched above him and about 10 feet
to the side. He did not know how much he had missed them by,
but it could not have been more than a few feet. His legs were
still numb, and his backside ached where he had fallen the second time. He touched his eyebrow and found that it was bleed-
ing. He felt all over his body for broken bones, but there
seemed to be none, and the fear and apprehension he had
felt on the descent were replaced by an extreme euphoria. He
felt giddy and drunk, exhilarated to be alive and in one piece.
"I am the greatest success the world has ever known," he said to
himself. "It was a piece of cake! What a way to make a living!"
He jumped up and executed a few steps of a jig and fell back
down on the soft earth laughing. He was laughing at the top of
his lungs and rolling over with happiness when he heard the
sound of a plane blowing up. He thought it was his own. When

the noise subsided, he was surprised to find that he could still hear.

A small polyglot armada of aircraft circled and whined over southeastern England as the Aphrodite project became operational. Lieutenant General Jimmy Doolittle and Major General Earle Partridge zipped from point to point in their fighters watching the action. Fabric-covered reconnaissance planes, L-2's and L-4's, flew in circles at low altitudes to spot the location of the jump crews and radio their fixes to ambulances waiting below. Sleek fighter planes, both British and American, snapped and spat at high altitude, maintaining a tight cover, and Mosquitoes and P-38 photo ships scrambled close to the drones and the mother ships to record each move for training purposes.

From their vantage points up high, the two primary mother pilots, Pappy Tooman and Foster Falkenstine, and the two back up mother pilots had a clear view of the show through skies unmarked by clouds or haze for the first time in weeks. They saw Pool take off and wondered why he used so much runway, and they saw Lieutenant John Fisher's B-17 waddle to the end of the flight line and turn into the wind for takeoff. "This is the one that worries me," Tooman said to his co-pilot. "This guy's been acting jittery all week, and I think he's a little flak happy."

Everyone watched nervously as Fisher slammed the power to B-17 No. 835, rolled down the runway, and made a perfect takeoff with 50 yards to spare. "Well, burn my hide!" Tooman said as he banked his B-24 mother ship for a better view, "did you see that? I know that kind of guy. He's nervous and raunchy all day long, but when somebody says 'Go!' he goes like a scalded dog!"

Both loaded drones were airborne, and the men in the sky flotilla watched them as they went around the rectangular course checking their equipment and setting up autopilot and Ace. They saw Enterline bail out of No. 342 and recon planes quickly spiral down in his wake to mark the spot of his landing. They saw 342 getting closer and closer to the earth, and they wondered if Fain Pool were ever coming out. Already he was several hundred feet below the briefed bailout altitude, and they could not understand what was keeping him. Then suddenly, like a man being shot from a cannon, Pool's form came spinning out of the navigator's tiny hatch and fell off behind the B-17, and a scanty 500 or 600 feet above the ground, his static line jerked the billowing parachute from his back and began to retard his speed. Another recon plane flew down to mark the spot of the pilot's landing.

Now Fisher and his autopilot man, Technical Sergeant Elmer Most, had entered the final stages of their short flight. Doolittle and Partridge gunned their fighters in close for a better look, and the mothlike reconnaissance planes quartered the sky below waiting for the bailouts. Everything seemed to be going smoothly when B-17 No. 835 went into an abrupt climb. At the top of the climb one man was seen to bail out, and then everyone with a Channel A radio heard the excited voice of John Fisher shouting, "Taxisoldier! Taxisoldier!" This was the code word for the mother ship to take control; it meant that the pilot was leaving his seat.

In Foster Falkenstine's aircraft high above, Major Henry James Rand began to work the azon control switches that would move the drone to left or right. Fisher's robot had been the only one equipped with television in the nose, and Rand had a clear picture of the earth below the drone and the course it was flying. Everything seemed normal, except for that sudden climb and the panicked cry of "Taxisoldier!"

A pilot far below in one of the recon aircraft watched as a pair of legs began to protrude from the navigator's hatch, but suddenly the drone went into another sharp climb, and the legs quickly disappeared back inside the fuselage. Once again the old bomber returned to straight and level flight, and once again a pair of legs came out the bottom. But this time the plane jerked into a sharp climb, stalled quickly, and fell off on the left wing.

Perched in front of his television set at 20,000 feet, Jim Rand had been watching a grove of greenish-white trees on the screen, but now the trees were whirling in tight circles. "She's going in!" he shouted.

The recon pilot far below saw that the B-17 was spinning toward the ground, and he boldly dived his little plane for a closer view. At about 100 feet, he saw a body fall from the open hatch, but body and airplane hit the ground almost at the same time and the same place, and B-17 No. 835 blew itself and its pilot to tiny bits in a loud explosion not far from where Fain Pool had parachuted safely to earth.

Generals Doolittle and Partridge were flying 500 yards astern when the plane blew up; both of them felt a sharp blast and had to fight to control their P-38's. Navigation B-17 No. 2, flying a quarter mile away at 1,500 feet, was tilted on its side by the force of the blast, and the tail gunner suffered a slight concussion. No one else was injured. "What do we do now?" said a voice over Channel A.

"Send another baby!" the voice of Henry James Rand broke in. "I'm up here. We might as well get the job done!"

When Pool had fallen clear of the belly of Drone No. 342, the only control over the vacant airplane became the tenuous double azon system operated from Pappy Tooman's B-24 high above. "Let's go!" Tooman said when Pool radioed his own "Taxisoldier!" "She's all ours!" Bombardier Glen Hargis began toggling the switches that would steer the radio-controlled drone across the Channel to its target. He had exactly three points of control over the 60,000 pounds of B-17 far below him. He could send out a signal that would turn the aircraft left, another signal to turn it right, and another signal to dive it into the target. He could not make the B-17 climb, but the radio altimeter, Ace, would automatically hold the robot at 300 feet for the entire run. Hargis was familiar with the equipment, although he had never before used it to steer an explosive-laden bomber. He was experienced with radio control of azon bombs, and for this reason he had been assigned to replace the regular bombardier in Tooman's crew. As he steered the drone out across the final land checkpoint at Orford Ness, he reviewed the mission in his mind, and when he saw that the drone was accepting control and maintaining altitude, he reached in his pocket and pulled out the target description to read it for the last time. "The target is situated on the southeastern edge of the Éperlecques Forest, 1¼ miles west south-west of the village of Watten," the paper said. "The site has been built in an excavation on the side of a hill which rises sharply to the north to a height of 250 feet. The construction works is approximately 350 x 330 feet, with the greater portion of the building area protruding above the ground surface. The most vulnerable part of the site is the 15 x 16 feet opening on the east side, at the bottom of the building. Attack is therefore necessary from the east. Analysis of both light and heavy flak indicates the best landfall to be in the area of 5112N-0248E. From that point to target, the best route for flak and target identification is to Poperinghe to target on a course of 269 degrees. Terrain contour presents no problem as the sharpest rise or fall is only 145 feet in 2¾ miles."

It took Hargis about ten seconds to read the entire description; during the long training and briefing sessions, he had read the information so often that he had all but committed it to memory. He found parts of the description almost amusing, especially the business about attacking from the east to hit an opening 15 by 16 feet. Hargis had sat in the plexiglass nose of many a bomber watching the million-candlepower taillight of an azon bomb twisting down toward a ground target and madly toggling switches to make it go left or right. As well as anyone, he knew the limitations of the azon bombing system. To be sure, a B-17 had more aerodynamics than a bomb; it could be steered more slowly and precisely, but 15 by 16 feet was still a microscopic target. Most likely, they would hit the huge concrete dome of the rocket site or maybe score a near-miss in the surrounding outbuildings and railroad tracks. Knowing what he did about the azon system of control, Glen Hargis would have been happy to settle for a near-miss.

"Son of a bitch!" Tooman was saying over the interphone. "Look at that!"

Barrage balloons were in position at 1,500 feet over the North Sea, and the robot was heading straight for the cables and chains that hung below to ensnare low-altitude German fighters and buzz bombs. "Nothing we can do about it now!" Tooman said. "They were supposed to be hauled in for this mission."

The robot flew straight into the screen of cables and chains and miraculously emerged from the other side. A navigational B-17 that had been flying above the drone cleared the balloons by inches. "Whew!" Tooman said. "That was dumb luck!"

A few minutes later, as drone and navigation ships steered a course just off the coast where the North Sea and the English Channel come together, puffs of British flak appeared. Tooman's aircraft was out of the effective range of light weapons, but he saw several explosions near the drone and the navigation ships. "It'll serve those bastards right if they hit that baby!" Tooman said. "They'll never fire on a friendly again!" Tooman and his crew had had vast experience dodging British flak, and more than once Tooman had threatened to wipe out an antiaircraft battery or two with leftover bombs.

"Who the hell are we fighting, the Germans or the British?" Tooman said. "Jerk that drone out to sea where those Limey bastards can't practice on it."

Hargis applied a slow and steady left signal, and the robot responded in a smooth, flat turn to the new heading. Soon the

APHRODITE: DESPERATE MISSION   114

puffs of ack-ack were well astern, and within a few minutes the
gray coastline of France appeared. "Let's hope the Germans are
as inaccurate as the Limeys!" Tooman said, and hardly had his
words died away in the intercom when the first black patches of
coastal antiaircraft fire began to appear around drone and
mother ship both. Tooman executed a few minor evasive maneuvers, but Hargis never lost sight of the high visibility wings
of the drone and kept it precisely on course. Soon the great
white roof of the rocket site at Watten came into view. The
bomb run was made precisely as briefed, from the east, and
Glen Hargis was delighted to see that the robot was steering a
perfect course for the huge rectangle of concrete.

"We've got a good one, Pappy," he said as the drone continued relentlessly for the target, and small puffs of light flak did
not seem to deter it. "If they don't hit her, we've got a good
one!"

When the robot was less than a mile from the target and still
dead on course at 300 feet, Hargis moved his fingers to the
switch that would apply full down elevator to the drone's autopilot controls and send it screaming into the target. He had
been briefed to dump No. 342 when it was 1,000 feet away, and
reconnaissance photographs had shown him the exact landmark
to use to aim the robot. The instant the landmark flashed
below, Hargis hit the dive switch, and everyone in Tooman's
crew watched through hatches and windshield to see the flying
bomb destroy the rocket site in a single blast.

But nothing happened. "Goddamn it, Hargis, hit that dump
switch!" Tooman snapped over the intercom. "We're passing
over!"

"I did hit it," Hargis said. "It's not responding."

Tooman empurpled the air with several more choice invec-
tives. "What do we do now?" the navigator said.

"We turn the stupid son of a bitch around and try again,"
Tooman snapped.

"There'll be a lot of flak this time," a voice put in. "They've got our number now. We gave 'em warning."

"Let's go!" Tooman said. "Screw the flak!"

Hargis checked the left and right controls of the guidance system, and each time the robot responded perfectly. Mother and baby, now 21,000 feet apart, but flying the same headings, curved in a long arc back over the Channel and over the same enemy antiaircraft batteries that had fired on them before and once again made a perfect run on the target from the east.

"It's no use, Captain," Hargis said into the interphones. "She won't respond to down control."

While the two planes flew around the target, miraculously surviving clouds of light flak, the alternate mother ship was called in, but the drone would not respond to this control either, and Pappy Tooman and his crew had to face the realization that they were in haphazard control of an undivable B-17 that was loaded to the roof line with nitrostarch. "What do we do now?" Hargis said.

"Let's just keep driving it around and around till it runs out of gas," someone suggested. "Then it'll go in on its own."

"Yeah," said Tooman with heavy sarcasm. "Great idea. Maybe we can wipe out Caen or St.-Pol, or maybe we'll just get some nice little French village."

"What's the alternative?"

"Be quiet," Tooman said, "I'm thinking." A few minutes later he said, "Dix, can you position that flak battery that almost got the baby before?"

Navigator R. W. Dix said, "Sure, it's about fifteen miles up the coast on the edge of a bluff. I got a good look at it when we came in."

"Hargis," Tooman said, "how about controlling that baby so she flies right in front of the flak battery?"

Hargis did as he was told, and the yellow-painted No. 342 made a perfect pass at 300 feet altitude about a quarter mile from the shoreline. Flak popped and snapped all around her, but the ancient aircraft hummed right through.

"Son of a bitch!" Tooman said. "Let's go again."

Hargis guided the drone in a wide 180-degree turn and brought it directly in front of the German flak battery again, but this time several hundred yards closer. For a few seconds the robot was obscured by the puffs of smoke around it, and then there was a great ball of yellow fire and a blast and a pillow of black smoke rolling away in the Normandy breeze. Tooman did another 180 and flashed back over the flak battery. This time there was no response.

Just below the control tower, the ready crews of Project Aphrodite sat in two large rooms, one for enlisted men and one for officers, and listened with dubious enjoyment as the events of the afternoon were relayed to them by radio. In the upper room, First Lieutenant Frank Houston sat among several of his peers and clucked softly to himself. "Tsk, tsk, tsk," he kept saying, "tsk, tsk, tsk," until one of the other pilots said, "For Christ's sake, Houston, keep your opinions to yourself. You sound like a chicken!"

"I feel like a turkey," said the twenty-three-year-old pilot from Montana, "the morning of Thanksgiving."

In his role as first supernumerary, Houston was fully dressed in jump gear—paratroop boots and flying fatigues—while most of the others wore the usual relaxed apparel of the air base and its easygoing CO, Roy Forrest. The day was clear but cool, even though it was early August, and Forrest himself sat at a desk in front of the room, booming orders into a microphone. He wore an OD sweater and a flying scarf and frequently made comments to the effect that England might be a grand country but back in Texas one did not have to wear long underwear during the heat spells.

There was a loudspeaker on the floor in front of Forrest, and through it the officers could hear every word of the day's radio conversations. The operations were not one hour old before they heard the frantic voice of Lieutenant John Fisher shouting, "Taxisoldier! taxisoldier!" followed shortly by the anxious voice of Major Henry James Rand calling for another robot. Forrest switched to a low-power frequency and talked to one of the tiny reconnaissance aircraft flying with the Fisher plane. "Why's Rand calling for another baby?" he asked.

The voice of the recon pilot came through the loudspeaker at a barely audible level, and the men rushed to the front of the room to crowd around. "It fell off on a wing and went in," the pilot was saying.

"Anybody get out?"

"Yes, sir, one man. The pilot got out, but the plane fell on him."

"And exploded?"

"Yes, sir. It blew a hole in the forest."

"No town nearby?"

"No, sir. We lucked out on that one."

"Roger and out," Roy Forrest said, and all at once Houston realized the import of the conversation. One of the B-17's had failed to get out of England. Now they would need the supernumerary.

"Andrecheck!" Forrest was saying into the microphone. "Shag ass! You're next." Houston was puzzled. Andrecheck was the third pilot scheduled to fly the mission. But in effect he would now be replacing Fisher, and all the timings and headings that had been so carefully worked up at headquarters would be mixed up. Surely the correct way to handle the mission would be to throw a supernumerary crew in Fisher's place and let Andrecheck and Cornelius Engel fly their missions later in the afternoon as briefed. Houston was puzzled, but relieved. He took up a place in the back of the room and counted his blessings.

Something like six weeks had passed since Frank Houston had volunteered to pick up his buddies in Russia and wound up in Aphrodite instead, and during this whole time his mood had varied between gray and black. Earlier on this day of the first operational missions, he had bicycled out to a remote hardstand to look over one of the loaded drones with Willard Smith, who would fly with him when the time came. The two men, a whole military caste apart, had become fast friends, and each had developed a healthy respect for the other. On their training missions, Smith had logged several hours at the controls, thus becoming one of the few enlisted men in the Army with stick time in a four-engine bomber. Of course, the time could not be entered in a logbook. Houston would say, "Here, Smitty, you take it for a while," and the heavyset staff sergeant would control the Flying Fortress while the regular pilot would sit and enjoy the scenery. After a while, Smith even learned to make turns and shallow dives and climbs, and Houston had no doubt that his autopilot man would land the B-17 and take it off with just a few more lessons. Smith was a quick study. By now Houston knew the stubby Pennsylvanian's whole military history, and it amused him that Smith had had to fight and bludgeon and wheedle and lie his way out of his original assignment in the Army, as a cook. "You should have stayed a cook!" Houston would kid his enlisted friend. "You'd have been the only cook in the Army with an IQ over sixty!"

But the conversation this morning, "way out in the tules," as Houston put it, had not been so pleasant. Houston liked to play the role of the frightened volunteer, even to exaggerate it for comic effect among his friends at the officers' club, but so long as he had known Smith, the autopilot expert had never expressed a single word of doubt or pessimism or fear about the mission. But as soon as the two of them had slipped into the drone through the navigator's hatch and observed the boxes of nitrostarch piled up like dominoes from the deck to the ceiling of the creaky aircraft, Smith had changed his tune. "Please, Lieutenant," he said, as the two men crouched down in the rearranged pilot's compartment, "I know you're the pilot and you're the expert, but look at this thing! This thing is absolutely unflyable! You don't have to be an engineer from MIT to see that."

Houston peered along the sides of the boxes toward the tail of the airplane, and he could see that the nitrostarch extended all the way through the waist and rearward as far as the eye could see. He had no doubt that the tail gunner's compartment was loaded with boxes, and a scene from his earlier bombing career came instantly to mind. He had fought and struggled and almost half lifted his loaded B-17 off the runway, nearly crashing in the process, and once in the air he found that he had to give the plane an enormous nose trim to keep the tail from dragging. When he had the bomber under full control at last, he turned the wheel over to his co-pilot and went back for an inspection trip. The tail gunner was sitting in a cocoon of armor plate, which he had smuggled aboard the airplane earlier, and off to one side were two or three extra, unauthorized boxes of ammunition. Houston said nothing to the gunner until the mission was over, but he had never forgotten the effect of a mere 300 or 400 extra pounds in the tail compartment. A B-17 was as stable as a Model A Ford—Houston knew that, and believed it—but no aircraft could stand a full load at the extreme tip of the tail. Something from high school physics called "force times lever arm" entered into the equation, and those extra pounds in the tail exerted a weight equal to several tons in the midsection of the airplane.

Now Frank Houston was looking around a B-17 that was loaded not only in the tail, but in the nose, the waist, the pilot's compartment, everyplace one looked. "Jesus Christ, did they even have to stack it where the co-pilot sits?" Willard Smith was saying. "Would it have washed out the mission to leave four or five boxes out?" Houston saw that several rows of stacked boxes began where the co-pilot's seat should have been and extended flush against the bulkhead to the rear. The effect was to halve the size of the pilot's compartment and totally block any passage rearward.

"Lieutenant," Willard Smith was saying softly, "I have been involved in some half-ass things in my life, but this is the all-time low. If my worst enemy had designed this system, it couldn't be worse. How can they expect to steer this airplane into a target when it obviously isn't even airworthy?"

Houston was trying not to comment aloud, for the benefit of morale, but he had to admit to himself that the enlisted man was absolutely correct. The aircraft was loaded high above the longitudinal axis; anyone who knew the rudiments of aeronautics must realize that the slightest list to one side or the other could send the craft spinning into the earth. Houston had seen the specifications, and he knew that the B-17 would be hauling a few pounds over its maximum gross weight, but that did not shock him. All experienced bomber pilots had hauled a few pounds over "max gross" at one time or another. But the difference was that a normal bomb load was concentrated in the *bottom* of the airplane, where it had the same effect as a keel on a sailboat, stabilizing the motion. This Aphrodite load was tucked into places that were four and five feet *above* the center of gravity. "Smitty," Houston blurted out, "whoever designed this method of loading must have been a shoemaker in civilian life."

"Wrong," Smith said. "It takes some brains to be a shoemaker."

"Let's get out of here," Houston said.

On the way back to their quarters in a borrowed jeep, the two men had spoken frankly. "I'll tell you the truth, Lieutenant," Willard Smith said as he guided the jeep around the potholes and cracks in the taxiway. "I've been looking for a way to weasel out of this practically from the beginning. At first I had the typical soldier's attitude. You know what I mean? It was inconceivable to me that ignorance could become entrenched in high places, especially in time of war, when everything you've got is right out there on the line, your life and everything. But I'll tell you: I've learned something. It's *exactly* in time of war when the dumbest asses rise to the top. Don't ask me why."

"I know what you mean," Houston said. He was thinking about the first day he had reported to the project, and found that one of the high muckamucks of Aphrodite was an officer who had been all but laughed out of Houston's old bomb group for incompetence and stupidity. Luckily this officer had been transferred away from Aphrodite in the interim, but not before his influence had caused several near disasters and given Houston and the other pilots a collection of sleepless nights.

"If I could have found a way to get out of this without being shot, I'd have taken it," Smith was saying. "I felt that there was absolutely no chance of success. I hate to say this, but it's the way I feel. There is *no* prospect of success! Now success involving great risk is something I wouldn't mind, but failure involving great risk is something else. And that's what we're facing."

"Well, we're in it, and we can't get out," Houston said.

"Agreed. We are deeply involved in a project that someday will be ushered into the Hall of Fame of Human Incompetence. But you're right. We can't get out. Lieutenant, I want to ask you just one favor."

"Ask," Houston said.

"I'm no pilot, but there are a few things I understand about physics, simple physics as it is taught in high school. *That load is bad,* Lieutenant. I guess it takes gall for me to say this to a hot pilot like you, but please do me a favor. Undercontrol this baby, will you? Play it 'way down. What you think is a normal turn could be a disaster!"

"Okay, Smitty," Houston said. "I'll bear that in mind."

Now Frank Houston was sitting in the back of the ready room remembering his conversation and reevaluating it in the light of Fisher's crash. All he knew was that Fisher had gone into a climb, stalled, and fallen off on a wing. To Houston, the crash meant one thing: Every gloomy, pessimistic, critical, accusatory word out of Staff-Sergeant Willard Smith's mouth had been absolutely correct. The missions were doomed; the planes were as airworthy as coffins. He thanked God again that on this day he was only the standby pilot. Then he heard Roy Forrest's voice booming out, "Okay, who's the supernumerary?"

Somebody nudged Houston.

"Who's the supernumerary?" Forrest shouted. "Come on, we haven't got all day."

Houston scrunched down in his seat. He knew he would have to go, but he was not going to hasten the process. Then someone piped up from a front row: "It's Houston!"

"Okay, Houston. Shag ass!" Forrest said.

"What happened to Andrecheck?" somebody asked.

"His controls are dead," Forrest said. "He just called from the hardstand. When they trussed up the boxes of nitrostarch, they bound up a couple of control cables. The whole load has to be defused and taken out."

Houston was numbed by this further confirmation of Willard Smith's theories. He stumbled down the stairs that led into the enlisted men's ready room. "Okay, Smitty," he said with mock cheerfulness, "let's go." Outside the door another enlisted man waited at the wheel of a jeep, and the next Aphrodite crew was driven at high speed toward the same hardstand they had visited early in the morning. Houston looked at Smith, expecting to see a quivering mass of jelly, but instead he saw a picture of calmness. Smith had his arm draped casually over the back of the seat and his feet propped up on the dash. He seemed to be viewing the situation with total equanimity, and Houston wondered if something had snapped in his friend's brain. Only a few hours before, he had been equating the Aphrodite project with every disaster in history.

Houston was all the more puzzled when Smith turned his head and said nonchalantly, "Well, if we gotta go, we gotta go, eh, Lieutenant?"

Houston was too shaken to answer. Smith slapped him on the knee and said, "Anyway, it's a nice day for flying."

Once again the two men shinnied through the navigator's tiny hatch and into the cockpit, now grown hot and stuffy from the afternoon sun and the lack of ventilation. The normal vent holes were covered with explosives.

Houston took his seat in front of the pilot's console, attempted to wipe a drop of perspiration from the tip of his nose, missed with his trembling hand, and poked himself in the eye. He turned and saw the chubby figure of Willard Smith watching him coolly. "Damn!" Houston said. "Stuffy in here!"

As he put the controls through the normal preflight checks, Houston could not keep his hands still. Perspiration rolled off his forehead and down across his eyes and onto the front of his flying fatigues. "Hot!" he said to Smith, and the sergeant answered calmly, "Sure is."

When the time came to switch on the power and begin turning over the engines one by one, Houston was a nervous wreck, and Smith's calmness was embarrassing him. Everything checked out, as far as Houston could tell through sweat-filled eyes, but when he began to taxi the overloaded airplane, he jolted it across a few of the larger holes in the asphalt, and all around him boxes of explosives clicked lightly as they jiggled together. Houston looked down and saw that his knees were shaking. Willard Smith was crouched alongside, still looking bored and nonchalant, and Houston found his fright being overcome by his shame and embarrassment at becoming so obviously nervous in front of his co-pilot. "Goddamn it," he said to himself. "I can't let Smitty see me like this." Then it occurred to him that Smith had not heard the news about Fisher; that would explain some of the calmness.

"You heard about Fisher, didn't you?" Houston said through gritted teeth.

"Sure," said Smith evenly. "We all heard it. Tough break."

Houston was more puzzled than ever, but he tried to forget

the inscrutable exterior of his friend and co-pilot and concen-
trate on the mission. His final checks went off smoothly, and exactly at eleven minutes after three he slammed the four throttles forward and aimed the lumbering old bomber straight
toward the end of the runway. Out of the corner of his eye he
could see Smith, a stopwatch in one hand and the other hand
already touching the spring-loaded switch that would lower the
flaps at the right instant. The plane gained momentum at an
extremely slow rate, and for a second or two Houston wondered
if he had lost an engine. But now they were going 40, then 50,
and Houston saw the flap indicator move to the one-quarter position. The aircraft was beginning to float; the tail wheel was
up, and with plenty of room to spare it seemed that B-17 No.
461 was going to reach flying speed. Houston hauled back on
the control column, and the aircraft wrenched itself free of the
runway, teetered slightly, and plopped back down with a re-
sounding thump. Once again Houston lifted the airplane off,
and again it returned to earth. "One more and we've had it!"
he shouted as he saw the patch of turnips and sugar beets coming up ahead. He pulled back, and the plane inched into the
air, tilted a few degrees in a gust of crosswind, and slowly began
to gain altitude. The tops of young pine trees passed beneath,
and No. 461 was away on its final flight.

Willard Smith was engaged in a tremendous act of will, and
so far he had been successful. In his entire life he had never
been so shaky, and in his entire life he had never concealed it
so well. He was happy to see that Frank Houston was scared.
Smith believed that in certain situations men should become
what he called "professionally frightened." He would have
doubted the mental stability of anyone who had taken off such
an airplane coolly. But if both of them had shown their nervousness, there might have been a sort of reciprocal hysteria, so
he glued his face into a look of repose, answered Houston's
questions in a monotone, and pressed his knees tightly together.

His takeoff assignment was simple, but he made a big project out of counting off the seconds on his stopwatch and applying the quarter flaps precisely when the indicated airspeed showed 60. Thus he was able to take his mind off the terror that threatened to overpower his emotions at any moment.

When 461 cleared the turnips and sugar beets and the young pines at the end of the runway, Smith remained in a state of concealed nervousness. The takeoff was only one of several procedures he would have to undergo, culminating in a high-speed, low-altitude parachute jump that would simulate a man running into the grille of a Mack truck. "Now remember, Lieutenant," he said to Houston, "we won't make any sharp turns, will we?" He spoke in the tone usually reserved for children—a soothing, gentle tone calculated to help Houston through his own highly visible nervousness.

"Don't worry about a thing, Buddy-o," Houston said merrily. "We're in the air now. It's all routine from here on!"

Smith turned and saw that Houston was his old, relaxed self again. Apparently he had doubted that the loaded airplane could negotiate the runway successfully, but nothing that remained in the routine worried him. Smith was just as glad. Houston had several crucial operations to perform, and he would perform them better in a relaxed frame of mind. "Professional fright" could be salutary, but not if it lasted too long.

"How you feeling?" Houston said.

Smith found that he could unlock his knees without trembling, and his hands had stopped perspiring. "Fine," he said. "The worst is over now."

Suddenly a B-24 came careening across the rectangles of visibility in front of the plexiglass windshield. "Jesus Christ!" Houston shouted, and just then a pair of the big Liberators came into view from the left, followed by what looked like a vast fleet of the big banana boats. Smith saw them at the same time as Houston, and he realized that 461 had bumbled into a group of B-24's, forming for a regular bombing mission. "Hang on!" Frank Houston was shouting, and the clumsy old B-17 went into a tight evasive turn.

Smith gripped the back of Houston's chair as the aircraft slowly banked off to the right, out of the line of travel of the forming 24's. When the plane had turned through 90 degrees, the G forces continued to hold Willard Smith to his kneeling position on the deck, and when the turn continued toward the 180-degree point and beyond, Smith knew that something was wrong. Fighting the centrifugal force of the tightly banked aircraft, he lifted himself into a squatting position and saw Frank Houston struggling to pull the B-17 out of the turn. The plane was falling off to the right, and Smith was horrified to see that Houston was straining to turn the wheel to the left and getting nowhere. "Hang on!" Smith shouted, and he muscled himself across the deck and into position in front of the co-pilot's controls. He grabbed the extra wheel and began applying pressure. "Heave!" Houston shouted, and the wheel began to turn slowly. At first the big airplane kept on careening to the right, but then the top wing dropped a few inches, and a few inches more, and at last old 461 was flying straight and level.

"Jesus!" Frank Houston said.

"We almost bought it, Lieutenant," Smith said. "And we knew it all the time, didn't we? *Not to make any sharp turns!*"

"Yeah, we knew it all the time," Houston said, "but it was a case of making a sharp turn or hitting a banana boat."

The B-24's were above them now, and Smith noticed that when Houston came to the first checkpoint and began his right turn to the southwest, toward Felixstowe, he did not bank the aircraft an inch. The plane went into a wide, sweeping skid turn, and Smith could see that Houston was accomplishing the entire maneuver on rudder only, keeping the wings straight and level. "I'd have washed out of flying school for this," Houston said as he deftly applied control and studied the turn-and-bank indicator.

Now the time had come for Willard Smith to inch his

190-pound frame into the hole below the pilot's compartment and crawl along the catwalk to the place where the autopilot had been relocated. "Okay, Smitty, this is where you earn your pay," Houston said. "See you in London!"

The two men locked their little fingers in the popular good luck rite of the era, and Smith dropped out of sight below. "Straight and level," he shouted up to Houston when he reached the autopilot, and to his surprise Smith saw that every warning light flicked out. Houston was flying a perfect course, and the autopilot tuning was accomplished in a few minutes. Smith slipped into his safety chute and moved into position alongside the open hole of the navigator's escape hatch. Barely two feet away, he could hear the No. 2 engine pounding, and he made a mental note to drop out of the plane with his arms and legs forming a straight line with his body, so that he could not present a random fingertip or hand or foot to the whirling blades of the prop.

The nylon strap of the static line lay alongside the hatch in gentle folds. One end of it was affixed to an eyebolt, screwed into an aluminum longeron. Smith snapped the other end of the static line to his parachute. Now he was ready to jump. He knew that his body would fall about 35 feet, and then the static line would jerk the parachute open automatically. All Smith had to do was jump. If something went wrong with the static line system and the backpack failed to open, he was to pull the red rip cord handle on his chest pack without delay, because the jump would be from a low altitude and there would be no time for indecision.

Smith went over the routine in his mind as he sat alongside the rush of air from the nagivator's hatch, and then he went over the routine again. The autopilot had been set up so quickly that he had ten or fifteen minutes to sit in his parachutes and think. He looked up at the place where the static line was connected to the eyebolt, and it occurred to him that any extra force would yank the eyebolt right out of the longeron. He thought that it might make more sense to wrap the end of the static line around the longeron itself, rather than clip it to the weak eyebolt, but he overruled his own judgment on the grounds that the men who designed the system must have known what they were doing. A shudder ran through him when he realized that the same men who had set up the faulty load of the B-17 might also have designed this weak eyebolt anchor for the static line. Or had they? Maybe somebody else had worked out the parachuting details; he hoped so. *"Somebody* on this project must know what he's doing," Smith said to himself.

He felt the airplane slide into another skidding turn, and if his calculations were correct, this would be the last one before they came back over the aerodrome at Woodbridge and made their jumps. Smith took off his glasses, put them in a case, and slipped them into his breast pocket. He checked the static-line connections for the last time and inched his feet through the hatch so that he was sitting sideways to the forward motion of the plane, his legs wobbling wildly in the slipstream.

"Go!" Frank Houston called, and Willard Smith shoved himself free of the airplane and into the blast of air behind the engine. He felt all the air being sucked out of his lungs, and he saw the bottom antenna support flash above his head. His whole body snapped violently, and he thought that his back must be broken, and then he felt himself catapulting through the air in a giant flip. When he opened his eyes, he saw yards and yards of white silk beginning to flash out behind him in a straight line, and then there was another jolt and he was swinging to and fro beneath the white canopy of the parachute. He wondered about that first heavy snap. He thought that a loop of the static line must have curled around his body, and when he had come to the end of the first 35 feet of free fall, the line must first have extricated itself from him in the violent snap and then jerked the cover off the parachute pack. "My God," Smith said as he decelerated below the chute, "one more loop and I'd have had it!"

He wondered how Houston was doing, but when he reached in his pocket for his glasses, he found that the static line had slapped across his chest with such force that the glasses were in shards. He knew that his nearsightedness would prevent him from getting the slightest glimpse of his friend Houston, and he turned his concentration to the feeling of euphoria that was beginning to ease through him now that he was unmistakably headed for a safe landing on the earth below. He closed his eyes and breathed in the cool summer air as it swept past his nose. He opened his eyes and looked at the fuzzy edge of the world below him. "Terrific!" he shouted in the giddiness of the descent. Every cell in his body seemed to him to be enjoying a blessed feeling of relief. He had triumphed over another Army fiasco. He had beaten the odds for a final time. All he had to do was land and step out of his harness and return to Fersfield and demand the pass that had been promised him.

Thinking such positive thoughts, Willard Smith reached earth in a mild crosswind, tumbled one or two times, jumped up to chase his parachute, and finally tackled the big white balloon and beat it into flat submission. Then he reached around and felt his back and realized he was well and whole and healthy. "Damn!" he said to the weeds that surrounded him in the open field. "I'll be seeing Doylestown, P.A., again!" It was the first time in weeks that he had been certain.

As he went about the final routine procedures of his first, last, and only Aphrodite mission, Frank Houston felt a strange calmness, in contrast with the stage fright that had gripped him so visibly at the beginning of the trip. "Jesus," he said to himself, "I wonder what Smitty thought?" But in the same instant he told himself that Willard Smith was a very wise soldier, and he would understand. Probably Smith had been scared himself, but he had done an unbelievable job of hiding it. No, Houston thought, he probably wasn't scared at all. He probably sat up late last night reading one of those books of his and learning how to overcome his own natural emotions.

"Well, it's all routine now," Houston said aloud after he shouted "Go!" to Willard Smith, perched on the catwalk below. "I just get out of this seat and pull the chain." Oddly enough, the prospect of yanking on a lanyard and arming 20,000 pounds of high explosives did not disturb him. He knew that at the end of a certain number of routine operations he would find himself landing gently in a farmer's field in southeastern England, and for him World War II would be effectively over.

Houston pushed a few final buttons, cut the power to 175 miles an hour indicated, and trimmed the four-engine airplane into the gentle dive that would ease it down to the 300-foot altitude where the automatic Ace altimeter would take hold and haul the plane into straight and level flight for the trip across the Channel to the target. Now there was nothing else to do in the pilot's compartment. He flipped on his Channel A transmitter and said, "Taxisoldier, taxisoldier." He wondered about the calmness in his own voice; it must have made quite an impression on the mother ship crew above.

"Roger," the equally calm voice of Lieutenant Foster Falkenstine acknowledged from the primary mother ship at 20,000 feet.

A second later Houston was sprawled on the deck of the descending airplane, clutching at his throat and emitting a strangled, gurgling rattle. Confused voices crackled in his earphones: "What happened? My God, what was that? What happened?" Houston shook his head a few times and drew himself up to a sitting position. His neck was sore, but he knew that he was otherwise in excellent health for a man who had jumped out of the pilot's seat without removing his neck mike or his headphones. Sheepishly, he climbed back into the seat and transmitted once again the code word "Taxisoldier." This time the voice of Foster Falkenstine acknowledged with a questioning "Roger?"

"That's right," Houston said. "Taxisoldier!" He would let them wonder what had happened. He would be the last person alive to admit such a damned fool mistake. He would blame his horrifying scream on static. "Gee, fellows, I didn't hear anything," he would say. "Must have been QRN, static. Or maybe one of those new German panoramic jammers." He would steadfastly refuse to discuss the matter any further.

Now he had to move fast. He estimated that the heavy trim had lowered the airplane to about 1,500 feet, and he wanted to get his work done and bail out before the 1,000-foot mark. He knew that a high-speed parachute jump below that altitude could be fatal.

He set the ten-minute clock on the instrument panel, checked the safety lights on the electrical fusing device, plugged in the two jacks that completed the circuit, and manually armed fourteen impact fuses with a mighty jerk on the lanyard. He estimated the total elapsed time of all these operations at one minute and the loss of altitude at 200 feet. That put him at about 1,300. He strapped on his chest pack and thought with surprise how undismayed and businesslike he was acting in these terminal stages. Then he dragged himself over to the navigator's hatch, hooked up his static line, dangled his feet into the slipstream, and looked down.

"Oh, my goodness!" he said to himself. "Oh, Jesus, I really don't want to do this! I don't want to do this! They can't make me do this!" He began to shake and look for ways out. Then he remembered his orders. Under no conditions was a loaded drone to be returned. Their presence was not desired at any air base in England. And even if he decided to stage a one-man mutiny and land the aircraft in defiance of his orders, the plane would almost certainly blow up on impact, now that he had fused and armed it both mechanically and electrically. "Son of a bitch!" Houston said to himself when he had considered all the possibilities in about three seconds flat. "There's only one way out of this, and that's straight down." He started hunkering forward on his backside, inch by inch, trying to get the feel of things, nudging his frame away from the booming sounds of the No. 2 engine. The slipstream was hauling at his paratrooper boots and tugging at his pants, and suddenly he was sucked out of the little hatch and flung flat out underneath the belly of the plane. He rolled once and saw blue sky above him, and then he felt a gentle, almost imperceptible jerk. "There goes the static line!" he said to himself, and braced for the shock of the opening parachute. But a few seconds later he realized that he was still seeing earth and sky in even alternation, and he was still falling downward at a frightful speed. He craned his neck to see behind him and spotted 35 feet of heavy nylon static line in trail. *My God,* he thought, *that's supposed to be connected to the plane, not to me!* and he knew that the static line had ripped loose from the innards of the B-17 without opening his parachute.

Houston looked straight down and saw details of the landscape with harrowing clarity. He wrenched at the red handle on his chest pack and watched as the canvas cover ripped away and nothing else. The silken folds of the pilot chute lay neatly folded, barely rippling in the airstream, and now Houston knew he was faced with a second defective chute. Frantically, he clutched at the filmy material and began pulling it out by hand. A few feet came loose, and then the air began to grab at the filmy white material. Houston was bracing himself for the full flowering of the parachute when he heard sharp noises, and light twigs and green leaves began to pass before his eyes in a streaky blur. Instinctively, he flung his hands up in front of his face, instead of covering his crotch and his Adam's apple as he had been instructed, and gave himself up. The branches became thicker, the leaves became larger and greener, and all at once Frank Houston came to a stop so shudderingly sudden that a bolt of pain shot across his shoulder and his legs went numb and for an instant he blacked out. Then he felt a sharp upward jerk and saw some of the same branches and leaves passing before his eyes in the opposite direction. When he stopped swinging, he found himself hanging in his straps six or eight feet off the ground, the risers of his still half-opened parachute caught in the branches above him, and he realized what had happened. The branches of the tree had acted like a giant spring, reaching out and catching the fluttering silk and cushioning his fall. If he had hit a few feet to either side of the tree, he would now be lying broken and dead. He was not sure if he had hit the ground, but whether he had or not, the springing action of the larger branches had hauled him straight back into the air, and now he would have to figure out a way to cut himself loose.

He was hanging at an angle, enmeshed in his risers, like a doll in a twopenny marionette show, and he twisted and turned in an effort to break loose. But the more he moved, the tighter the risers wound around him, and by the time he thought of his penknife, tucked away in one of the pockets in the pant leg of his flying fatigues, he had bound himself so tightly that he could not reach the knife no matter how he wriggled. He tried to swing his body in wide arcs, to catch hold of the tree, but the maneuver failed to get him closer than 10 feet to the trunk. Then he tried to climb up the risers to an overhanging branch, so that he could pitch himself backward out of his leg straps, but this maneuver also failed. Finally, he abandoned all his plans and only flailed and thrashed about in a near panic of claustrophobia, cursing a blue streak in the process. He kept this up for what seemed like fifteen or twenty minutes, until he was so fatigued that he could hardly move a muscle, and then he let his head fall back and saw an elderly man in overalls standing not 10 feet away.

"Hey!" Houston yelled, but the man continued standing immobile, his mouth hanging slack. Houston screamed, "What the hell are you looking at, you idiot?"

The old man took a tentative step forward and said, "Are you a Yank?"

"You're goddamn right I'm a Yank!" Houston said.

The man stopped again, continued his closer examination of the dangling figure, and appeared contented to spend the rest of the afternoon gazing.

"Goddamn it!" Frank Houston said. "Can't you see I'm stuck? Now help me get out of here!"

"Are you quite sure you're a Yank?" the old man said.

"Yes, for Christ's sake, I'm quite sure I'm a Yank!" Houston shouted. He rattled off his name, rank and serial number, his hometown, his mother's name and address, and the address of his old commanding officer and bomb group, everything that came to his mind in the inverted position.

"If you're a Yank, what are you doing in that tree?" the old man said.

"I'm picking raspberries!" Houston roared. "Now will you get me down or do I have to call the constable and have you put under arrest?"

The man seemed impressed by the warning; it apparently did not occur to him that there was no telephone service in the tree from which Houston hung like an overweight fly in a spiderweb.

"Well, what can I do?" the man said.

"You got a knife?"

"Yes." The man produced an ancient pocketknife.

"Pass it up!" Houston said. He slashed at the risers and straps and descended six feet to earth with a rousing thunk. He stood up, gave the man his knife and a scathing look, and started to stride off through the woods, but he had only taken a few steps when his knees turned to water and he fell over. When he opened his eyes, the man was standing over him as lethargically as before. Houston closed his eyes, opened them again, and saw the same sight. "I'm still a Yank," he said.

The man knelt down beside him. "Stay here, Yank," he said slowly, "and I'll try to find some help for yer."

Houston let his head sink back to the soft earth and decided to allow others to control the future course of the day's events. Above him, the sun dappled the green leaves of the tree that had saved his life, and the pilot from Montana looked up and saw that it was an oak—a grand, thick, noble English oak. A light breeze brushed across his face, and a gradual sense of well-being began to suffuse through his tired body. For him, Mission Aphrodite was over, and in this happy realization he could even forgive the old man. Certainly the proper Englishman had been standing there watching him for fifteen minutes, and certainly he had done nothing to relieve Houston's misery. But there were venerable English traditions to be observed. Old Sam Houston chuckled aloud. How could the farmer have helped him down? They hadn't even been introduced.

The mother ship piloted by Lieutenant Foster Falkenstine had almost reached the coast of France, and the interphones were still alive with conversation about the terrifying noise that had come from the drone below. "I can't figure it out," Falkenstine said to Rand, who was sitting in the plexiglass nose, controlling the baby 20,000 feet below. "It sounded like somebody getting a knife in the neck, like somebody's last death rattle."

"Well, if it was a death rattle," Rand said, "then who came on the air a minute later and said, 'Taxisoldier'?"

"That's what puzzles me."

For a few minutes, Falkenstine and Rand and the co-pilot discussed the ghoulish possibility that something indeed had happened to Frank Houston and that he was lying unconscious in the drone below. "He'll be killed when we dive it in the target," the co-pilot said.

For a moment there was silence over the intercom, and then Rand spoke up. "He's not in the baby," he said. "It's impossible. In the first place, somebody said 'Taxisoldier' on Channel A, and at that time there was nobody in the baby to say it but Houston. In the second place, there's a dozen different airplanes flying around down there, and if the jump pilot didn't get out, we'd have heard about it."

"Makes sense," Falkenstine said.

"The thing to do now is get on with the mission," Rand said. He was busy handling the controls that moved the drone to left or right and trying to remember the details of the briefings on the target. He was not as much in the dark as some of the other crew members, and he knew that this particular target, near a place called Wizernes, was one that terrified British intelligence. He remembered the last report on the rocket installation in the Pas-de-Calais. Two sites were listed as "ready to fire." One was Watten, the target that Tooman had been unable to hit, and the other was Wizernes, the one they would reach in a few minutes. Rand took another look at the description furnished by U.S. intelligence:

"The target lies $3\frac{1}{4}$ miles s.s.w. of the center of St. Omer. It is constructed within a quarry which has been excavated into the hillside from the flat floor of the valley formed by the river Aa. The ground on the south side of the site rises sharply 240 feet above the valley. The only part of the site which protrudes above the ground surface is the prominent dome, the remainder being within the confines of the underground quarry excavation. The only vulnerable part of the target is the opening approximately 40 feet below the lip of the dome and on the northwest side of the site. Attack is therefore necessary from that direction."

Rand had studied mock-ups of the target and movies of the approach until he felt he could handle the entire mission blindfolded. He knew exactly where the railroad track exited from the concrete dome and where the outbuildings were and how to

avoid a few minor hills that might interfere with the drone's
bomb run. He had spent long, sleepless nights thinking about
Wizernes, and more than once he had dreamed of seeing the
great circular mass of concrete erupt straight into the sky. Rand
had attended all the high-level briefings in London; he knew
that the V-2 was coming and that it was a rocket with an inde-
terminate-sized warhead, and he had heard that the Germans
were also working on a V-3, a long-range superrocket that could
level the cities of eastern America. He had read top secret intelligence reports that described how Nazi strategists were zeroing
in on New York, Boston, Pittsburgh, and Washington and were
in the final stages of assembling their mighty V-3 rockets deep
in the insides of the large sites in France. The problem was said
to be one of engineering and fabrication; all the scientific obstacles had been removed.

Rand doubted it. He was a scientist, and he was well aware
that V-2 was certain to become operational almost any day. But
there was a vast technological gap between a V-2 with a range
of a few hundred miles and a V-3 with a range of thousands. On
the other hand, Rand also knew that the Germans were far advanced scientifically. The great brains of the *Reich* had been
concentrating on war technology for more than two decades,
while scientists in the free world had been going about their
studies to the exclusion of such matters as rocket construction
and ordnance capabilities and the inner strengths of ferroconcrete bunkers. Rand had spent most of his peacetime career
working on cancer research, a subject that fascinated him.
But now he wished he knew a little more about rockets. In his
mind there was only one certainty: *If* the Germans had a V-3, *if*
it was almost ready to send supersonic bombloads into down-
town Manhattan and the Golden Triangle and DuPont Circle,
then Wizernes *could* be its launching point. Of all the large
sites laid out in northwestern France by the Germans, the
round dome of Wizernes looked the most menacing. Rand
knew the dimensions of the V-2; he had read them on intelli-

gence reports. But this mass of concrete at Wizernes was plainly constructed to handle something of much larger size, perhaps double the size of the V-2. Such a target had to be taken with the utmost seriousness. Doolittle had told Rand that there were as many as 400 antiaircraft guns surrounding Wizernes, and more ack-ack guns stationed along the logical routes toward the target. Rand thumped his hand on the armor plating that now protected him from three sides and below. He looked down at the robot and saw that it was flying straight and level. Both mother ship and drone were making their landfall now, just southwest of Calais toward Cap Blanc-Nez, and Rand was pleased to see that no coastal flak greeted either aircraft. He knew that reconnaissance airplanes had been studying the area for several weeks and plotting the flak-free corridors for Aphrodite. Mother and drone would fly from the coast to Ardres and then to the target, a few minutes' flying time to the southeast, making a tight 180-degree turn at the last minute to approach from the northwest.

All the way from the last British checkpoint at Orford Ness, Rand had not seen a single cloud, but now he was annoyed to see that small puffs were beginning to appear far below the mother ship, and occasionally they would come between the mother ship and the drone, and Rand would hold his breath until he could regain visual control a few seconds later. "What the hell are those puffs?" he said into the interphone.

"Clouds," Falkenstine said. "Where did they come from?"

"I don't know," Rand answered, "but they're not making things any easier."

"Are we on course?" Falkenstine asked the navigator.

"Dead on, sir," the voice came back. "We should reach the initial point in about three minutes."

For a second, the late-afternoon sun glinted off the high-visibility wings of the drone below, and Rand breathed a silent request that the robot would continue to remain so plainly in sight. He made a few adjustments and saw that the drone was passing over the briefed checkpoints with perfect regularity. Now the great white dome of Wizernes came up in the distance, and Falkenstine said, "There it is!"

Rand worked the control switches carefully, and the loaded B-17 below responded. It was still at 300 feet, held there by the automatic radio altimeter, but in a few seconds the Ace would be overpowered by a strong signal to the autopilot, and the drone would go crashing into the dome of Wizernes. "Steady," Rand said as the concrete top came into his sights. "Steady!"

For an instant Rand wondered when the 400 antiaircraft guns were going to open up, but he had no time to worry about such minor matters. Now the drone had almost reached the pre-planned point, 1,000 feet short of the target, where he would apply full down elevator through his azon controls. "Steady!" he said once more, and then his heart sank as the drone entered a small cloud and disappeared from sight. Calculating madly, Rand tried to estimate the robot's location, and when he guessed it should be directly over the aiming point, he threw the switch to dive the huge flying bomb on target.

"There she is!" Falkenstine said. The drone had passed through the cloud and appeared to be headed downward. The mother ship went into a steep bank, and Rand had to hold on tight to keep from being pitched against the plexiglass windows in front of him. He saw the drone and the target in perfect alignment, and he held his breath, waiting for the explosion. But now the drone seemed to be moving away, passing over the concrete dome. "Get down!" Rand screamed. "Get down, you son of a bitch!" The robot flew on, the large sites at Wizernes plainly behind it now, and exploded in a huge yellow balloon of flame.

"Missed, goddamn it!" Falkenstine said over the intercom. "We went over."

"How far?" Rand said.

"I don't know," Falkenstine answered. "Maybe a quarter of a mile."

APHRODITE: DESPERATE MISSION   140

"What's the difference?" Rand said disconsolately. "We missed, that's all." He did not speak on the trip back across the Channel.

> *Time of attack—Aug. 4, 1600 hrs., height—300 meters. Aircraft shot down by flak. Attack was directed against a construction work. Aircraft exploded upon impact into tiny fragments, which were scattered over a radius of 500–1500 meters from the point of impact, creating craters of various diameters (one measuring 20 meters). Aircraft maintained course even while attacked by flak and no counter-measures were observed. Whether or not there were accompanying aircraft flying above could not be determined. No traces of a crew or aerial guns were found. A great quantity of explosives must have been used, based on complete destruction of aircraft.*
> —German Air Force intelligence report

One robot remained, and it took off at 4:02 P.M., seconds after the code word denoting another failure had been flashed from Falkenstine's mother ship high over Wizernes to the operations office at Fersfield. Pappy Tooman and his bombardier, Glen Hargis, took control of the No. 4 robot after the pilot and the autopilot man had jumped. They steered the ancient B-17 straight across the Channel toward another German large site buried in the ground at Mimoyecques, about seven miles inland from the tip of Cap Gris-Nez. Midway across the Channel, Hargis reported that the drone was acting up.

"What's she doing?" Tooman asked.

"She's climbing," Hargis said. "She's coming up too high. Everything I do at the target is based on that plane staying at three hundred feet, but she's easy at six hundred now and still coming up."

"Well, you'll just have to improvise," Tooman ordered.

Hargis tried to comply, but now the robot was flying more and more erratically, sometimes nosing upward until he thought it would stall and sometimes leveling off as though to gain speed for another attempt to haul itself into the air. Hargis was still fighting the drone when Tooman reported the French coast dead ahead and told him to get ready for the final run to the target.

"There's no way to control!" Hargis said. "I'm going to try to dive her back to Ace altitude."

"It won't work," Tooman said, "but you might as well try."

With the target visible a few miles ahead, Hargis applied full down control, and the robot's nose dipped toward earth. When the plane had reached Ace altitude, Hargis turned off the dump switches, hoping that the radio altimeter would take hold and level the drone out. But the clumsy, heavy-laden B-17 kept on descending and crashed short of the target.

"Look at the head on that!" Tooman shouted over the intercom, and the crew rushed to the ports for a look. A ball of greenish-yellow fire had rocketed up from the detonation like a giant Fourth of July firework, and when it reached a point almost two miles from the earth, it flattened out on top.

"That's the biggest explosion you'll ever see," Tooman said. "Too bad it didn't hit something." Desultory flak began blossoming around the B-24, and Tooman dropped a wing in a tight turn and poured on full throttle for the run home, losing altitude and gaining speed with every mile. He passed Dover at some 6,000 feet, and he heard a gasp over the intercom and the voice of the tail gunner. "Hey, we're in the goddamn middle of a goddamn buzz bomb attack!" Tooman looked out and saw the flaming exhaust of a German V-1 passing to the right, headed straight for London. Another came by, and a third, and then the B-24 mother ship shuddered in midair as a burst of flak went off nearby.

"The Limeys are firing at the V-bombs!" Hargis called out from his vantage point in the nose.

Tooman flicked on his radio switch. He was white with rage, compounded of previous encounters with British flak and the disappointment of missing his target at Mimoyecques, and he said evenly and loudly into the microphone: "Can you please shut off the goddamned artillery? You're down there nice and safe. We're up here, and there's flak all over the place. This is supposed to be friendly territory."

The flak continued, but no more immediate bursts upset Tooman's equanimity. He flew north-northeast along the coast, out of range of the Dover gunners, until he reached Great Yarmouth, and when he turned inland toward Fersfield at an altitude of 4,000 feet, the British opened up on the B-24 with 40-mm automatic weapons. Tooman had been homing on a "splasher" beacon and had radioed his estimated time of landfall and had turned on his IFF loud and clear, but now once again he had to contend with friendly flak. He put the four-engine bomber into shudderingly violent evasive maneuvers, dived to gain speed and pull clear of the coastal antiaircraft stations, and finally burst into peaceful air south of Norwich.

The intercom was silent, and Tooman was just as glad. He was no more profane than the next man, but he knew that his vocabulary would singe the wires and burn out headsets if he ever gave vent to his true feelings about the antiaircraft defenses of the British Isles. He reached the little town of Diss, a few miles from Fersfield and put the aircraft into his own patented all-weather approach—straight down the railroad tracks, hard right turn over the church steeple, then level out and drop the wheels just in time to catch the tip of the runway. The Liberator was almost to the end of the taxi strip when Tooman realized that his crew was keeping silent in deference to him. They were like children hiding their faces in their soup because they knew the father was in a bad mood. "All right, men," he said in the most stentorian voice he could summon. "I've just got one thing to say. When you fly over these British gunners, you really learn what combat is!"

Somebody opened up his microphone and laughed, and Tooman gunned the B-24 to its hardstand and eased it into the parking space. The crew assembled outside the main door of the plane, and Tooman said, "Okay, men, the fun's over," and the crew dragged its parachute packs and its flight kits toward the debriefing room.

Tooman's crew was the last to check in from the long, unrewarding day. His men were tired from four hours and fifty-four minutes in the air, and they gave short answers to the intelligence officer who scribbled their remarks on prepared forms. The forms were four routine bombing missions, and they called for such information as "position in formation," "bombs; type, no. & size," "mag heading," "IAS," "enemy fighter opposition," "time, place, duration and type of attack." Not all the requested information applied to an Aphrodite mission, and the first debriefing was quickly over. Then Tooman and the rest of his crew trooped into a larger room, where all the other men who had flown on the mission waited to be interrogated by Lieutenant Colonel Roy Forrest, project officer Frank Holbrook, and a few other officers of field grade. When everyone had made his report and the questioning had stretched out close to the two-hour mark, a dimly outlined picture of the day's events came into focus.

The parachuting had been a debacle. Five of the jumpers had been injured and two were still in the hospital. The pilot of the No. 4 robot, an outspoken Midwesterner named Cornelius Engel, had experienced seat-pack failure *and* chest-pack failure, and only by tearing the silk out of the chest pack by hand had he been able to put a slight brake on his descent. He landed hard, and when he regained consciousness, he found that some of his teeth were pushed back into his throat, his back was sprained, and there were severe rubbing burns on his thighs. Frank Houston confirmed that he had suffered the same experience and had been saved by a mighty oak. Engel's autopilot man, Technical Sergeant Clifford Parsons, told a bizarre story of confusion and courage. He had still been working on the autopilot controls, trying to tune out some warning lights, when Engel had shouted down that they were being fired on by friendly flak. Their orders were to bail out if they were fired on, but Parsons' kept plugging away at the potentiometer dials on the autopilot until it was nearly ready to function. Then Engel shouted down, "Goddamn it, Sergeant, they're firing on us. Get out of that hole!"

The pitch dials still had not been set up to Parsons' satisfaction, but there was a note of urgency in the voice from above, and he wriggled into his chest pack and thrust his legs through the navigator's escape hatch and slowly began to lower himself on his arms. The slipstream had shoved his legs almost parallel to the belly of the B-17, and he was about to lose his grip and fall away into the air when he remembered that he had forgotten to hook up his static line in all the excitement. He was not an overly powerful person, but he managed to lift himself back onto the catwalk and make the connection. Then he dropped through the hole and felt the blast of air and the twin jerks of the static line and the blossoming of the parachute. "I thought my troubles were over," Parsons told the audience at the briefing, "but I came down on the roof of a house, and I fell two stories after my chute collapsed. I guess I sprained my ankle."

Some of the parachutists had experienced tense moments on the ground. Staff Sergeant Philip Enterline had sat across the road from seven or eight menacing members of the Women's Land Army for thirty minutes, trying to talk them out of attacking him with their pitchforks and rakes, before a jeep of the American military police arrived and took him to safety. "I think on the next jumps you should keep everybody in uniform or paint American flags on them," Enterline suggested. "In these flying fatigues and paratrooper's boots, we look just like German paratroopers."

Enterline's pilot, Fain Pool, told how he had heard an ear-splitting explosion just after he landed and how he had made the assumption that his aircraft had blown up (in reality it was Fisher's). "But then these English field hands came running up," Pool said, "and they wanted to know what happened. I thought about security, so I just said, 'I don't know. My aircraft caught fire, and I had to bail out.' More people came running up and they said, 'Was that your plane that blew up?' and I just said, 'I guess so.' They had formed a ring around me, and then a constable came along and drove me to Woodbridge."

Everyone fell silent when it came time for the report of the co-pilot of Aphrodite's only fatality. Technical Sergeant Elmer Most, a heavyset man well over six feet tall, told how he and Lieutenant John Fisher had fought to set up the bulky drone, but no matter what they did, the radio altimeter would not function. Even when they were at nearly 2,000 feet, it indicated 300, and when Sergeant Most attempted to set it right, the airplane began a series of abrupt climbs. "Lieutenant Fisher told me to get out, and I headed out the hatch with him right after me," Most reported. "But there wasn't room for me and both my chutes through that hole, and I stuck there, and Lieutenant Fisher put his foot on my shoulder and shoved me through. I banged my head and I don't know how long I was floating in the air, and then I heard this explosion and I could see trees smoking and a big hole in the woods."

"Was the ship armed when you left it?" Colonel Forrest asked.

"No, sir, I don't think it was," Most said. "I think Lieutenant Fisher had set the safety clock and plugged in the tumbler jacks, but I don't think he had pulled the lanyard yet."

At the close of the briefing, Forrest wrote up his report. Four drones had been dispatched. One had blown up almost immediately; the cause was unknown. One had failed to respond to down control and had been shot down by a now-defunct German antiaircraft battery. One had gone into a cloud and responded too slowly to down control and crashed well beyond the target, and one had failed mechanically and blown up

APHRODITE: DESPERATE MISSION   146

short. "Ain't that beautiful?" Forrest said to his operations officer. "Four up and four down, and nothing near a target. The end of a perfect day."

A search team reported back from the scene of Fisher's explosion just after nightfall, and a young lieutenant was hanging onto a short piece of metal. "Major Rand told me to find this if I couldn't find another thing," the officer told Forrest. "It's the receiving antenna, cut to exactly the right frequency. If anybody found it, they'd know what wavelength we were transmitting on, and they could jam the mission."

"Tell the ordnance officers to wrap those antennas in prima-cord on all missions from now on," Forrest said. "That way they'll blow up with the rest of the load. We don't want to be leaving any precut antennas around for the Krauts."

Forrest asked the young officer what else they had found at the site of the explosion. "Well, the first thing we found was a British farmer who said we blew up eighty of his cows," the lieutenant reported. "I told him we'd look into it."

"Probably lost an old sow and a blind dog," Forrest said, "and now he's trying to get rich off it."

"Yes, sir," the young officer said. "Far as the general scene is concerned, he crashed in the middle of the Thetford Chase Forest. Most of the trees are firs and white oak. Most of them are a foot or two in diameter, but there are some old specimens five and six feet through the trunk. Across an area of about one hundred and twenty yards wide, every one of those trees was pulverized, and there was less damage as you fanned out from there."

"How deep was the hole?" Forrest asked.

"The main crater's about twenty-five by thirty-five feet, kind of rectangular-shaped, and maybe five feet deep. Then there's a secondary crater going out from that for another fifty feet, maybe three feet deep on the average."

"Did you find anything identifiable besides the antenna?"

"Yes, sir, we found fragments of engine and some pieces of the fuselage."

"Any traces of the pilot?"

"No, sir. None whatever. He must have been incinerated, sir."

Forrest dismissed the efficient young officer and went into his room to write Fisher's next of kin. He had written dozens of such letters, but this time he did not know what to say. The project was still supersecret. Finally, he settled on a short statement of sympathy and a vaguely worded message to the effect that the young pilot had died in action. As he scribbled the letter by the light of an old, yellowing lamp tucked beneath his blackout curtains, Forrest remembered how Fisher had dangled his legs from the escape hatch and then climbed back into the bucking aircraft to set it straight and level, ultimately sacrificing his chance to parachute safely. He felt a sadness that he could not write more about John Fisher's devotion to duty.

At last the disagreeable task was done, and Forrest whistled up the operations officer and said, "John, I think I can say without any question of a doubt that we deserve a drink."

"We do, Colonel," the ops officer said, and the two men made the long walk in the darkness to the combination officers' mess and saloon on the far side of the apron. A few of the jump pilots were bellied up to the bar, and Forrest recognized Frank Houston and gave him a mighty clap on the back.

Houston spat his drink out and said, "Colonel! Please don't interrupt me, sir. I will be drunk in a few minutes and ready for action."

"Why are you getting drunk, Sam?" Forrest said, winking sideways at a few of the others.

"Because I have to kill a man with my bare hands tonight, and I've never killed a man before, and I'm getting up my courage," Houston said thickly.

"Who you gonna kill, Sam?" the commanding officer said.

"The parachute man."

"You can't kill him, Sam," the Texan said. "I've already shipped him out."

"To where?"

"Never mind, Sam," Forrest said. "Now listen, I've got a proposition for you. You've entered into this project with the proper spirit. You've never griped or complained about what you would have to do, and I appreciate that."

A look of incredulity came across Houston's face, but Forrest talked right through it. "Yes, sir," he said, "I want you to know I appreciate an officer like that, Sam, and I've asked Major Rand to rig up another baby for you. So you go enjoy yourself in London for a few hours and come back here, and we'll have another one ready for you."

Houston drew himself up in a mock brace. He said in a cadet-school flat monotone, "Sir, I appreciate your kind offer. Sir, I joined the Army Air Corps because I love my country. Sir, because of my intense love and devotion for my country, I wish to tell you what I think of your kind offer. Sir, kindly take your kind offer and shove it up your ass!"

At first, there was a stunned silence, but when Forrest threw back his head and emitted a bellowing cow-country laugh from the depths of his Texas soul, everyone else at the bar fell into raucous laughter. "Goddamn you, Sam," Forrest said, giving poor Houston another mighty clap on his sore shoulder, "I wouldn't take that from anybody but you, but from you it's a pleasure."

"Thank you, sir," Houston said, "and now, sir, with your kind permission, I would like to leave this godforsaken place and get a ride back to my old outfit."

When Houston had disappeared, Forrest drank a few more gins than customary and bought round after round from his personal bankroll for Fain Pool and Pappy Tooman and Foster Falkenstine and some of the other veterans of the first Aphrodite mission. But he declined a final toast proposed by Fain

Pool. "Sir," Pool had said, raising his glass of bourbon high above the fresh bandage on his sliced eyebrow, "I have made a decision, and I'd like you to drink to it. Sir, I'm going to jump again."

"You're what?" said the astounded and slightly tipsy commanding officer.

"With your permission," Pool said, "I'd like to volunteer for another mission."

Forrest put his arm around the eager young officer and said, "Pool, I like you, I've always liked you, but Pool, there is one very basic reason why I don't drink to that, and why you won't fly another mission."

"What's that, sir?" Pool said.

"Because you're demented, that's why!" Forrest roared. "Any son of a bitch that volunteers to do this twice has got to be crazy. If I ever hear you mention flying another mission, I'm putting you into the flakhouse for a year, is that understood?"

"Yes, sir," the chastened young pilot said. "Yes, sir." He paused. "I'd have liked it, though," he said meekly.

When Forrest wended his way back to the orderly room some time after midnight, he found the intelligence officer wrapping up his own final report on the events of the day. "What's taking so long, Joe?" Forrest said.

"Tough to get the wording just right," the G-2 officer said.

"What's so tough about the wording?"

"We had a lousy day, and I'm trying not to say so."

Forrest brushed the intelligence officer aside and positioned himself in front of the old typewriter and began flailing away with two fingers and a thumb. "Here," he said, "just put down all the statistics and conclude it with this."

Forrest read aloud from his own work: " 'Mother and robot crews feel that the equipment is good and are satisfied that they can make successful attacks. They derived good experience from the missions and have gained a great deal of confidence in the project.' How's that?"

The intelligence officer said that it was a very fine piece of writing.

The official report on the missions of August 4 went through channels, higher and higher, until it reached Washington, D.C. A few days later there was a return message from General H. H. "Hap" Arnold, commander of the U.S. Army Air Corps: "PRELIMINARY REPORT ON YOUR AUG. FOUR EFFORT VERY ENCOURAGING. ALL PERSONNEL CONCERNED ARE TO BE COMMENDED. WE ARE FOLLOWING PROJECT WITH GREAT INTEREST AND ARE COUNTING ON BEING KEPT INFORMED. ASSUME YOU ARE DOING EVERYTHING POSSIBLE TO INCREASE ACCURACY."

A copy of the message worked its way down to Roy Forrest, and when the salty Texan read it, he laughed and told Loyd Humphries, "Well, well, Humpy, nothing succeeds like failure."

By the time the Aphrodite project became operational, the Allies had lost 2,900 men and 450 aircraft in the effort to knock out the menacing rocket-launching sites across the Channel. More than 7,000 tons of bombs had been dropped on the four big bunkers, and yet a measure of activity had never ceased at the sites, nor was there any evidence that the bombing had been more than mildly effective. The RAF, with its 12,000-pound "tallboy" bombs, had knocked off a corner of the huge concrete rectangle at Watten, but every reconnaissance flight confirmed that the Germans still appeared to be stirring at Watten and its three sister sites at Wizernes, Siracourt, and Mimoyecques. To be sure, no one could see through the thick ferroconcrete domes, but there was enough peripheral activity to convince the Allies that whatever had been going on under the massive white panoplies was still going on.

"So you can see, Forrest," the brigadier general said over the post prandial cigars at Spaatzhouse, where the commanding officer of the U.S. Strategic Air Forces in Europe maintained his headquarters, "a direct hit by Aphrodite would save a lot of lives and do a lot of good."

"Not to mention forestalling any V-3 attack on London and New York," said a visiting British colonel.

"We're doing everything we can, sir," said Forrest. "The main thing is the weather. We've scrubbed something like twenty-five missions, and that's hard on everybody."

After the informal dinner at Lieutenant General Carl Spaatz's headquarters, the men moved into an anteroom for more cigars and brandy and conversation, and after an hour or so Forrest found himself hemmed in by a team of nettling officers. At first, he had thought he must be turning supersensitive at the old age of thirty-one: Whenever Aphrodite was mentioned, there would be a snicker, or a telltale glance, or some other form of subtle belittling. To Forrest, the colonels and majors and captains around him seemed to be alternately humoring him and patronizing him. At last his Texas good nature failed him.

"Excuse me, gentlemen," Forrest said, "but just what is all this smart-ass joking about? If you're trying to tell me something, why don't you try English, if that language is spoken around here."

Several of the junior officers turned red and silent, but a few of the colonels were not reluctant to tell Forrest that the Aphrodite program *was* a joke to them, and its miserable opening-day record of zero hits in four attempts had surprised nobody.

"If the project's a joke," Forrest said evenly, "then how come it's got the top priority in the theater and everybody keeps telling us how important we are?"

No one answered.

"Look, fellows," Forrest went on, "if that's the way it is, then let's act like honest people. If your feeling is that we're not doing the job, then let's scrub the son of a bitch, and I'll go home and meet my new daughter."

Forrest still believed in Aphrodite, but he could not allow a small clique of desk pilots to backbite or undermine the project, and he knew the bluff would have to be called right now. "How about it, gentlemen?" he said.

A lieutenant colonel spoke up. "Forrest," he said, "there's something you don't know. To tell you the truth, we'd all *love* to scrub this damned fool model-airplane program you're running, but we can't."

"And why not?" the angry Texan asked.

"Because it's the Old Man's baby!" the officer said. "It's the Old Man's pride and joy and consuming interest. He's like a kid about it."

Roy Forrest was not a close friend of USSTAF's commanding general, Carl "Tooey" Spaatz, but he knew enough about the general's reputation for realistic judgments to find this new information surprising. "You're kidding me!" he said.

"No, we're not," the other officer said. "He's always after us for reports, and he's always encouraging us to keep the project going. He says this Aphrodite nonsense is the wave of the future. We've reached the point where we wince every time there's a message from the War Department."

"From the War Department?" Forrest said. "You mean you're not talking about Spaatz?"

"We're talking about Hap Arnold," the officer said.

Forrest flew back to Fersfield late that night with a new optimism. If General Hap Arnold, chief of the U.S. Air Force, was squarely behind Aphrodite, nothing could stop them. His priorities would not be toothless formalities, and his demands for necessary equipment, fighter cover, bombing support, men, and matériel would be answered. Indeed, something that had been puzzling him for several weeks was now resolved by this new information. He had always wondered why a pair of nearly identical units from the Army Air Corps Signal Division and the U.S. Navy's assault-drone program had arrived at the secret base at Fersfield demanding shop space and quarters right at the height of Major Jim Rand's attempts to get his own program off the ground. Aphrodite was top-secret, and yet within a few weeks of the onset of the program, teams doing similar work had checked in from Wright Field in Ohio and the Navy's assault-drone station at Traverse City, Michigan. How had the news reached them so quickly that experiments with radio-controlled "babies" had now reached the operational stage? The answer had to be Hap Arnold. Forrest surmised that the Aphrodite secret had been shared at the top levels in Washington, and now everybody wanted to get into the act.

Major Henry James Rand and his fellow technicians hardly slept in the two days after the abortive missions of August 4. Conference followed conference, and no idea was too amateurish or too naïve to be discussed. Rand seemed almost frantic. "If I make a stupid design, that's one thing," the cigar-smoking major screamed at Roy Forrest at one of the endless postmortems. "But if some dumb son of a bitch lashes the nitrostarch to the control cables, I say that's so stupid as to be worth a court-martial!" Unfortunately, no one knew which ammunition loader had tied up Lieutenant Joe Andrecheck's control cables. A dozen enlisted men had packed the airplanes under the supervision of an Army ordnance lieutenant, and any one of them, including the lieutenant, could have made the mistake.

Certain conclusions were reached firmly and quickly and acted on with dispatch. Everyone agreed that the loads had been stacked too high for stability. New designs for loading were drawn up, and more of the weight was snubbed into the bomb bays, where the original Boeing designers had intended the bulk of the aircraft's payload to be carried. The British agreed to supply 500 tons of a new explosive called Torpex, nearly twice as powerful as TNT and about half again as powerful as nitrostarch. With this new formula, first developed by the Germans, the drones could carry a lighter load and achieve the same effect.

The mother ship crews had returned from their frustrating

missions with certain suspicions about the plotted trajectories of diving B-17 drones. Pappy Tooman was especially annoyed. "Major Rand gave that baby down control, and it cruised and cruised till it was maybe two thousand or three thousand feet over the target," he said. "I'll admit that the major can make a mistake, but not that big a mistake!"

"Well, if you're so sure of yourself," Roy Forrest said, "go run some tests and see what you can find out."

Tooman rallied his whole crew and a couple of baby crews, installed an improvised driftmeter and a mirroring device in one of the drones, and flew all day, measuring angles of descent, gliding speeds, estimated impact points, and such matters. At the end of his experiments, he thought he had discovered the fatal flaw in the computed dump distances. He reported to Rand and Forrest. "It's like this. The estimated distance of one thousand feet between full down control and impact is just about right, give or take a few feet. But that's if you apply full down elevator and *hold* full down elevator. But we found out what happens when that baby goes down and starts picking up airspeed. Pretty soon she's going so fast that the forces on the elevator surfaces are too great for the autopilot servo to handle, and the elevator comes up and so does the glide angle. These damned B-17's, all they want to do is fly straight and level! They got a million ways of bringing themselves back to even."

The three men had a long discussion about how to hold full down elevator as the plane picked up speed. "Two men can do it, by leaning against the control columns," Tooman said. "We found that out. Two men are a hell of a lot stronger than the C-1 servos."

For a while, the engineers were set on a clever solution. They would put a heavy downspring on the elevator bell crank arm, and the instant the controller ordered the baby to descend, the C-1 servos and the heavy spring would combine to put a powerful pressure on the dump controls, a pressure equal at least to the combined power of a pilot and co-pilot leaning into the columns. But Jim Rand saw the flaw. If the downspring should accidentally take hold over England, he said, the loaded baby would go into an uncontrollable dive. The certain loss would be a baby pilot and co-pilot, plus whatever was at the impact point below. Since this could conceivably include Ipswich or Norwich or Great Yarmouth or any of dozens of British settlements, the idea was abandoned for reasons of safety, and Tooman went out to continue his experiments and try to learn more about the control of an unmanned B-17.

On the ground, the studies continued night and day. Fain Pool and Frank Houston were called back and questioned, and a team of interrogators visited Cornelius Engel in the hospital, where he was recovering from the effects of double chute failure. All three of the men had slashed their fingertips, and the interviewing showed how. Each had reached out for the lip of the navigator's hatch while plummeting through, and there was a sharp ridge around the edge. Since there was no practical way to train jump pilots not to make this last-second instinctive grab, Rand ordered the maintenance crews to smooth off the ridge, enlarge the hatch for easier exit, and install a wind deflector on the front edge.

There remained the actual problems of parachuting. Seven men had jumped; five had experienced parachute trouble of one sort or another. "I think I know the answer," said a prospective jump pilot named Glen Barnes. "I think your problem is the static line."

"The static line isn't the problem, Lieutenant—it's the solution to problems," one of the older engineering officers spoke up. "You can't expect a pilot without parachuting experience to jump out of a B-17 at a thousand feet and pull a rip cord."

"Why not?" Barnes asked.

"Because he's already got a million things to remember, and because he's not a parachutist by training in the first place. With the static line, all he does is jump, and everything takes care of itself."

Barnes said, "Sir, I couldn't disagree more. The record of the missions shows that the static line system doesn't work under these conditions."

"Well, tell me why," the engineering officer said. "My mind's open. God knows we've got to get to the bottom of this."

Glen Barnes was a scientific farmer in Kansas by trade. He had the metabolism of a hummingbird, and he had been keeping busy around Fersfield by test-flying the Aphrodite airplanes. He was known as a devoted student of the B-17.

"Sir," he said, "that static line is thirty-seven feet long, and it's heavy nylon, with a breaking strength of something like three thousand pounds. Now consider the jump pilot as a projectile, which is exactly what he is. He comes out of the hatch of that B-17 at just under two hundred miles an hour, and maybe he's tumbling or rifling and maybe he's not. Now he's got to fall thirty-seven feet before the static line starts pulling his chute out. But what happens if that static line loops around him? What happens if a single loop of it has caught around his foot, or his hand, *or his neck?* There's no reason to assume that this can't happen. And when it does, the jumper gets about a twenty-G jerk and the chute doesn't open. In my opinion, that's what happened to Lieutenant Houston. Somehow a length of that static line crossed over his shoulder, and the shoulder took the force of the jerk instead of the parachute. It pulled the static line right out of its anchor."

There were some who agreed with Barnes and some who loudly disagreed. Then Lieutenant Colonel Dale Anderson, the technical leader of the group from Wright Field, spoke up. "Gentlemen," he said, "I know that jump techniques are none of my business, and they won't be until my group is ready to put a drone in the air, but I've been talking to a few people and I'd like to point something out. You're depending on sensitive radio equipment to control this drone, and the first thing you have to be absolutely certain of is your receiving antennas. They must be in perfect working order. But what happens after two men bail out and leave two thirty-seven-foot lengths of heavy nylon line flapping and lashing in the slipstream? Gentlemen, it doesn't take a genius to see that one of those heavy lines could snap those short antennas right off, or short them, or just bump them a little, enough to ruin your control."

"Maybe that's why the Ace failed on us a couple times," said one of the mother ship bombardiers. "It worked over and over again in practice, but as soon as we went operational, it responded inaccurately or it didn't respond at all."

All were agreed that the static lines were a problem, but a senior engineering officer said that he was not convinced that they should be eliminated. "I recognize the problems," he said, "but I think we'd be getting into more problems without the static lines. Let's wait and see. We'll try a few more missions and see what happens." There the matter stood.

On August 6, Project Aphrodite was ready to take the air again, thanks to forty-eight hours of nearly continuous work by crews under the whiplashing Major Rand. "You're a hard man," Roy Forrest had said one night when he wandered into the shop area and found a full crew beginning its third straight eight-hour shift.

"I'm hard on myself at the same time," Rand said wearily, "and right now while we're talking, people are getting killed in the front lines. And if we don't get those rocket sites out of there, civilians will die by the thousands in London."

"Wait a minute," the commanding officer said. "You talk like I was criticizing you. I'm proud of you and all your guys, Jimmy—let's be straight on that."

Rand turned contrite. "I've been edgy lately," he said. "We should have hit those targets the first day. Now the Germans have had warning. This time they'll be throwing all kinds of flak at us."

"Well, don't work your way into the hospital," Forrest said, patting the dumpy major on the shoulder. "We need you around here, and I don't give a rat's ass what anybody says!"

Forrest was remembering the talk at Third Bomb Division Headquarters about the "mad scientist" and his "insane ideas," and he knew that some of the criticism had reached Rand and troubled him. It all seemed unfair to Forrest. Rand had not pushed his system on anyone. He had simply agreed to try to adapt it to these pressing new wartime needs. He had promised nothing except a good effort, and he was providing the good effort around the clock. To Forrest, it seemed that the complainers at headquarters might better have spent their time putting Rand in for a decoration instead of carping about him.

The missions of August 6 were scaled down to a more manageable size by the planners at Elveden Hall. Only two drones were to be dispatched, and each would be controlled by its own primary and secondary mother ship. The mother ships would take off first and climb to 20,000 feet. At 10:50 A.M. the first drone, *Franklin Yellow,* would take off, followed by the second drone, *Franklin White,* ten minutes later. Both robots would fly the same rectangular course over East Anglia while the mother ships checked control and the jump crews bailed out. Both drones would have the same target: the massive casing of ferroconcrete at Watten, a few miles north of St.-Omer in the Pas-de-Calais area. If everything went according to plan, the first baby would explode its nine tons of Torpex directly on the rocket site, opening up cracks and fissures for Drone No. 2, which carried a mixed load of inflammables: 9 incendiary bombs in the nose, 35 in the pilot's compartment, 116 in the radio operator's compartment and 20 in the ball turret, plus 830 gallons of jellied gasoline in the bomb bay tanks. The planners had based the operation on the results of the tests at the Air Corps' experimental station at Eglin Field, Florida, where rats in bunkers had been suffocated in a few minutes when gasoline had been poured over the exit holes and ignited. Even if the most powerful load of explosives ever carried aloft by man failed to destroy the rocket site, the theory was that enough damage would be done to enable the napalm of Drone No. 2 to kill the personnel working far beneath the earth, sheltered by the slab of concrete. Thus the two drones were considered to be working in tandem, and there was no prospect of total success unless both functioned perfectly. To help smooth out the operation, Eighth Air Force Headquarters had requested RAF diversionary assistance, and the English had agreed to send over 100 bombers at 14,000 to 16,000 feet, to occupy the German gunners and fighters and to shake up the antiaircraft artillery batteries before the highly vulnerable robots reached the scene of the attack. A heavy cover of American P-38 Lightnings would shelter the mission, and B-24 Liberators of the Third Bomb Division would mop up at thirty minutes after zero hour with raids of their own on the rocket sites.

The briefings went faster than those of two days before, and the crews hopped into jeeps for the ride to their aircraft, scattered in hardstands at the farthest corners of the base. "Hey, fellows, just one thing!" Pappy Tooman called to the jump crew of Robot No. 2. "What are you guys hauling again?"

"Eight hundred gallons of jell gas and two hundred incendiaries," the pilot answered.

"Well, I'd like to leave you with one little message," Tooman said. "No smoking!"

First Lieutenant Joseph Andrecheck, the same pilot who had found his control cables lashed to the fuselage two days before, was scheduled to be the pilot of the first drone, and he had made a personal vow to carry out a perfect Aphrodite mission. Andrecheck was a wiry little B-17 pilot with thirty-four missions behind him and a record of never having aborted for any reason, mechanical or otherwise. "Shit in the neck," his co-pilot had said about the former dairy farmer from upstate New York, "is a disease Joe ain't got!" Andrecheck volunteered for Aphrodite on the mistaken premise that he would have to parachute behind the lines in Poland, where his command of his parents' native language would be helpful, but when he had learned that he would be flying a planeload of high explosives, he had shrugged his shoulders and said, "So what? A flight's a flight. I fly airplanes for a living. Nothing connected with flying airplanes should bother me." And nothing did. To perform his job of flying airplanes better than the next man, Andrecheck neither drank nor smoked. He was twenty-six years old, and he was no prude, but he did not want to lose any of the sharpness of reflex that might someday save his life or the lives of his crew members. Occasionally he would sit in on the jump pilots' red dog game, and among the others he was known as the morale builder for his cheerful personality and friendly manner. A hitch in the prewar Army as an enlisted man had given him pride in his officer's uniform, and he spent hours polishing the buttons and shining his shoes. Pappy Tooman, who loved a pun, used to single out the friendly Polish-American pilot and say, "Look at old Andrecheck—all spit and Polish!"

Even now, on the day of his first Aphrodite mission, Andrecheck had buffed his jump boots to a high gloss. "It'll never hurt," he told his autopilot man, Sergeant Raymond Healy, as they climbed into the parked drone. "Might be some broads where I land!" Later he was to remember the remark and wince.

The two drone crewmen looked carefully at the load of Torpex that was scattered all about them inside the stifling pilot's compartment of the B-17. "Looks a little better than the other day," Andrecheck said. "Not piled quite so high. Now let's see if they tied up our controls again."

He sat in the pilot's seat, unlocked the controls, and turned the wheel; the ailerons were moving. Andrecheck pumped the control column back and forth and saw that the elevators were operating. He touched the rudder pedals, and there was a perfect response. "Great!" the pilot said. "Now if we can just turn over the engines, we're in business!"

Everything checked, and exactly on the tick of ten minutes to eleven on the morning of August 6, robot aircraft *Franklin Yellow* was off and running and lifting from the asphalt runway in a perfect takeoff.

"How'm I doing?" the exhilarated pilot said to his temporary co-pilot. "I tell you, Ray, nothing can stop us today. It's a great day for the Polish!"

"Thanks a lot," Healy said wryly.

"Oh, excuse me," the cheery pilot said. "It's a great day for the Irish, too!"

If there was ever a case of an air crew triumphing over obstacles by the sheer force of personality, *Franklin Yellow* was going to be it. The autopilot check took only a few minutes; the warning lights snapped off in one-two-three order, and the C-1 was clutched in with a minimum of bother. Andrecheck flicked on his transmitter and said, "Flyball," the new code word to indicate that they were beginning bailout procedures. When he received an acknowledgment from Foster Falkenstine's mother B-17 high above, Andrecheck cupped his hands and shouted down to the catwalk: "Go! Have a nice trip!"

After Healy jumped, the pilot transmitted "Change pictures!" to tell the mother ship that he was abandoning control. He slipped off his radio gear, set the ten-minute safety clock on the control panel, and slid out of the pilot's seat. Now he had two remaining assignments: to pull the cables that would arm the Torpex manually and to plug in the jacks that would complete the circuit for the electrical arming system. He checked the warning lights that would show whether the tumbler switches in the electrical system had already fallen, in which case the plugging of the jacks into the system might detonate the whole load in midair. The lights were out, and Andrecheck knew that it was safe to pull out the dummy jacks and insert the live ones. Or was it?

He took a closer look at the safety lights to see if there was the barest glimmer of electrical activity in the bulbs. There was none, but he knew that a man's eyes could play tricks on him when he was under pressure, and he brought his eye so close to the lights that they were almost touching and peered deep into the innards of the bulbs. Still he could see nothing, but he could feel his heart pounding and his face dripping with sweat, and he knew that he was being confronted with something that he had never expected: a numbing panic. Plans for self-preservation spun through his head. He realized that he could skip the electrical connections and let the drone go over to the target with only the mechanical fuses armed. Who would ever know? Even if the plane failed to blow up, it would only be dismantled by the Germans. Who would *ever* know?

"My God, what am I saying?" the pilot who had never aborted said to himself. "I must be losing my marbles. How the hell would I live with myself if I did a thing like that?" He fingered the two jacks that would complete the circuit to the live fuses. "Well, it'll blow up or it won't blow up, one or the other," he said aloud, "and it won't take long to find out, that's for sure." He rammed the two jacks into place. The only sound was the air rushing up through the open navigator's hatch a few feet away. Without wasting another second on soul-searching, the little pilot grabbed the lanyard leading to the mechanical switches and pulled with all the force of his 150 pounds. The lanyard came free in his hands, and he knew that now the B-17 was doubly armed and fused and ready for the target. "Good-bye, you poor bastard!" he said as he slipped into his chest pack, lying alongside the scape hatch, and snapped his static line to the eyebolt above. "Don't go near Poland!" He gripped the sides of the hatch and swung himself out in space till he was directly above the middle of the hole and fell through in a ball. A minor appendage of the airplane's underpinning passed about a foot over his nose, and then he felt a jerk, and a big expanse of white silk was rippling above him.

"Perfect!" he shouted as he floated through the air. "Perfect!"

He sailed into the outer branches of a small pine tree, hit the ground feetfirst, and fell off to one side, exactly as he had been taught by the paratroop officer at Fersfield. He spilled the air from his chute and was stepping out of his harness when a dozen wood nymphs in uniform were around him at once, talking madly. "Who are you?" "Where are you from?" "Where is your aircraft?" "What are you doing here?"

Andrecheck looked around and saw an antiaircraft gun poking into the sky, and he recognized the females as British military personnel. When he had told them the usual prepared story about his aircraft catching fire and forcing him to bail out, the woman in command of the troops said, "Well, Lieutenant, we'll just have to have a spot of tea together!"

"Twist my arm!" Andrecheck said, and went off to enjoy the company of the first women he had seen since being restricted to the base at Fersfield six weeks before. The women led him into a shack adjoining the antiaircraft gun, and the first round of beverages had just been poured when a jeepload of American military police came screeching up and told Andrecheck to climb in. "Damn it, Sarge," he said, "what's the matter with you guys anyway? You didn't give me a chance to get a single phone number!"

The drone B-17, its autopilot set up perfectly by Sergeant Raymond Healy and its controls trimmed perfectly by Lieutenant Joe Andrecheck, left the coast of England at Orford Ness under the perfect control of the mother ship piloted by Lieutenant Foster Falkenstine at 20,000 feet. At the first turning point over the North Sea, latitude 51 degrees 50 minutes north, longitude 2 degrees 37 minutes east, Falkenstine's bombardier flicked the switch that would turn the robot to the right and place it on a heading for the target. The drone responded by turning left, rolling over on its back, and falling 500 feet into the sea.

Ten minutes behind, in the other primary mother ship, the prevailing emotion was dismay. The pilot of the second robot had radioed that the autopilot was set up, and Pappy Tooman's bombardier, Glen Hargis, had taken control and started to steer the drone toward the next control point. The sky was cloudless and bright, but there was a silvery haze between Tooman's B-24 at 20,000 feet and the robot far below, and it seemed to Hargis that the robot was veering toward the right. He applied a slight correction, but the drone continued right, and when he sent the signal for a full left turn, the baby would not turn back past the straight and level. "The autopilot's not set up right!" Hargis said through the intercom.

"*Franklin White,*" Tooman called on Channel A, using the predesignated code name for the robot. "*Franklin White.* How do you read me?"

There was no response.

"*Franklin White!*" Tooman called. "Do you read me, *Franklin White?*"

Again there was no answer. Then an anonymous voice crackled into his headset, and Tooman knew that it must be one of the recon pilots far below. "*Franklin White* is empty," the voice said.

Tooman looked at his watch. "Son of a bitch!" he said. "They both bailed early."

Up in the bombardier's compartment in the nose, Hargis was having his hands full. He could make the drone fly almost straight and level by applying full left control, but at the slightest pause in the left impulse, the drone would flutter off to the right. "It's no use, Pappy," Hargis said. "She's not responding."

"We'll try the alternate mother," Tooman said. "Pass the control off!"

Hargis flicked his own radio switch to Channel A and called out, "New umpire, new umpire," the code word instructing the alternate mother ship to attempt control.

A voice answered, "New umpire. Roger!"

"She's got it, Pappy," Hargis said, and everyone on Tooman's crew relaxed. The drone appeared to be midway through a

360-degree turn, and Hargis figured that the bombardier in the alternate mother ship must be attempting to put it on a new heading. But as he watched through the plexiglass bubble, he saw the drone straighten out and take a course in the general direction of London. He flipped on his Channel A switch and cried out, "New umpire! New umpire!" This time there was no answer.

"I guess they didn't take control," Hargis said in the intercom.

"Where's the baby?" Tooman said.

Hargis peered into the silvery haze. The drone had vanished. "I don't know," he said.

"Everybody get to a window and start looking!" Tooman cried. "Karrels, you see anything back there?"

"No, sir," the tail gunner answered.

"Well, keep looking till you do!" Tooman said.

He banked the mother ship into a steep turn and straightened it on a course toward the southwest, approximately in the direction the robot had been flying. "See anything?" Tooman kept asking over the intercom, and voices kept answering, "No, sir."

After about ten minutes, Tooman said, "Hargis, I'm gonna tell the fighters to find it and shoot it down."

"May as well," Hargis answered.

Tooman ordered his radio operator to change frequencies, but when he asked the "little friends" to find the robot and destroy it, a voice crackled back: *"You* find it and destroy it!"

Tooman unleashed a string of expletives, interrupted by the voice of the tail gunner. "Sir, there's a B-17 doing 360's below us."

"Where?" Tooman said.

"Off to the right," the gunner answered. "Just over the outskirts of Ipswich."

"Jesus Christ!" Tooman said.

He stood the B-24 on its nose for a better look, and when the aircraft had dived about 5,000 feet, Hargis said, "That's it, Pappy. The wings are bright white!"

"Well, start controlling!" Tooman said. "She's about to wipe out the town!"

Hargis applied full left rudder. The robot, which had been making tight 360-degree turns, straightened momentarily and headed once again toward the southwest. Hargis decided to let the biggest fire bomb in the history of warfare go back into its turn and try to level the airplane out on another heading. He could not tell whether the baby was flying at 500 feet or 50, nor did he know whether it was on the verge of stalling and crashing into the city below. He had to take his chances. Hargis released the left-turn switch and watched the robot resume its tight turn to the right. This time the bombardier resumed full left control earlier, and the robot straightened out on a new heading and flew out of his line of vision. "Where is she?" he called into the interphone. "I've lost contact again."

"Headed out toward the water," the tail gunner said. "No! Wait! She's turning back inland!"

Again Hargis picked up the dim outline through the haze below, and again he saw that the drone aircraft had resumed its sharp right turn and was circling over the eastern edge of Ipswich. "Well, we gained a few miles," he said, and prepared to begin the tedious process again. Six turns later he had nursed the reluctant baby to the seacoast, but a broad swath of fog rolled in from the North Sea, and neither the bombardier nor the tail gunner nor the pilot could see the slightest trace of the plane loaded with napalm and incendiaries. "Keep looking," Tooman ordered. "She's got to be somewhere around here."

There was silence over the intercom for several minutes. The crew members were congregated at the windows, wiping their breath fog away and squinting into the haze below for the slightest indication of the baby. "Anything?" Tooman said.

"Nothing," a voice said.

"Well, get your head out of your ass and look!" Tooman snapped. "That goes for everybody."

"Wait!" Hargis called from his position in the bombardier's compartment. "I thought I saw something over the estuary. Wait! I think it's the drone!"

"Are you sure?" Tooman said.

"No, I'm not sure," Hargis said. "All I saw was a flash of white."

"How far out?"

"A few miles."

"Clear of the coast?" Tooman said.

"Yes, sir. I think so."

"Then dump it!" Tooman barked. "We've got to take the chance."

Hargis hit the dump switch and held it down. He peered out through the fog covering the estuary that ebbed into the North Sea and saw nothing. Seconds went by, and more seconds. "There!" the tail gunner said, but before he could make his directions more explicit, everyone in the mother ship could see a ball of yellow flame ballooning into the air from the tidal mud flats.

"The whole North Sea's on fire!" the radio operator cried out.

"Yeah," Tooman said laconically. "Better than Ipswich." The Liberator circled the wet holocaust below for a few minutes and then headed back toward Fersfield. Everyone aboard was braced for another explosion, this one from Tooman, and it was not long in coming. "Hargis," the veteran pilot said in even tones of anger and annoyance, "can you tell me in a few simple words how you managed to lose that baby? Just a few simple words will do, you sad sack!"

"It was a mix-up, Pappy, that's all," Hargis said. "I thought the other ship had it, and he thought I had it, I guess."

"You guess?" Tooman roared at the top of his lungs. *"You*

ess! Well, we don't guess in this business, Hargis. We don't guess when we're running nine tons of bombs and jell gas, Hargis. We don't guess when General Doolittle and General Partridge are both up in the air watching us!"

"I wasn't guessing," Hargis said, "I was—"

"I don't give a good goddamn what you were doing," Tooman said. "You were supposed to control that baby, and you didn't control it, did you? You had a job to do, and you didn't do it, did you? *Did you?*"

"No, sir," Hargis said.

"Hargis," Tooman said, "everybody in the Air Corps knows the three most useless things in the world. Number one: a runway behind you. Number two: gasoline down in the truck. And number three: a bombardier. *A bombardier!* I never saw a one of you guys that could find himself in the dark with both hands, let alone a target!"

Glen Hargis, probably the most skilled double azon bombardier in the Air Corps, did not see fit to comment on this ancient Air Corps canard. When they were up in the air, Tooman was the supreme high exalted ruler of their lives and their destinies. The bombardier made a mental note to explain the whole matter to Tooman at some future date; he knew he had not been guilty of human error, that the whole unfortunate result of Aphrodite Mission No. 6 was the result of a radio mix-up compounded by ground haze and a balky control system. But he also knew that it would be ridiculous to try to make his explanation over the interphones, with all the other crewmen listening in, and Tooman steamed to the ears anyway. Hargis knew that failure drove Tooman to violent rages and that they ended as quickly as they began. Later his friend Pappy would cool down, and he would understand.

On the ground, everyone was ordered to report to the briefing room for critique. Generals Doolittle and Partridge would be waiting to conduct a complete interrogation of the participants in this second day of total failure. When the crews reached the building, they found Doolittle striding up and down angrily, sputtering and fuming, and the usually placid Earle Partridge standing white-faced and grim behind him. Doolittle rattled off a string of questions, but none of the answers seemed to satisfy him. Once he pointed a finger at Rand and said, "Explain one thing to me, Major, just one thing, and I'll leave here happy. Why is it you fly these things day in day out under perfect control, and the second you take off on an operational mission everything goes blooey! Why? It doesn't make sense, Major!"

"I don't know, General," Rand said to his old friend.

"No, you're goddamn right you don't know," Doolittle said, "and until you can find out, you're finished here!"

Before Rand could comment, Doolittle was demanding to know what had caused the failure of the second robot, and one of the reconnaissance officers explained that the bailout crew had jumped early, before the autopilot was set up properly.

"How early?" Doolittle said.

"The autopilot man went out fourteen minutes early, sir, and the pilot four minutes," the recon man said.

"Why?" said Partridge.

"I'm not sure, sir," the officer answered. "Somebody said that they were fired on, but at this point I'm not sure."

"That's the whole trouble!" Doolittle said. "Nobody's sure of anything around this place!" He paced back and forth. "How'd the parachuting go today?" he said. "Any better than the last time?"

One of the project officers said, "Sir, the first jump crew got out okay. The second one had a little trouble. The autopilot man hurt his leg and his ankle, not too bad, maybe sprains or ligaments. The pilot of the second plane lost an arm."

"Lost an arm?" Doolittle said.

"That's what I understand from the hospital, sir," the officer said. "The static line caught in his arm, and gled so bad they had to take it off."

"My God!" Doolittle said. He walked over to Partridge and the two men conferred in low tones. Then Doolittle turned and looked out over the group of officers and men. "Gentlemen," he said, "I've asked you a lot of questions, and you've given me very few answers. It seems to me that this whole project is put together with baling wire, chicken guts, and ignorance. You're returned to training status indefinitely!"

A few hours later, word came from Third Bomb Division Headquarters that Rand's double azon system was to be abandoned. "The double azon method of control was not designed to do this type of work and was merely an expedient until the proper control equipment could be brought from the States," a report noted. "Malfunctions and failures of equipment occurred because it was not designed for this use. However, valuable information was obtained from this operation as far as tactics, technique and loading were concerned."

With double azon discarded, the success or failure of Project Aphrodite would now depend on the FM-TV control system of the Navy, standing by for its first mission, and the Castor system of the Army contingent from Wright Field. Jim Rand, frustrated and dejected and bone-weary from two months of nonstop effort, accepted a Bronze Star and climbed into a transport plane for a flight to the 388th Bomb Group Headquarters at nearby Knettishall. The plane crashed on landing, split open, and slid across the apron into a gasoline truck. Rand pulled a dazed crewman to safety, but before he could go back for another, the wreckage burst into flames. When the medics arrived to administer to the only two survivors, they found Rand in a state of nervous breakdown. Soon afterward a doctor ordered him to the hospital for a rest.

2. Anvil

JIMMY," Lieutenant Colonel Roy Forrest said to the commanding officer of the Navy contingent at Fersfield, "I hear your boys are squabbling among themselves. It's a hell of a time for that."

Commander James Smith, USN, a 1933 graduate of Annapolis from Springfield, Missouri, bore a rank exactly equal to Forrest's, but the Texan was nominally in charge of the air base and therefore Commander Smith's temporary superior, although he tried not to show it. The two men had been acquainted for a week, but they had been on close terms from the beginning. Smith had arrived with his unit and reported to Forrest with a snappy salute and said, "Here are my orders, sir!" and Forrest had said, "Stick your orders back in your pocket, Commander, and tell me what you want. Whatever you Navy boys want, you'll get."

Interservice cooperation was no bugaboo to Forrest. He had felt a surge of patriotic pride as he watched the Navy men come aboard his base in a color confusion of flying greens, dress whites, and regulation black uniforms, bespeaking the evident haste with which the outfit had been called to war, just as he had nothing but the kindliest feelings for the U.S. Army target-drone team from Wright Field, led by a crusty colonel named Leon "Sparky" Hoffman and braintrusted by a brilliant Regular Army lieutenant colonel named Dale Anderson and a civilian electronic genius named Peter R. Murray. They were all welcome; Forrest would take help from any point of the compass. The common denominator was the threatening bunkers across the Channel.

But others apparently felt differently. The Navy had hardly been on the base at Fersfield for twenty-four hours before Forrest answered a telephone call from Third Bomb Division Headquarters at nearby Thetford and listened to an earful of invective from a staff officer about "the goddamn Navy sticking its nose into our business." The voice went on to say that the officers of the small naval detachment had spread the word around that they were being called in to bail out the Army, "and they're treating the whole goddamned thing like a goddamned Army-Navy Game!"

Forrest ended the conversation with a feeling that the Navy was not the only outfit with a rah-rah feeling of competition about the Aphrodite program, but he was not disturbed. Interservice rivalry could work miracles if it were harnessed properly. The problem was how to harness it. Already he had heard from some of the Army men on the project. They complained that the Navy men would not pay them the slightest courtesy. "Why, we went out to look at one of their drones, and they had a sentry on it!" said one of the mother ship pilots. "So we told the sentry who we were, and he told us it didn't matter, we weren't going inside, and when Jonesy took a step forward, the goddamn sentry actually lowered the gun on him!"

"Boys," Forrest said, "I can cut through red tape and I can speed things up and I can even get you a bottle of bourbon once in a while, but there's one thing I can't do: I can't change human nature. The Navy guys are competitive, and so are you. Admit it! You want to get inside the Navy drone because you want to see what the Navy's got that you ain't got! And you know that's the truth!"

"I don't know what the hell's the matter," Smith was saying now, "except that they've never been in combat before and they're having trouble getting used to being in a war zone, and there's been some hot feelings about that."

Within less than twenty-four hours after a few hurried midnight telephone calls in July, 1944, an elite force of eleven naval officers and sixteen enlisted men had been tumbled out of bed, led to waiting airplanes, and flown to the Naval Aircraft Factory at Philadelphia to begin a crash program. Since 1937 the United States Navy had been working on remote-controlled drones, but the program had remained experimental. Now they found that they were to adapt their radio-control systems to a B-24, the four-engine bomber that the Navy used for submarine patrol and designated PB4Y. These twenty-seven men of the Navy's drone program, selected from the 5,000 sailors involved in the project, had long and varied experience in radio-controlling target drones, FU-4 biplanes, low-wing Vultee Vibrators, and assorted other aircraft into targets, and they entertained no doubts that they would be able to adapt their highly sophisticated system to the bigger PB4Y. The Navy's long-range goal had been to send robot planes into Japan, controlling them by FM and television from mother ships 40 and 50 miles back and arming, diving, and detonating them all by remote control. Compared to Jim Rand's modified azon system, with left, right, and dump controls only, and jump pilots jerking wires to arm the aircraft, the Navy was light-years ahead.

In less than a week, the silvery Liberator had been stripped of all nonessentials including the co-pilot's seat, a control system and arming panel had been installed, the bomb bay had been shored up inside by timbers, and the brand-new aircraft was ready to be ferried to England. Just before the departure for the European theater, a senior officer called the group together and told them that he would pass along what he had learned at a high-level briefing in Washington. There were four mysterious bunkers across the Channel from England, the officer said, and the British feared that they were going to be used to launch giant rockets with 10- and 20-ton warheads. Most of the sites were lined up on London, and a few were believed capable of launching rockets to the United States in the future. Winston Churchill had discussed the problem with President Roosevelt, and the President had called in the Chiefs of Staff and asked them to apply their intelligence to the problem. The large sites were impervious to normal bombing; something would have to be improvised. The Army was already improvising, but its system was primitive, and no one expected much of it. The Navy would have to take over the task. They would have the highest priority, and their mission would be supersecret. As though to emphasize his point, the officer pointed out the window to where the PB4Y was parked. Full lieutenants, pistols strapped to their sides, were walking plane guard.

The Navy contingent had straggled into the air, headed for the tiny, secret air base at Fersfield. There were two twin-engine Ventura mother ships, the silver PB4Y with the hollow interior, and a four-engine R4D transport, full of technicians. The R4D hopped almost straight across to England, but the PV Venturas were grounded for nearly three weeks at Greenland when storms swept across the airstrip called Blooey West One, and the Navy mother ships were found to lack adequate deicing equipment. By the time the whole Navy contingent coalesced in England, it was nearly August, and the Navy men were beside themselves with frustration and annoyance. They had the best guidance system and the most experience. They were good and they knew it, and they were eager to show their superiors—and the Nazis—what they could do. Like overtrained thoroughbred horses, they wanted to get out on the track. But now they had to wait around this godforsaken abandoned RAF air base while an inexperienced group of Army handymen tried to carry out the vital mission with a Rube Goldberg system that had "failure" chalked all over it. By the time the entire Navy contingent bedded down in the clammy cots at Fersfield, tempers had grown short all around, and the sailors were snapping at everyone except one another. Soon they had crossed even that line, and petty quarrels and some not so petty had begun to rend the crack Navy detachment from one end to the other.

Forrest had heard about a nightmare ride by one of the Navy crews a few days before. The crew had taken off in a PV-1 with a faulty compass and accidentally flown over the strategic Portsmouth area, where thousands of tons of matériel and thousands of troops were waiting transshipment to the battle zone across the Channel. No one on board the Navy plane had the slightest idea of the proper code words of identification, and the deep-bellied twin-engine Ventura was not a well-known silhouette on the aircraft recognition charts of the English gunners. The inevitable result was a cloudburst of flak. The pilot of the PV, an iron-willed hot-tempered lieutenant named Wilford John "Bud" Willy, dipped away from the gun positions and put the plane on a new heading. Soon a persistent buzzing came into his earphones, but he had not been in the war zone long enough to learn that this was an automatic warning signal, telling him that he was approaching barrage balloons. Thinking that his radio was defective, Willy tore his phones off and flung them on the deck. Suddenly, the PV was passing through a curtain of long steel cables, and every man aboard was lined up at the escape hatch, making last-minute adjustments to his parachute. Willy skillfully steered the PV through the maze of cables and put the ship on still another course, this one northeasterly, toward London, where he was a certain bet to be hit by the sharpshooting antiaircraft crews of the world's largest city. At that point two younger officers had threatened everything but a full-scale mutiny unless Willy accepted their navigational instructions, and an hour later the PV had landed safely with everybody on board in a white rage. To make matters worse, superior officers had called Willy in and read him the riot act, having followed his disorderly route by radar and telephone all afternoon, and less than twenty-four hours later another officer of the Navy detachment, a veteran combat flier, had flatly refused to accompany Willy on a flight.

"You'll go with me, and that's an order!" Willy had said.

"I won't go with you unless I can fly the airplane," the other officer said.

"I'm flying," Willy said, "and you're my co-pilot."

"Listen, Willy," the pilot said, "I've been in combat zones before, and you haven't, and you have no idea how dangerous it can be. I heard what you did yesterday, and I'm not flying with you, even if it means a captain's mast."

"We'll see what it means," Willy had said, and stalked off grumbling. "You're flying with me tomorrow." That night the other officer took a cold shower and dried off in the chill air, thus giving himself a cold and making himself eligible for sick bay the next morning.

Forrest shared the story with the good-natured Jimmy Smith, and the Navy commander said, "Yes, I heard something about that, but there wasn't any talk about a captain's mast."

"No," Forrest said, "I heard that Willy cooled down. But I'll tell you, Jimmy, *all* your hands had better cool down now. Fun is fun, but we Army guys have already struck out, and everybody's depending on you to clobber the targets. And you can't get 'em by fighting each other."

"You don't know the half of it," Smith said, shaking his head wearily. "Now they're arguing about the control system and the arming system and everything else and trying to make me order changes in the arming system. But how can I do that? I'm an administrator, not a technical man. I just told them to leave things the way they were designed in Philadelphia."

Forrest thought for a moment. "Smitty," he said, "I know you guys are real tight on security, but would it be okay with you if the commanding officer of this air base took a look at your airplanes?"

Smith laughed. "I'll see if it can be arranged," he said, and disappeared toward the flight line.

Roy Forrest lit a cigarette, propped his feet up on his desk, and mused about the armed services of the United States. In his lifetime he had had little contact with the Navy Air Corps, but it had always seemed to him that the Navy pilots had a built-in superiority. For one thing, their standards had always been higher. When the Army Air Corps had been requiring two years of college from its would-be pilots, the Navy was demanding a degree. When the Army reduced its requirements to a high school diploma, the Navy was still demanding two years of college. The Navy flying training lasted longer and was said to be far more rigorous than the Army's. One heard all kinds of stories about the Navy Air Corps' phenomenal navigational techniques, in comparison to the Army Air Corps, where not even every navigator could navigate. The Navy pilots looked better, with polished gold wings and olive-green flying uniforms and pure white dress uniforms, and their air bases were slicked-up establishments like Corpus Christi and Pensacola, with straight lines of palm trees and long rows of neatly laundered clamshell roads. By contrast, Forrest thought of certain Army bases he had seen, where thousands of men lived in the mud and huddled under tents at night. The Navy treated its personnel better. Why, they even had a wine mess! Forrest was in the Army, and he was not interested in trading places with anybody, but facts were facts: The Navy Air Corps was an elite outfit. The Army Air Corps was a bunch of guys named Joe. *Good* guys named Joe, to be sure, but somehow lacking the charisma and esprit of their counterparts in olive green.

Commander James Smith, USN, returned to the room and told Forrest that the PB44 drone was ready for his inspection, and the two senior officers jumped into Forrest's seven-passenger Austin and rode out to the remote hardstand where the doomed airplane was sitting under camouflaged netting, inside a perimeter of sandbags. Two guards in gray puttees were walking rings around the plane, but they snapped to when Smith stepped out of the Austin, and one of them opened the door of the plane. Forrest ducked inside and began to look around. He was highly aware of his own limitations; he was neither electronics expert nor demolition specialist, but he had always had a knack for machinery and wiring, and he wanted to satisfy himself that there was nothing obviously wrong with the Navy equipment. Of course, there wouldn't be, but he had his *pro forma* responsibilities as commanding officer. At first glance, nothing struck his eye. He spent a half hour fiddling with the control equipment, and it seemed to him to be highly sophisticated, leagues ahead of the rickety double azon gear that had fouled the Army missions. He saw that the Navy could perform about ten different functions by remote control, including changing the speed of the drone, steering it, diving and climbing it, and turning on the Ace altimeter from the mother ship. Forrest could see no problems here. Then he turned to the arming panel, a plywood "breadboard" with all sorts of switches and terminals jutting from it. To the meticulous Forrest, the man who had designed the finest latrine in the European theater, the arming panel looked curiously out of phase with the other equipment. "Jimmy," he said, "this looks like something you'd make with a number two Erector set and Lincoln Logs." He thought he saw several cold-soldered joints and other evidences of untoward and dangerous haste, and without being able to put his finger precisely on the trouble, he did not like the way the plywood board was bolted to a metal bulkhead, which could have the effect of joining the arming and firing systems via a common ground. It seemed to Forrest that such systems should be kept scrupulously apart and that transient currents could now enter the circuit from any of several directions.

"Where'd they do this arming panel, Jimmy?" Forrest said.

"At the Naval Aircraft Factory in Philadelphia."

"Doesn't it look a little sloppy to you, compared to the other stuff?"

"Roy, I just can't say," Smith answered. "Offhand it's obvious that it's not as carefully thought out as the other equipment, but then we've had the other gear for years, and this arming panel's had to be improvised fast."

"Why'd you need a new arming panel?"

"Because this is the first time we've been called on to blow up ten tons on impact. The old arming panels were for different jobs."

"Well, to tell you the truth," Roy Forrest said, "I don't think this one will work. It might be good for blowing up stumps in a meadow, but that's about all."

That night Forrest had dinner at Elveden Hall, Third Bomb Division Headquarters, and once again found himself in conversation with the acerbic little colonel with the knack for rubbing him wrong. "How's the Navy coming?" the colonel asked.

"Arguing among themselves," Forrest said. "Carrying feuds and rumors. Flying over combat zones without combat experience. Screwing up, in other words."

The colonel did not seem disturbed by the news. "Well," he said, "that's their problem."

"Well, it's my problem, too," Forrest said. "The whole program's been going lousy. Now the Navy's getting ready to kill their jump pilot. I looked at their equipment today, and there's not a doubt in my mind that they're gonna fail."

"Roy, you've always had a healthy imagination," the colonel said, becoming unusually familar. "But you're wrong this time. You know how long those Navy boys have been working on this kind of equipment? Since 1937, out in the Hawaiian Islands."

"I don't care how long they've been working with the stuff," Forrest said. "It's a matter of conscience with me, and goddamn it, they've got it wrong. They're gonna try to blow a load of ten tons of Torpex with an arming system that's about as safe as a basketful of rattlesnakes."

The colonel and the lieutenant colonel refreshed themselves with ready-poured martinis carried on a tray by a comely WAC. The colonel lifted his glass. "Here's to you and your wild imagination, Roy," he said, lifting the glass. "When the Navy blows up its drone, give me a ring. Nobody wanted the Navy here in the first place."

The boys at headquarters were still playing the Army-Navy Game, and so far as Forrest could tell, the Navy reciprocated the feeling.

Nevertheless, he had worked hard to achieve harmony among the competing groups. The Navy men were now friendly and warm toward him personally, and indeed he had spent more time socializing with them lately than with the men of his own outfit. One night he had walked into the tiny officers' club to find six or eight of the sailors engaged in friendly banter with the others.

"That one over there," Loyd Humphries told Forrest, pointing to a hawk-faced, sturdily built Navy lieutenant of some twenty-nine or thirty years, "that's Joe Kennedy, Jr. His father was the Ambassador to England."

"Oh, yeah?" Forrest said.

Forrest had arrived at the bar just as one of the jump pilots was telling Kennedy, "Well, by God, if my old man was Ambassador to England, I'd have my ass transferred right out of this outfit!" Kennedy's response was a wide, lopsided grin and then a loud laugh, and Forrest took an instant liking to the young man who did not seem to take himself as seriously as some of the other Navy personnel. "My name's Roy Forrest," he said, sticking out his hand, and the lieutenant flashed a warm smile and said, "I'm Joe Kennedy, sir, and I'm happy to meet you."

"What's your role in this big can of worms?" Forrest asked, "or ain't I supposed to know things like that?"

"I'm just the dumb kid on the block," Kennedy said. "I'm not with the radio-control outfit. They recruited me from sub patrol at Dunkeswell to take their drone off and bail out."

"You're a jump pilot?" Forrest asked, and before Kennedy could answer, one of the Army jump pilots said, "Yes, sir, he's the jump pilot, the only one the Navy has. Deranged, just like the rest of us."

Forrest, who still had paper work to do in the orderly room, said good-bye to Kennedy and a few of the other Navy officers. "Come over to my quarters any time," he said, "and I'll show you what good liquor tastes like." Thus had begun a nightly institution. Commander James Smith would pick up Kennedy and one or two other key personnel and drop by Forrest's quarters in the old dispensary for a shot or two of bourbon before dinner. One night Forrest confided to his friend and aide, Loyd "Humpy" Humphries, "I love these guys, Humpy, but they're drinking me out of house and home. You know that bourbon costs me eighteen, twenty dollars a fifth. I'm halfway through my poker money already!"

Soon afterward the young lieutenant named Kennedy came to Forrest's quarters alone and said, "Colonel, would you like some good whiskey?"

"Would a rattlesnake like mice?" Forrest answered. "I'm almost down to drinking that scotch-type stuff that they make out of latrine drippings."

"Well, if I can just get transport," Kennedy said, "I can go to London and bring back a case of good, mellow scotch."

"For how much?"

"A buck forty a fifth."

Forrest knew when he was being kidded. "Sure, Joe," he said, "and you'll throw in the Tower of London if I act fast, right? Now listen, Joe, I like you and I like Jimmy Smith, but if you Navy guys want a free ride to London, why don't you just come in and say, 'I want a free ride to London'? Don't come in here with all that horseshit about getting scotch at a buck forty a fifth!"

"No," Kennedy said. "You've got it wrong, Colonel. I can *really* get it at that price. I've still got connections at the embassy."

"You're not kidding?"

"Word of honor on it."

"Humpy," Forrest said to his sidekick, "shag ass over to the flight line and get one of those unloaded babies and fly it over to London for a new set of plugs! And hurry up! We've got to have those plugs by tonight!" He turned to Kennedy. "Lieutenant," he said, "I just learned of a flight leaving right away for London. Maybe you can catch a ride."

"Yes, sir!" Kennedy said.

About six hours later, Forrest was writing a report when there was a tap at the door to his room. "Who is it?" the Texan called out.

"Delivery boy!" Joe Kennedy and two sailors came into the room under a heavy load of bottles and deposited them on the commanding officer's bunk. "That'll be sixteen dollars and eighty cents for the scotch," he said. "The other stuff's on the house."

Forrest counted twelve bottles of the finest scotch and two full cases of Pabst Blue Ribbon beer packed in sawdust, plus a few random bottles of gin and bourbon and a bottle of crème de menthe. "Pabst Blue Ribbon beer!" Forrest said reverently. "I had almost forgotten the name."

When Kennedy had collected both money and thanks from the astounded lieutenant colonel and taken his leave, Forrest could not resist opening one of the warm cans of beer and taking a deep draft. The liquid tasted strange to him. "Goddamn!" he said, and tried another swig. It was still strange. "Son of a bitch!" the commanding officer said. *"I've gotten used to British beer!"*

Later that night Forrest thought once again about the

conversation with the colonel at headquarters and the trouble-
some arming panel, but he still could not decide precisely what
it was that disturbed him, other than the general homemade appearance of the plywood strip and the grounding system. "It's
trigger-happy," Forrest said to himself. "It's a trigger-happy son
of a bitch, and I know it, and I wish I could change it." He fell
asleep and dreamed about a great big incandescent flash in the
sky, and the face of his new friend, Joseph P. Kennedy, Jr.,
smiling out of the middle.

Special Attack Unit No. 1, as the Navy contingent at Fersfield had been designated, was discordant but functioning. In
a sense, the men were like siblings, capable of engaging in fearsome brawls with one another but presenting a solid front to
any outsider. They resented each other's idiosyncrasies and defects, but they resented strangers more. The Army technicians
from Wright Field were especially nettling, and the Navy men
suspected them of everything up to grand larceny. All one had
to do was compare the Navy PB4Y drone with the new B-17's
being prepared by this Castor unit, and one could see as-
tounding similarities, ranging from the Ace altimeter to the television cameras protruding from both noses at the same angles.
The Army explanation was that the old-timers in the radio-
control business had shared secrets from the beginning, wing-
ing back and forth between Wright Field and the Navy installations at Traverse City, Michigan, and Clinton, Oklahoma. But
younger men in the Navy program chose to disbelieve this history of friendly interchange. "They'll steal us blind," one of the
young lieutenants told his guard detail. "Keep 'em off our
gear!" So the two projects, nearly identical in theory and using
similar techniques and equipment, chugged along at their separate paces, and cross-fertilization and impartial criticism were
thereby denied to both. Only the commanding officer, Lieutenant Colonel Roy Forrest, had been permitted a peak at the
Navy equipment, and this because he had become a fast friend

APHRODITE: DESPERATE MISSION 186

of Commander Smith and because he was not a technician. Word had leaked back that Forrest was critical of the Navy arming panel, but no one paid attention. Forrest was an amateur.

The Navy technicians were doubtful that anyone with less than years of experience in electronics could begin to understand their complex arming system. The Navy would have no simple mechanical arming for the sophisticated special attack unit, no jump pilot clambering back on the catwalk to tug on a bunch of cables strung haphazardly along the ceiling. The Navy would arm remotely, from the mother ship, by transmitting an FM signal. Long after the jump crew had bailed out and the drone was safely over water, the signal would be transmitted, and a solenoid would pull a lever arm that would yank the safety pins out of the inertia switches, cocking the system and rendering it explosive on impact. The safety features were obvious, and the Navy prided itself on its concern for its men. No one was a digit in the Navy. If it took thousands of dollars' worth of gadgets and hundreds of hours of design manpower to work up a device like the Navy's remote arming, it was reckoned to be worth it. The Navy was not going to subject its jump crews to the added danger of mechanical arming before bailout.

Of course, remote electronic arming presented a few minor problems, the most obvious of which was that a stray FM signal that coincided with the arming system's frequency could actuate the solenoid and arm the airplane. Back at Philadelphia, when the drone PB4Y had been undergoing tests, the plane had accidentally armed itself three times on a flight over the city, and for an hour or two Navy electronics specialists had been mystified. There were simply not enough scattered FM signals in the relatively uncluttered air above the City of Brotherly Love to account for even a single accidental arming, let alone three on one afternoon. But the ground officers laughed off the incident; they explained that radiomen must have been transmitting matching FM signals from their own shops in the course of routine equipment checks. Everyone had breathed a sigh of relief, but the executive officer of SAU No. 1 had ordered a "safety" pin installed in the plane just in case. Now, when a spurious signal reached the arming system, the pin would hold the long arming bar firmly in place and keep it from wrenching the switches into the "hot" position. The plane could not be armed until the jump pilot pulled the pin, just before bailing out. Some of the lower-ranking members of the group looked at the "safety" device and proclaimed that it was more dangerous than the unsafetied system, for various complex electronic reasons, but the exec was adamant, and the hastily improvised "safety" gadget remained in the circuit.

As another check against accidental arming, now that the project was in England and ready to fly against the German rocket sites on twenty-four hours' notice, frequency-search aircraft flew twelve and fifteen hours a day, seeking the slightest indication of stray FM signals that might trip the equipment. Day after day, aircraft ranging from lumbering old Navy weather planes to crackling F4U Corsairs roamed the skies over England, their receivers wide open to all FM signals, and recorded that the supersecret arming frequency was all clear. Reconnaissance airplanes like the high-speed P-38 Lightning and the British Mosquito were sent on sorties over France and Germany, looking for the itinerant signals, and other aircraft flew low over the powerful navigational and radar beacons that lined the British coast, measuring their electrical emissions and their possible effects on the FM band. Still there was no detectable interference. The channel was clear. In three weeks of this Operation Ferret, the only measurable interference that turned up on the Navy's frequency came from test emissions at Fersfield. Apparently the Germans, for all their skill in panoramic jamming, were concentrating their man-made static on the AM bands used by the thousands of bombers that were coming over the fatherland daily. Military FM was still in its infancy.

Unlike the Army, which had acted in haste and now was repenting, the Navy double-checked its procedures all along the line. Lieutenant J. P. Kennedy, Jr., was flying routine daily tests with a fully loaded drone, learning every nuance of the PB4Y's behavior under strain. Some of the Army technicians said wryly that the Navy was simply benefiting from the Army's mistakes. Army jump pilots had flown dozens of hours in unloaded, feather-light drones and then gone off to war in overloaded B-17's with totally different sets of characteristics. The Navy jump pilot would fly his operational mission in a PB4Y that was as familiar to him as his own motorcar back in Boston, Massachusetts. Joe Kennedy had flown fifty missions in Liberators already, on sub patrol over the Bay of Biscay in all kinds of weather and under all kinds of conditions, and now he was taking up a brand-new PB4Y loaded with 15,000 pounds of sand almost every day. When he was satisfied that he knew the aircraft and its characteristics, he would turn over control of the drone to the PV mother ships above and relax in the pilot's compartment while the controllers steered the loaded aircraft around eastern England. One day a mother ship controller did some quick calculating and reckoned that he was controlling Kennedy's drone from a distance of 70 miles. "How'm I doing?" he radioed to the twenty-nine-year-old jump pilot.

"Right down the pike!" Kennedy answered enthusiastically.

More than once the drone Liberator returned with twigs or other foliage affixed to its undercarriage, but this was interpreted only as an indication of derring-do and confidence in the equipment by mother and baby crews alike. A bespectacled ensign named James Simpson was riding with Kennedy when the robot began mushing down and clipping the tops of a grove of oak trees. "Get up!" Simpson shouted. "We're going to crash!"

Kennedy made a simple adjustment, and the PB4Y climbed steadily out of danger. "Just checking different prop pitches," he said to the terrified Simpson. "Don't worry. You're as safe as in your mother's arms." Simpson, an autopilot expert, flew with Kennedy more often than any other of the Navy men, and he soon learned that no matter what seemed to be happening, the robot was under full control of the experienced pilot.

But if the drone tests were proceeding routinely, Special Attack Unit No. 1 was still having its problems adjusting to the new situation that had catapulted them out of their comfortable beds back at Traverse City and deposited them, green and untutored, in the middle of a bustling theater of operations. There were frequent encounters between SAU No. 1 planes, out on routine flights, and big bombers of the Eighth Air Force, forming up for raids on Germany. The Navy men, their minds brimming with radio-control data and performance details, were slow to learn the proper identification codes, IFF procedures, and other techniques for staying alive in a war-oriented environment. Sometimes they would be chased back to Fersfield by friendly but suspicious British fighters, which would circle around until satisfied that the heavy-bellied PV's were indeed on the right side. Sometimes the Navy pilots would look out their windows to see flak exploding around them. The PV engines were as hard to keep synchronized as the engines of the German JU-88, and both planes emitted a kind of pounding noise when they were not in perfect tune. British gunners would hear the familiar *vroom-vroom-vroom* and peg a few rounds just to be on the safe side. One afternoon a young ensign named John Demlein found himself fired on repeatedly as he flew his PV from Fersfield to South London to pick up a part. When he returned, he said to his fellow pilots, "Look at me! Do I look like a Kraut? Do I look like a Luftwaffe pilot? Does that PV look like a Messerschmitt? What the hell is this all about, anyway?" No one was able to provide an answer.

All of the Navy pilots were ready and eager for combat, but soon the top officers of SAU No. 1 were finding it difficult to round up pilots for the dozens of routine hops that had to be

made during the standby training period (including the routine hop to the big Navy base at Plymouth for five-gallon cans
of ice cream and other flights to replenish the wine mess) .

"I'm damned sick and tired of flying dangerous missions in
England!" one of the pilots snapped when he was asked to pick
up a PV part at Dunkeswell.

"But you'll go, won't you?" said the executive officer of the
little unit, Lieutenant Wilford J. Willy, the same officer who
had become hopelessly lost in an earlier flight over the British
Isles. Willy phrased the remark as a question, but the younger
pilot knew an order when he heard one.

"Yeah, I'll go," he said, "but don't expect me to like it."

"I didn't ask you to like it," Willy said sharply.

When the Navy pilots were not risking their lives to British
gunners and fighters, they were risking their lives to weather.
The most ordinary flight could turn into a nightmarish adven-
ture in blind flying, and even when the weather would break
for a few minutes and the pilots could fly down on the deck to
make a landfall, they would find the same checkerboard of
farms and villages below them and the same droning armadas
of B-17's and B-24's and Halifaxes and Lancasters above
them. Under such circumstances, no flight could be regarded as
routine.

One bleak afternoon a mother ship pilot named Harry
Wherry was ordered to pick up some material at the Pratt and
Whitney office in London. Ordinarily, Lieutenant Harry
Wherry was the most jovial and easygoing of men, but he was
beginning to grow annoyed at Bud Willy's tendency to send
senior members of the program gallivanting all over the
treacherous skies of England on errands that could just as easily
have been handled by jeep and courier. "Goddamn it, Bud," he
said, "there's a storm coming up, and I just flew one of those
half-assed missions yesterday. Can't you get somebody else to
go?"

As the Navy's big day approached, the normally affable Willy had grown more and more short-tempered himself, and it seemed to some of the others that he had let his temporary appointment as executive officer go to his head. Both Willy and Wherry wore the twin gold stripes of lieutenants, senior grade, and Wherry found it annoying to have to take orders from this former aviation mechanic. Wherry had to fight to control his temper when the little executive officer said, "You're going, Lieutenant, and you're going right now. That's an order!"

Wherry collected his crew and climbed into his PV for the flight into the heavily defended London area. " 'That's an order!' " he mocked. Lately the phrase had come more and more to Willy's mouth, and all the officers had found it annoying. "That's an order" was a remark usually made by officers to balky enlisted men. Officers spoke in a gentlemanly manner to each other. The merest suggestion by a senior officer to a junior was sufficient; one officer did not have to "order" another.

But in the air Wherry cooled down. The sky had cleared of all but haze, and it seemed like only a few minutes before the massive low profile of London appeared ahead. Wherry carefully identified himself and his plane on the radio, and under orders from the British military controller began to seek a flak-free corridor into the aerodrome on the outskirts of the city. Suddenly the PV was rocked by a blast. Wherry looked out the port window and saw a big ball of fire and the little fingers of smoke that signified shrapnel, and he shoved the plane into an evasive turn to get out of range of the gun battery as quickly as possible. More flak appeared around him, and five or six bursts were fired before the plane settled into a landing pattern and angled down toward safety.

Wherry hit the ground in a towering rage, and his drive into London in the middle of one of the worst V-bomb attacks of the war did nothing to calm his spirits. "Goddamn that Willy!" he said to himself. "He's got ten guys over there could have flown this mission, and another twenty that could have driven here in a few hours, and he's got to send me!" In his heart, Harry Wherry was not the least concerned about the dangers of flying a mission over enemy territory, but his mother had not raised him to be shot down by friendly flak or blasted out of an automobile in the middle of Piccadilly.

By the time Wherry had picked up the part at the Pratt and Whitney office and reassembled his crew for the return to Fersfield, it was night, and the classical mushroom-soup fog had descended upon London. By order of the RAF commandant in the London defense area, routine flights were canceled. Wherry called Fersfield and talked to Willy. "Tell 'em that your flight isn't routine," Willy insisted. "Give 'em our priority number. We've got to have that part the first thing in the morning."

"Don't tell me, let me guess," Wherry said. "That's an order?"

"That's an order!" Willy said.

Wherry slammed his gray-white Ventura down the runway as though trying to bore a hole in the weather, and he was relieved to see that the skies were almost clear above the ground fog. He gunned the PV northeast toward Fersfield, hoping to find his home airport bathed in moonlight for a nice, easy landing. But Fersfield was drenched in North Sea fog. At higher altitudes, the sky was clear and the stars were shining, but at 1,000 feet the air began to look like wet cement, and from the 500-foot level down to the ground, the sky was a giant slab of pitch. Wherry called the control tower and asked for instructions on an alternate landing site.

"We'll land you, sir," the voice came back. "We've been instructed to land you. Stay above the field, and we'll turn the perimeter lights on."

Wherry ordered his crew to keep a tight lookout, but no change appeared in the skyline below. "Are they on?" Wherry radioed.

"Yes, sir."

"Well, they're no help," he said.

"Stand by," the tower operator said. "We're going to turn on the searchlight and point it at you, and you can come in on that."

Wherry turned to his co-pilot. "Did you ever hear anything so ridiculous? I'm supposed to glide down through this fog on a searchlight beam? Who the hell's stupid idea do you suppose that is?"

To the tower, Wherry radioed, "I'm diverting," and he spun the PV around and headed toward the south of England. Within a few minutes, fiery bursts of light flak had come out of the darkness and gone off like firecrackers around the PV. "The British radar must have us," Wherry said. He ordered the radioman to keep up a continuous broadcast of identification signals. After twenty-five minutes of buzzing familiar air bases and finding them socked in and fleeing in a hail of flak, the harassed pilot finally found a broad elliptical hole in the overcast and began descending toward an American fighter base. The control tower operator called for the daily identification signal, and all that came to Wherry's busy mind were codes he had been taught for the approach to England from Greenland, three weeks earlier. "I don't recognize those signals!" the tower operator said. "Can you identify yourself further?"

Wherry put the aircraft into a tight circle and began to think hard. The Aphrodite mission was supersecret, and he knew he could not name his home air base or his home unit even if it meant his life. Only 30 or 40 miles away, German radio operators would be listening in on every word. So Wherry began giving his name, rank, file number, hometown, and everything uniquely American that he could think of, including the most recent batting averages of several of the Cleveland Indians.

"Clear to land," the control tower operator said at last, and Wherry brought the plane down in a perfect three-point landing on the wet and glistening asphalt runway.

"For your information," a weary duty officer told him as the bedraggled Navy crew trooped to its temporary overnight quarters, "you've been tracked by radar for the last hour, and you've been fired on all the way. The gun crews were told that you were probably a JU-88, and they underestimated your speed by about fifty miles an hour. That's the only reason you're alive."

"For *your* information," said an angry Harry Wherry, "stick it up your ass!"

The next morning at dawn, he hustled his crew out of bed and into the PV. "Hey, what about breakfast?" a crew member said.

"You'll get breakfast soon enough," Wherry snapped.

Fifteen minutes later the plane set down at Fersfield, and Wherry gunned it up to the flight line, slammed on the brakes, and jumped out in a rage. "Where's that son of a bitch Bud Willy?" he shouted.

Another mother ship pilot, Lieutenant Hugh "Rosy" Lyon, came up and said, "What's the matter, Harry?"

"Nothing's the matter," Wherry said, "I'm just looking for Bud Willy."

Lyon and several other officers finally wrestled the enraged pilot off to one side and talked to him. "Look, Harry, it's all over now," Lyon said. "You're safe, and you did a good job. Now don't go doing anything you'll be sorry for."

Finally Wherry began to calm. "Okay," he said. "I won't punch Willy. But I won't talk to him either."

A few minutes later the Navy pilots were still standing in a group alongside the main hangar when a P-51 Mustang zoomed out of nowhere and careened into a spectacular wheel landing at about 100 knots. The little fighter plane taxied in at a high speed, spun around on a wheel when it reached the apron, and jerked to a stop, still quivering. "Those Army pilots don't care about a thing, do they?" Harry Wherry said. "Just blast in and blast out!"

"Yeah," said a red-haired controller named Lieutenant John Anderson. "Look at that. He's walking away from the plane with the flaps down." This was strictly antiprocedure in the

Navy. The fragile flaps were supposed to be tucked into the wings for their own protection; otherwise, they could be damaged by gravel or other flying matter.

"Hey!" Anderson shouted. "Hey! Your flaps are down!"

The pilot kept on walking.

"Hey, fellow," Wherry cried out. "You forgot something!"

"Flaps, stupid!" Rosy Lyon shouted. "Flaps!" The Army pilot seemed to hesitate, then disappeared into the hangar.

A few minutes later the skipper of SAU No. 1 came bustling out of the hangar door and over to the group. "What's all the hollering about?" he said.

"Some dumb-ass Army pilot parked with his flaps down," Harry Wherry said.

"Yeah, I noticed," Commander Jimmy Smith said. "Do you know who the dumb-ass pilot was?"

"No," Anderson said.

"James H. Doolittle."

One man, above all others, had a terrifyingly clear picture of the future of Special Attack Unit No. 1. Earl Olsen did not possess the gift of prophecy, but he knew basic electronics frontward and backward, and this made him unique among the men of the Navy detachment. At twenty-nine, Olsen was a curious combination of dedication and naïveté. A lowly lieutenant (jg), he was known among the wilder types of SAU No. 1 as a pitilessly hard worker, a plodder with no time or interest in extracurricular activities. One of the pilots jokingly called him "that square from Delaware," even though Olsen had been brought up 2,000 miles west of Delaware, in Montana, and 3,000 miles east of Delaware, in Norway. By all the definitions of wartime society Earl Olsen was indeed a square. He did not smoke or use foul language, he would take a drink only rarely, he showed no interest in the constant poker game that went on in his Nissen hut, and he eschewed the company of British females, having become happily married three years before. His skipper, the likable Jimmy Smith, described him as "a quiet Sunday school type, more interested in work than anything else." Night after night, while the others were making the best of a frustrating social situation at Fersfield by drinking and playing cards and telling tall stories in the officers' mess, Earl Olsen was at work. He thought of himself as reserved and conservative, anything but messianic, but he had a mission. He was going to save the project.

At first, Olsen had been respectful of the others. Wilford Willy had selected him from among dozens of electronics experts to join the special attack unit in England, and the beetle-browed, slimly built Norwegian-American had been dazzled by the honor. Earl Olsen had come aboard Project Aphrodite with the impression that he was joining an elite unit; the impression had not lasted more than a few days. He was making a routine check of the circuit in one of the robot aircraft's FM receivers, and he discovered that it did not conform to the specifications in the manufacturer's handbook. At first he assumed that the wise old heads at the Naval Aircraft Factory in Philadelphia had improvised some improvements that would add reliability and safety to the system. But when he studied further, he found that someone in Philadelphia had deliberately misaligned the intermediate-frequency stages and turned the FM receiver into a broad-spectrum catchall for FM signals, desired *and* undesired. The effect of the tinkering was to widen the path through which spurious signals could enter the receiver. Because of the misalignment, the intruding signals would have to be relatively strong, but Olsen knew that German jamming stations were not lacking in power.

His first inclination had been to get out his tool kit and his instruments and realign the intermediate frequency (IF) stages, but first he talked it over with a Navy chief named Orlowski, for whom he had deep respect. Orlowski asked to see the receivers, and after a short inspection, he said, "Mr. Olsen, that thing needs selectivity. It's just plain screwed up." That night the two men worked till long past midnight, narrowing the gate through which FM signals could enter the receiver. When they had reduced the band width to a bare minimum, they cut down the radio frequency gain, and the result was a circuit that would reject any signals that were not strong and precisely on the intended frequency. When they had finished, Olsen turned to Orlowski. "What do you make of all this?" he asked.

"I hate to say, Lieutenant," the chief radioman answered.

"Well, say it anyway."

Orlowski paused and lit a cigarette. "Okay, Mr. Olsen, you asked for it," he said. "I think somebody back in Philadelphia is stupid. I think whoever ordered the changes on this receiver ought to be busted to apprentice seaman and sent to cooks and bakers school."

"You realize you're probably talking about a high-ranking officer?" Olsen said.

"I don't care if I'm talking about the Secretary of the Navy," Orlowski said. "Their setup procedures stink. I bet they thought they were working up some clever antijamming adjustments. Instead, they just screwed it all up."

Olsen said nothing, but he agreed. He was slowly coming to the realization that his previous respect for rank had been misplaced, that men in high station could make the same atrocious errors as men in low station. Time and again he had seen evidences of faulty planning at higher levels, but he had chosen to disregard it. He had told himself that there were things he did not know, that he was not privy to all the facts of the situation, and above all else, he hated to judge others. But now he realized that he no longer had a choice. As electronics officer of SAU No. 1 he had been told that his assignment consisted simply of maintaining the radio gear. He was not to bother himself with the basic designs, which had been made by others, and he was not to tinker with any of the circuitry. The whole matter was too delicate; lives would depend on it, and the success of the mission was in the balance.

"Chief," he said to Orlowski, "I'll tell you what this means to me. This means that you and I have to go over every single inch of the circuitry. Nothing in this design can be trusted."

"I agree," Orlowski said. From then on Olsen and Orlowski and their assistants had worked long into the night behind the blackout curtains of the shops at Fersfield. They checked signals and inputs and trace currents and random impulses, and they polished up the circuitry in the radio-control equipment until it was as foolproof as humanly possible. "Let the Germans try to jam *that!*" Olsen said late one night. "If they're half a kilocycle to one side or the other, they're gonna miss it. And if they're a milliwatt off in their power, the set isn't even gonna hear them. I don't see what else we can do."

With the radio-control equipment now perfectly adapted to the special needs of the mission, Olsen turned his attention to something else that was technically not his business: the electrical arming panel. By now the Navy detachment had finished its training at Fersfield and was on twenty-four-hour alert for a mission. Any day now Lieutenant Joe Kennedy would take the robot into the sky with a full load of Torpex, and his life or death and the success or failure of the mission would depend on the safety of the remote-controlled arming system. Olsen went over the arming panel and its radio receiver with galvanometers and voltmeters and ammeters and magnifying glass, and when he had completed his check, he was in a high state of excitement and anxiety. He raced back to the Nissen hut where he lived with three others and found his friend Ensign James Simpson, the autopilot expert. "Jimmy!" Olsen said. "Get out here quick and look at something with me."

For an hour the two men went over the arming panel and the FM receiver that was integral with it, while Olsen excitedly pointed things out. Simpson kept shaking his head and making sounds of amazement. When Olsen had finished his guided tour of the arming system, he said, "Well, Jimmy, what about it?"

"I'm no authority, Oley," Simpson said. "I'm an autopilot man, and you're the electronics man. But there's a twelve-year-old girl at the pub down the road that could have done a better job of designing this system!"

"It's the worst piece of junk I've ever seen," Olsen said softly. "It's got to be changed, or the mission's a failure."

Olsen and Simpson hurried off to get Orlowski, and as the three men jeeped out to the drone for still another study of the arming system, Olsen explained what was at stake. The arming panel was hair-triggered. The slightest eddy of random radio energy could set it off, and there were numerous eddies of energy throughout the set, just as there always are in FM receivers when the transmitted carrier is off. As though to guarantee failure, the designers of the system had inserted a holding relay into the circuitry, and the holding relay was irreversible. Once an electrical impulse reached it and caused it to close, it stayed closed, and electricity coursed through the system, heating up resistors, energizing solenoids, and producing wildcat electrical pressures that could be dangerous. When the three men clambered back into the PB4Y and the receivers had been warmed up again, Olsen held a tiny test light across various points in the circuit, causing it to flicker from transient currents that should not have been there. "Now put your head down and listen!" Olsen said. "Hear that chattering? That's some of the relays reacting to radio energy—plain old white noise. Most of them will just chatter and stay open, but that holding relay will close and stay closed if enough energy reaches it."

"And if it closes, then the circuit is completed all the way to the fuses?" Simpson asked.

"That's right," Olsen said.

"What about that safety pin that Willy installed?" Simpson asked.

"Take my word for it, Jimmy," Olsen said, "that pin is less

than useless. It keeps the impact switches from arming, but it doesn't keep the fuses from arming. All that safety pin does is give the pilot a false sense of security."

"But what if the fuses arm?" Orlowski said. "That won't explode the load; it'll just arm it."

"Theoretically, yes," Olsen said, "but you never can tell what fuses will do if current is left on them too long. Tell you the truth, I wish I knew more about these damned fuses!"

"Well, what do we do now?" Orlowski asked. "Remake the whole thing, the way we did the control receivers?"

"This time it's a little different, Chief," Olsen said. "This arming panel isn't our baby; it's the ordnance officer's. I'll go talk to him."

Olsen hunted up the ordnance officer, a young lieutenant who had been assigned to the project by the Navy. The lieutenant had always been a source of puzzlement to Olsen. The man was a Navy pilot, a likable sort, with extensive combat experience, but so far as Olsen could determine, he had no background whatever in matters of ordnance and electronics. Once again Olsen had assumed that he lacked some of the facts, and had withheld judgment on his fellow officer. But now that he had seen the arming panel he realized that emergency changes had to be made, and he could no longer assume that the ordnance officer had the slightest idea what he was doing. Their conversation was brisk and bristling.

"Lieutenant," Olsen said, "excuse me for intruding on your affairs, but there are some things I'd like to point out to you about your arming panel."

"Go ahead," the ordnance man said.

Olsen explained in detail what was wrong with the circuit. He minced no words, and he ended by saying that the arming panel was the weakest and most dangerous part of the whole system.

"I suppose you know this was designed by experts," the ordnance officer said when Olsen had completed his explanation.

"No one who knows anything about electronics could have designed this," Olsen said.

"Well, someone did," the lieutenant said. "Smarter people than you put all this together in Philadelphia."

"Does that include you?"

"It does."

Olsen waggled a finger under the nose of the man who was one rank his senior. "Lieutenant, you and your buddies in Philadelphia have designed a piece of crap," he said, surprised at his own audacity. "This arming panel is unstable. All by itself it can undo years of work that we've put into radio control."

"Olsen," the lieutenant said, "I've heard about all I want to hear. That arming circuit is staying the way it is. It was designed by experts, and by God, it's not going to be touched by you or anybody else. Willy's already messed it up with his damned fool safety pin. If you mess around with it, you'll *really* foul it up!"

"Do you concede that the holding relay could close and stay closed and apply current to the fuses?"

"I concede nothing," the angry ordnance officer said. "Those fuses are safe."

Olsen came away from the conversation with a feeling that the ordnance officer did not understand the situation. "I still think he's basically a good man," he told his friend Simpson, "but I don't think he has the slightest idea what he's designed —if he *did* design it."

"Well, he told me he made the whole thing himself," Simpson said. "He stood right here and he said, 'I designed it, and if it works, my career is made, and if it fails, I may as well commit suicide.'"

"And take a few others with him," Olsen said grimly. "Well, all I can do now is go to Bud Willy and get him to order the changes. Bud's aware of the situation. He'll listen to me."

Having kept himself almost exclusively in the company of ground technicians like Orlowski for several weeks, Olsen was only vaguely aware that there was discontent among the flying crews, and much of it related to Willy and his sudden authoritarianism. Olsen had heard reports about the newly appointed executive officer playing the dogmatist, but he felt they must be exaggerated. He had known Willy for several years, and he was well aware that Willy could be as bullheaded and stubborn as the next man. But Lieutenant Wilford John Willy had much to commend him, and Earl Olsen was uniquely aware of his strong points. The two men were close. They were bowling partners and coffee partners; they both were devoted family men, and they sometimes went on liberties together, visiting such dens of iniquity as USO poolrooms and doughnut stands. They were both "mustangs," chief petty officers commissioned at the outbreak of World War II, Olsen in electronics, Willy in aviation. Both had been associated with the Navy drone program since its early years, although Willy had seniority, and they had a healthy respect for each other's talents. When it had fallen to Willy to assemble a crew of experts to take on the important assignment in England, he had unhesitatingly chosen Olsen as the electronics officer. Olsen, in turn, admired Willy's ability to get the job done, whatever the job. He was the kind of officer who thought nothing of rolling up his shirt sleeves and digging into the greasy insides of an airplane engine to see what was wrong. Willy was not the most imaginative or creative of men, but he had a way of blending disparate groups together, of making new men feel at home. As long as he lived, Olsen would never forget what Willy had done on a night at Cape May, New Jersey, two years before. Olsen's commission as an ensign had just come through, and the other chief petty officers responded to an old Navy tradition by heaving him bodily out of the chiefs' quarters. When Olsen tried to go back in for his clothes, the chiefs shoved him into the hall and flung his clothes out after him.

Olsen was not a highly emotional person, but he had been upset by the rude ceremony, and he wandered disconsolately over to the officers' quarters. "What's the matter, son?" Bud Willy said. "You look like you just got back from a shipwreck." The two men sat and discussed the Navy and its traditions for several hours, and at the end of the time Olsen felt a warmth toward this officer who had taken the time to console him. He sensed, as he put it later, that "Bud Willy wasn't the brightest man alive, but he had feelings for others. He cared about people. He was honorable, he was a decent human being."

On the other hand, Olsen soon learned that Willy, despite the maturity of his thirty-five years, was insecure in the strange new world of commissioned officers, after a long career as an enlisted mechanic and later as an enlisted pilot. Sometimes it seemed to Olsen that Willy spoke louder than necessary, as though unsure that his orders would be carried out. Willy seemed to lack respect for his own knowledge, built up over a long and honorable Navy career, and he would insist stubbornly that problems he handled strictly according to regulations, even when it was obvious that the regulations needed bending. Nevertheless, Olsen considered Willy a good officer. He knew no perfect ones.

Now he was walking into Willy's little office, nervous with the knowledge that he must enlist his friend's all-out assistance if the Aphrodite program were to be saved. He knew better than to approach Bud Willy brusquely, demanding a yes or no answer. He broached the subject delicately, told how he had had misgivings about checking the work of others, and tried to outline the circuitry and its defects with a pencil and paper. Midway through his technical explanation, he began to sense that Willy was not following him, and he interrupted himself to say, "Bud, do you see what I'm getting at?"

"Hell, Oley, my safety pin takes care of any arming malfunction," Willy said.

Olsen knew that he would have to express his disagreement calmly and rationally or the strong-willed little executive officer would shut off the whole conversation. "Bud," he said gently, "sit down and let me tell you something." He told Willy that the safety idea was an excellent one, but that it had an essential defect: It was a mechanical solution to an electrical problem, and electrical problems did not resolve themselves so easily. He told Willy that the safety pin would not change the fact that all sorts of electric currents would be coursing through the system. "Look what happens if the system gets an accidental signal to arm and that holding relay closes," Olsen said. "The bar that swings down and arms the impact switches is locked in place by your pin, so nothing happens to the impact switches. But your safety pin doesn't keep current from reaching the fuses and the solenoids, and so they'll get hotter by the second. There're twenty-eight continuous volts on those solenoids. They're not meant to operate that way, and something could burn out."

"And then what happens?" Willy asked.

"I don't know, Bud," Olsen said, "but I do know it's an unhealthy situation. I know it's not electrically sound."

Willy was willing to discuss the matter, but as the talk went on, he seemed to harden about the safety-pin device, and Olsen began to get the sickening feeling that Willy had developed pride of authorship and was going to hold out for his gadget at all costs. "Bud," he said diplomatically, "I don't have any objection to your invention. It's a fine idea. But not unless we straighten out the electrical problems in the circuit."

"Like what?" Willy asked.

"Let me explain again," Olsen said, and once again he led his superior officer through the explanation. "So you see, Bud," he said at the end, "it's a very dangerous situation. That holding relay puts the whole mission into jeopardy, and all we have to do to solve the problem is snip the jumper wire on the booster relay. Do you see what I'm talking about?"

"Yeah, Oley," Willy said. "It's clear enough, but you don't seem to know what you're asking me to do. You're asking me to make changes in the field, and that's just like telling me to go

over the heads of all those commanders and captains and ordnance and electronics experts that designed this stuff."

"Bud, if you have any respect for me at all, believe me, none
of those guys were electronic experts," Olsen said. "They
couldn't have been. Look, *you're* not an electronics expert, but
you can see what's wrong with this circuit, can't you?"

Willy said he thought he understood, and asked Olsen to give
him time to think about it. "Bud," Olsen answered, "that mission can be called on twenty-four hours' notice. If you have to
think about it, okay. But don't think too long, or this whole
project's gonna go up in smoke."

Later in the day Olsen had a chance to approach his friend
once more, and this time Willy said, "No, Oley, I'm sorry, I
can't see it. I think you're making a big deal out of nothing. If
we have my safety pin in there, I'll be perfectly happy to fly the
airplane."

"*You'll* be happy to fly the airplane?"

"Yeah," Willy said, "I've been on the skipper to let me go as
co-pilot."

Olsen stood up. "Okay, Bud, then that's another reason for
you to let me make these changes," he said emphatically. "If
you don't, you'll be risking your own life and Joe Kennedy's,
too, and the whole darned project."

Willy put his arm around his friend's shoulder. "Don't worry
so much, Oley," he said. "You act like you're fighting the whole
goddamn war by yourself. Did old Bud ever let you down?"

Olsen said, "Not till now. Don't you see what you're doing,
Bud? You're safetying one part of the system and completely
ignoring the other. It doesn't make sense."

"Look, Oley," Willy said in tones of annoyance. "Don't *you*
start telling me what makes sense and what doesn't. I didn't get
to be executive officer of this outfit by being stupid. I've got all
the responsibility and pressure that you've got, and a little
more, so do me a favor and stow it. Scientific experts in Phila-

delphia designed the arming panel; we're not changing it over here."

"You mean *you're* not," Olsen said.

"What the hell's that supposed to mean?" Willy said.

Olsen held himself in check. "Oh, nothing," he said.

Willy put on his hat. "Oley," he said, "you stop playing your games. That's an order!" He stalked outside.

Olsen chased Willy out and grabbed him by the arm. "Bud," he said, "you're making a mistake!"

Willy pulled away. "Bud!" Olsen called at the disappearing figure. "I don't care what you say. I'm gonna clip that jumper wire!"

Willy jerked to a stop. "If you do," he shouted, "I'll court-martial you!"

"I can do it without you ever knowing about it," Olsen said.

"You do, and so help me Christ I'll court-martial you, Olsen! By God, I'm not kidding you. You leave that damned thing alone! Don't you go near it!" Olsen turned to go back into the shop, his mind made up. Willy's voice screamed after him. "Don't ever let me hear that you went near that thing, is that understood? I'll throw the goddamned book at you! Listen, this is important business you're fooling with. This thing was designed by experts, and you're not gonna touch it! You leave it alone! You just take care of your goddamned radios!" Olsen slammed the door.

Several hours later he was slumped at his desk pondering the situation when the bespectacled autopilot expert, Jimmy Simpson, walked in and asked how things were going. Olsen told the whole story to his friend and asked his advice. "Well, it's simple," Simpson said. "You can snip the jumper and risk a court-martial, or you can go to the Old Man."

"Over Willy's head?" Olsen said. "That's always popular."

"Then go ahead and snip the wire, if you know you're right."

"I do."

"Then why don't you do it?"

"Look, Jimmy, that's easy for you to say," Olsen said. "But you know Bud as well as I do. He's a very hard-nosed guy. He says he'd court-martial me, and he would! I have no doubts about it. I'm all alone in this thing. Orlowski is with me, but they'd just say what the hell does he know, he's only an enlisted man. You're with me, but you're an autopilot man, and they're not going to listen to you either. If I go out and snip that wire, I'll make the circuitry perfectly safe, and I'll spend the rest of the war in the brig."

"Okay, then," Simpson said. "Let's go see the Old Man."

"You'll go with me?" Olsen said.

"You need some moral support."

The ensign and the lieutenant junior grade caught up with Commander James Smith in his office, where he was working on a stack of papers. Olsen told the whole story in the mildest terms, blaming no one and taking no potshots at the designers of the original system. "It's just one of those things, sir," Olsen said, "and one snip of a wire would solve it."

Jimmy Smith, friendly and pleasant as ever, said, "Oley, I appreciate your interest, and I don't want you to get me wrong, but I didn't design those circuits, and I didn't design those damned electrical fuses either. I'm just as leery of the whole thing as anybody. But I'm not qualified to judge things like this. I can't say what's right and what's wrong. I'm not a technician."

"Yes, sir," Olsen said, "but I *am* a technician, and I can tell you that our operation is being jeopardized by this design. The work that we've put into the program, Skipper, the work that you've put into it yourself—it's going to be wasted if we don't make a few minor corrections."

"Oley," Smith said, flashing the pleasant smile that made him so popular with his men, "I'll tell you what to do. You go ahead and work it out with Willy. He used to be an aviation mechanic. He knows more about things like this. Whatever you and Willy decide, it's okay with me."

"Sir, I've talked to Willy already, and he doesn't want to change anything," Olsen said.

"Well, I'm sorry then, Oley," Smith said. "I can't do anything else. I'm depending on Willy, and whatever decisions he makes are final."

Olsen and Simpson went back to the shop, and Olsen said, "That's it, Jimmy. That's as far as I can go. I've done everything humanly possible. That robot is a deadly thing. It'll blow up long before it gets to any target. I just hope to God that nobody's in it when it goes."

"Nobody will be in it if you take just one more step," Simpson said. "There's one thing you can still do."

"What's that?"

"You can tell Joe Kennedy."

"Tell him what?"

"Tell him that he's crazy to fly that robot unless it's fixed up. He's the ambassador's son. He's got fifty missions. That's fifty more than anybody else around here. They'll listen to him where they won't listen to you."

"Jimmy, I can't go crying on Joe Kennedy's shoulders," Olsen said. "He's just an innocent bystander in this thing."

"Yeah," Simpson said wryly. "If you don't go talk to him and get that arming panel fixed up, he's just an innocent bystander, all right. An innocent *dead* bystander." He paused. "Oley," he said softly, "I know what you're going through. Let me talk to Joe for you. He's a sharp guy. He won't fly in a plane that's not right. I'll talk to him and let you know what he says."

"What makes you think he'll listen to you?" Olsen said.

"I fly with him every day, don't I?" Simpson said. "I've flown twelve hours with him already, checking that autopilot. He's even let me handle the wheel. And I'll tell you something else that's strictly classified, friend to friend. He says there's a chance that I'll fly co-pilot on the mission. Now do you think he'll listen to me?"

Olsen was stunned. "You're a sap if you go! If you go now, knowing what you know, you're a raving lunatic!"

"There's a lot of honor in flying this mission, Oley," Simpson said softly. "Look at me. I've been in the Navy for eleven years, and I'm almost thirty years old, and I just made ensign a year ago. My eyesight's not too good, and I've always wanted to be a pilot. How the hell else am I going to win a DFC? The way I figure, this is my one chance to do something really worthwhile. Whatever the risk, I've got to take it."

"Even if you know you might get killed?"

Simpson nodded.

Later that afternoon the two friends were walking toward the galley when Olsen stopped and said, "Look! What are those trucks doing around the drone?"

Simpson peered into the farthest corner of the air base, where there seemed to be an unusual amount of hustle and bustle around the robot PB4Y. "I don't know," Simpson said, "but we'd better find out." They dashed toward the orderly room and almost knocked Lieutenant Colonel Roy Forrest down as he was walking out the door.

"Excuse me, sir," Olsen said. "What's all the activity around the baby?"

"You mean you haven't heard?" Forrest asked. "You're on for tomorrow. They're loading the drone."

Ensign James Simpson, USN, formerly Warrant Officer James Simpson and Chief Petty Officer Simpson and Ordinary Seaman Simpson, and before that a poverty-stricken boy living under an overturned shrimp boat in Port Arthur, Texas, was in dead earnest about flying the mission with Joe Kennedy. Indeed, he had thought about little else since coming to Fersfield. Apart from the natural desire of every sailor to make a splash in the war and earn the respect of his shipmates, Jim Simpson knew that there were compelling reasons for him to make the flight. A few routine tasks had to be performed in the air—an apprentice seaman could have done them—but there was one critical assignment that required skill and knowledge, and that was the setting up of the autopilot. The Army had had reason to believe that faulty autopilots had caused two or three of their drones to crash, and the Navy was not going to make the same error. Ensign James Simpson had graduated No. 1 in his class at Sperry gyroscope school, and he might well have been the best at his craft in the whole U.S. Navy. Certainly he was one of the few autopilot experts to win a commission and the only one assigned to the Navy unit in the Aphrodite project. Who else could logically fly with Kennedy to troubleshoot the autopilot if anything went wrong?

It disturbed Simpson that his good friend Olsen had found the arming equipment defective and dangerous, but it did not sway him a degree away from his intended course. He had more respect for Olsen's intelligence and skill in electronics than for all the rest put together, and if Olsen said that the plane might arm accidentally and blow up in midair, there was every reason to believe him. So be it. Ensign James Simpson would fly the mission. They did not give DFC's for routine flights, and there was a risk in everything. In his daydreams, he could see the looks on his shipmates' faces when he returned to Fersfield after his successful parachute jump, and everyone would cluster around and say, "How'd it go, Jim?" and he would answer, "Routine, nothing to it," and go off to wash up for the awarding of the medal. That would put an end to Commander Jimmy Smith's wisecracking once and for all. Simpson liked the skipper—everybody did—but sometimes he wanted to tell him outright to "stow it." Smith was fond of saying, "Well, well, how is our raw ensign doing today?" and Simpson took this as a commentary on the fact that it had taken him years of hard work to reach the lowest rung on the commissioned officers' ladder, while most of the others had reached higher ranks with far less effort. Only once had Simpson dared crack back at Smith.

"Our raw ensign is doing fine, thank you, sir," he said, "and he wishes to remind you that he may be a raw ensign, but he has twice as much time in this program as any other two men."

The group had fallen quiet, but Jimmy Smith was not a man who saw mutiny in every offhand remark. "Well, more power to you, Ensign," the skipper had said, "and don't take me too seriously."

After that, some of the other men had started calling him "our raw ensign," and Simpson did not like it. He was a conscientious officer, and he did not think it was anyone's business that it had taken him eleven years to win his gold stripe. The breakthrough from chief to warrant to ensign was no mean accomplishment; other men with his shortness of stature and thick glasses would still have been down in the engine room, shoveling. He was proud of his rank, and he wanted to make his shipmates proud of it, too.

On the evening before the scheduled mission, the air was clear and cool, and Ensign James Simpson watched the smoke from his cigarette ascend in a straight vertical line as he sat outside the briefing room waiting for his friend, Lieutenant Joseph Patrick Kennedy, Jr. Inside, important decisions were being made. The most important, so far as Simpson was concerned, was the selection of co-pilot. He was convinced that Kennedy wanted him to go on the flight; the two men had made almost daily trips in the drone, and they worked well together. If it were entirely up to Joe, they would fly together on the mission —Simpson was convinced of it. But he also knew that the decision was not Joe's alone and that his wealthy friend from Massachusetts was meticulous about such matters as chains of command and areas of responsibility. "Let's get one thing straight, Jimmy," he had said to Simpson in a marathon bull session late one night, "I'm all for taking you on the flight. It wouldn't make sense to take anybody else. But I'm just an interloper here—you know that—and I don't make the final decisions. If we were back in my regular squadron, it'd be different. I don't cut any ice around here, and I shouldn't. I'm just the hired help."

"Yeah," Simpson had said, "hired to do the most important job in the project."

"Hired to do a job, that's all," Kennedy had said, "and to do it the way they tell me. Now lately they've been telling me that maybe I should fly the plane alone and clutch in the autopilot by myself. It can be done. And your skipper's hinted a few times that maybe he should fly with me, and Lieutenant Willy has hinted the same thing, and so has the ordnance officer. He's a pilot, too, you know. One of the radio controllers came up to me the other day and he said, 'Joe, I think they can do without me in the mother ship if you just say the word. Then I can fly with you.' *Everybody* wants to go. So I'll just sit around and wait and see what develops. If anybody asks me, I'll say there's only one job to be done up there by a co-pilot, and that's to get the autopilot and the Ace running right, and you're the best man for that."

"Fair enough," Simpson had said, "and if I get passed over, I won't beef about it or send a complaint to the Secretary of the Navy. No, sir, Joe, I won't do anything stupid. I'll just go out to the corner of the field and shoot myself."

Both men had laughed, and Kennedy had said, "Shut up and go to sleep. I want you to be well rested so your aim'll be good!"

Now little Jimmy Simpson, twenty-nine-year-old ensign, sat outside the room where the most important decision of his life was being made by others, and tried to ready himself emotionally for a turndown. "Well, what the hell," he said to himself. "If nothing comes of this, at least I've met Joe Kennedy and made a good friend. It's a rare thing to meet a guy like that."

The friendship between the polished socialite from Massachusetts and the poor kid from Port Arthur had developed quickly, partially out of proximity (they were bunkmates) and partially out of certain common denominators. Both were deeply religious, Simpson a Protestant and Kennedy a Catholic, and both were eager to talk about it. They did not subscribe to the adage about never discussing politics or religion, and whenever either subject came up, Simpson knew he was in for a long night. Kennedy had been around the world; he had kissed the Pope's ring and attended masses in the great cathedrals of Europe, and Simpson would beg him for details and listen avidly.

Usually there would be a poker game going on in the middle of the hut under a single bare light bulb, and Kennedy and Simpson would sit on bunks in the shadows at the end of the room and try to ignore the outcries and complaints and the loud clichés. Only once had Kennedy allowed the racket to get under his skin, and Simpson thought he had never seen so graphic an illustration of the innate power to command. At two o'clock one morning, Kennedy had suddenly sat up in bed and shouted, "You people put that light out and get to bed!" At the time there had been several Navy lieutenants, an Army major, and two Army captains in the game, and within five minutes of Kennedy's "order" they had folded up and stolen away.

Simpson often wondered what Joe would do if he overheard any of the snide remarks about his practice of putting on pajamas and kneeling in prayer before going to bed. The Nissen hut was small, and the cardplayers could not fail to hear Kennedy pray, and sometimes Simpson would see them exchange glances of superiority or disdain. One night when the regular players had brought some new blood into the game, Kennedy knelt in prayer, and a few of the new men began snickering. "Watch out, guys!" a Navy lieutenant whispered. Kennedy continued with his prayer, and when it was over, he stood up, turned slowly, and stared hard at the two newcomers for a full minute or two. Then he climbed into bed and went to sleep, while the card game continued *sotto voce*.

Jim Simpson did not kneel in prayer each night, but he respected Joe Kennedy's ritual, and he thought that he had never known so noble a person. Now and then Simpson and Earl

Olsen would talk about the temporary member of SAU No. 1, and they found that they agreed completely about him. Once Olsen read aloud a passage from a letter he was about to mail to his wife. " 'I've found a man who is quite a man,' " he read to Simpson. " 'I wish I could model myself after him.' "

"I feel exactly the same way," Simpson said. "The funny thing is that the three of us are within a few months of the same age, and yet I feel so junior to him." Olsen agreed. They decided that the explanation lay in Kennedy's curiously full life: his audiences with the Pope and all the crowned heads of Europe, his service in the Massachusetts legislature, his job as a courier for the State Department during the Spanish Civil War, and his double tour of duty over the bloodied waves of the Bay of Biscay. Discussions of these subjects were never initiated by Kennedy. Indeed, in the beginning of his term with the unit, the information had to be pried out of him. But now he had loosened up, at least to a few men in his hut. He told about his father's hopes that he would return to politics after the war, and he said that his own feelings were mixed on the subject. Sometimes he said he agreed, and sometimes he said he did not. More than once he hinted that personal matters might change his whole future. Simpson knew that Kennedy had been seeing a British woman; hardly a night passed when the two men did not cycle the half mile down the country lane toward the down of Diss so that Kennedy could drop coins in a roadside pay phone and talk in low tones for twenty to thirty minutes at a time. Simpson stayed off the subject; he knew it was none of his business, and Joe Kennedy was not the sort of man who traded intimacies. One night Kennedy, half-asleep, said something about marrying and going to Scotland on a honeymoon. No one had pumped him on the subject, and it had not come up again.

Sitting outside the door of the briefing room, musing on the past and hoping for the future, Ensign James Simpson looked at his watch. It was almost eight; the briefing had been going on for an hour. He wondered what there was to talk about for such a long time. Certainly there was no further need to discuss the target. The mother ship crews had spent days studying papier-mâché mock-ups of the rocket site buried in the ground at Mimoyecques; they knew their headings and their timings backward, and they had been engaged in the remote radio control of airplanes for years. Whatever his personal differences with the other members of the unit, Jim Simpson knew that they were a superior force, trained and ready and eager to go. To be sure, his friend Olsen had cast a slight pall over the project, and lately Bud Willy, for one, had been acting jumpy and bossy and unlike himself. But this was only because he was human; he was like an actor who had been in rehearsal for months and months and at last was to step on the stage and play his role. Who wouldn't be nervous and jumpy? As for Olsen, Simpson had decided to put his friend's warnings out of his mind until the mission was over. Everything that Olsen had said had made sense, but nothing was being done about it, and the best thing to do was to fly the mission and hope for the best. Given a choice between a continuation of his safe, anonymous career and a crack at perilous glory, Jimmy Simpson would opt for glory. He only hoped that he would get the chance.

Now the door to the briefing room came open, and the important figures of Mission Aphrodite began to stream out in a loud procession of talk and banter. There were Harry Wherry and Hugh Lyon, pilots of the mother ships; SAU No. 1 skipper, Jimmy Smith; Fersfield commanding officer Roy Forrest; the young first-string controllers, John Anderson and John Demlein; and the various project and operations and intelligence officers who made the plans and laid the groundwork. Joe Kennedy was one of the last to leave the room, and unlike the others, he was not laughing or joking or deep in conversation. He walked over to Simpson and put his hand on the ensign's shoulder. "It doesn't look good for us, Jim," he said. "They're talking about Willy flying with me instead of you."

"What the hell can Willy do that I can't do?" Simpson snapped, and at once regretted his tone of voice.

"Nothing," Kennedy said. "Not a damned thing. But if he decides to go, and Jimmy Smith decides to let him, then he's going and that's that."

Something in Kennedy's tone of voice made Simpson drop the subject. "Whatever you say, Joe," he said softly. "You're the boss."

"I wish I was," Kennedy said. "Then you'd go and no doubt about it."

The two men wandered outside the office and saw that it was not yet dark. The sun was gathering itself for its nightly plunge down the other edge of England, and far out on the field a group of men cast long skinny shadows as they worked on the drone. "They're loading," Simpson said, in a barely audible voice, as though the sound waves from his mouth might detonate the volatile cargo. "Want to take a look?"

Kennedy nodded and the two men climbed on their bicycles and pedaled the mile or so to the robot PB4Y. Negro troops had formed a line from the ammunition carriers to the aircraft's after entrance, and they were slowly passing along wax-lined pine boxes full of packages that looked like wrapped blocks of butter. "Torpex!" Kennedy said softly. Each box of the powerful new explosive looked as though it might weigh 50 or 60 pounds, and the men were handling them gingerly. At the end of the line, the last man would heft the box up to his chest level and slide it into the aircraft, where another pair of hands would haul it away for stacking. As Kennedy and Simpson watched, this last man grabbed a box and snagged it on the lip of the hatch as he struggled to lift it up. The explosives teetered on the edge and then dropped toward the asphalt. At the last split second, the Negro loader stuck his foot out and took the full weight of the Torpex on his toe, and the box fell off to one side.

"Let's get out of here!" Kennedy said. "I know that stuff's

supposed to be stable, but I'd rather be someplace else!" As the two men cycled away, they saw an officer leading the limping loader to a jeep. "Probably a broken toe," Kennedy said. "The guy ought to get a court-martial and a medal." Simpson laughed.

Inside the small officers' club, the two friends saw a knot of Navy men drinking together, and they ordered fruit juice and gin cocktails and joined their comrades. The conversation turned, as it often did, to Lieutenant Colonel Roy Forrest, who apparently had spoken with his usual Texas bluntness at the briefing. "The boy colonel!" one of the Navy men said derisively. "Ain't a thing he don't know, is there?"

"He seems pretty competent to me," Kennedy said.

"Competent?" the other man said contemptuously. "He doesn't know his ass from second base. If he was in the Navy, he'd be a seaman second. I don't know what makes the Army Air Corps think a punk like that can hold command."

"Well, in the first place, he's not such a punk," Kennedy said. "He's thirty-one or thirty-two years old, and he's flown a mess of combat missions. In the second place, he's been a squadron commander for two years. He led the whole air force on the third Berlin raid."

"That's *his* story," one of the others said. "I don't believe he could lead a platoon of niggers to a watermelon patch." Several of the men snickered, and several looked at the speaker with contempt.

Kennedy nudged Simpson and said, "Let's go, Jimmy," and the two men put away their drinks and walked into the gathering night. "I had to get out of there," Kennedy said. "That talk was all wrong. That kind of talk makes me want to fight, and wouldn't that be lovely? A big brawl on the night before we all take off on the mission!"

Simpson laughed. "One big happy family," he said. "C'mon, let's go get something to eat."

"By that I assume you mean let's go eat some more of my

eggs?" Kennedy said. Several days before, Kennedy had received another of the presents that kept pouring in from his dot-
ing family. Often he would get fancy boxes of his favorite
glass-encased fifty-cent cigars, but this new package had contained a miniature pirate's chest lined with satin and bound
in brass straps and full to the brim with fresh eggs, a gift from
his sister, Lady Hartington. Kennedy and Simpson and a few of
the others had been nibbling at the rare and precious gifts, and
now there were only a dozen or so left.

"I've got an idea," Simpson said. "Will you do me a favor?"

"Sure."

"Get yourself in a long conversation with the galley cook at
the officers' mess and make sure you keep him going for at least
five full minutes."

"What the hell for?"

"None of your business," Simpson said. "Look, would you
trust me to set up your autopilot tomorrow if I got the chance?"

Kennedy nodded.

"Well, then, trust me tonight," Simpson said. "Meet me back
at the hut in fifteen minutes." The two men walked toward the
officers' mess and Simpson disappeared into the shadows. A
short time later he entered the Nissen hut with a uniform that
bulged in several places.

"What the hell have you been up to?" Kennedy said from a
dark corner.

Simpson reached under his shirt and removed a bulge that
turned out to be a pound of butter. Another bulge became a
package of bacon, and what had appeared to be a potbelly
turned into a loaf of bread. "Now get out your eggs, and we'll
have a feast!" Simpson said.

"You mean you had me engage the cook in conversation and
then you—"

"Never mind," Simpson said. "What you don't know won't
hurt you."

Kennedy delivered a short lecture on morals and ethics, but

Simpson let it bounce off. He noticed that his friend's eyes kept flicking toward the edibles, and Simpson let him ramble on. Finally, the "raw ensign" said, "Okay, Archbishop, are you finished?"

"Yes," Kennedy said.

"Then let's eat!"

Kennedy produced a small frying pan from his gear and said, "Start the fire!" Simpson went to the coke tins and found them empty. The one-pound-per-day-per-man ration was all used up, as usual.

"Go ahead and get the stuff ready," Simpson said. "I'll be right back."

He picked up a large GI can and slipped out the door and into the shadows. He skirted around the backs of the Nissen huts and worked his way toward one of the large piles of coke that were guarded by a British sentry. He waited a few minutes for the proper timing and then began inserting coke into the GI can, one piece at a time to cut down the noise. Then he tiptoed back to the hut carrying five pounds of coke, or one night's ration for the hut. "When do we eat?" he called out triumphantly as he entered the room.

A half hour later the two friends were dining on bacon and egg sandwiches dripping with butter, and when the feast was over, Kennedy pulled out a bottle of embassy bourbon, and poured each of them a nip. "Cigar?" he said, offering Simpson a Havana Special in its own glass case.

"No, thanks, I don't smoke cigars," Simpson said. "I never had a chance to develop expensive tastes." It occurred to him that this might be a good time to bring up Olsen and his worries. "Joe," he said, "there's something serious I want to talk to you about."

"Serious about you, serious about me, or serious about the mission?"

"Serious about the mission," Simpson said.

"Is it something we can do something about?"

"Maybe *you* can."

Kennedy was silent. "Jimmy," he said, fixing his narrow eyes on the other, "I've been all around Robin Hood's barn about the mission. People have been asking me all kinds of things, suggesting all kinds of things, and I've developed a policy about the whole matter. And you know what that policy is."

"To keep quiet and obey orders?" Simpson said.

"That's the way it is."

"And you won't change now?"

"Nope," Kennedy said. "Not for you or anybody else."

For a moment, Simpson thought of pressing the point, but his friend's expression, fixed and stern through the cigar smoke, made him change his mind. Above all, he did not want to put any misgivings about the mission into Kennedy's mind, and he realized that he would have to cover his tracks. "Oh, well," he said with mock calmness, "it probably wasn't important anyway."

Jimmy Simpson and Earl Olsen went to breakfast together on the day of the scheduled mission, August 11, 1944, and both men were unusually glum as they sat in the little English-run mess hall. Olsen had studied the dummy arming panel until late the night before, and he was more convinced than ever that the mission would be a failure. The question kept running through his mind: *When* will it be a failure, before or after the jump crew gets out? He felt that there was a fair chance that Kennedy and his co-pilot would survive, a slight chance that the robot PB4Y might reach the English Channel, and hardly any chance at all that it would destroy its target. But what could he do? He had run through his list of possible allies, and all but Simpson and Orlowski had refused to take him seriously. He felt that he had reached the end of the line. "Did you say anything to Kennedy about the arming panel?" he asked Simpson.

"I started to," Simpson said, "but he didn't want to talk about

it. Then I realized that I might just be making him nervous, so
I dropped the subject."

"Well, he's better off nervous than risking his neck with that
haywire ordnance panel," Olsen said.

Simpson gave his friend an impatient look. "Now isn't that a
hell of a remark to make to the man that may fly co-pilot?" he
said. "Don't you think I have any nerves?"

"I think you're crazy if you go in that plane, Jimmy," Olsen
said. "I think you're a sap for trying to go on this mission, and
I'm asking you as a friend not to go."

"No," Simpson said. "I'm going, if I can, Oley, and that's all
there is to it."

At nine thirty in the morning, the air crews went into another
briefing session, and once again Simpson was told to wait outside. Olsen waited with him, and after a few minutes the door
of the briefing room popped open and Joe Kennedy came out
alone. "Jimmy," he said, "I believe Bud Willy's going with me.
They're discussing it in there now."

"He doesn't know the drill, does he?"

"I don't know. Somebody suggested that you type up a list of
instructions one by one, and he'll just follow them."

"But wouldn't it be simpler—"

"Look," Kennedy said sharply, "I've got to go back inside.
Bud Willy's going, and that's that. He's the exec, and if he says
he's going, he's going." Kennedy lowered his voice and took his
friend by the arm. "Jimmy," he said, "I know how you feel.
The next time *you'll* go. I'll have more time to argue. I'll make
them see it my way. But there's no time now." He disappeared
inside.

Soon after, the meeting broke up. Willy ordered Simpson to
type up the list of instructions and "stick it on the control
panel where I can see it."

"When's the mission?" Olsen asked.

"I don't know. We're on four hours' notice."

Simpson hurried off to type up the list, and Olsen fell in with Willy on the way to the hangar. "That's a tough break for Jim," Olsen said to his old friend. "He had his heart set on winning the DFC."

Willy strode out ahead, and Olsen could see that the senior man was making an effort to leave him behind. He doubled his pace and came up alongside. "Bud," Olsen said, "we're old friends. Tell me something as old friend to old friend. Why are you going on this mission? What can you do?"

Willy's face was grim, the muscles taut across his cheekbones. "It's none of your damn business what I do, Olsen," Willy snapped.

"You can fly the plane, but Kennedy will do that," Olsen went on. "You can trim the autopilot, but that's Kennedy's job, too. You could pull out that fool pin of yours, but that doesn't belong in the system in the first place, and in the second place, Kennedy can pull out a pin as well as you."

Willy stopped and turned. "Olsen," he said, "cut it out or I'll court-martial you!" Olsen could see that Willy was trembling, and he could not remember ever seeing him so visibly out of control. "On second thought," Willy said between clenched teeth, "I think I'll court-martial you anyway. Goddamn you, Olsen, you've made everybody aboard a nervous wreck."

Olsen held his tongue, and Willy bustled off. Then Olsen found that he was trembling himself, and he felt like crying or fighting or both. No one would listen. The PB4Y was almost fully loaded now; there would be 20,570 pounds of Torpex and 600 pounds of TNT demolition charges aboard, and on four hours' notice the whole deadly load could be ordered into the air, safetied by an amateurish arming panel and an improvised "safety" pin that only made the device more dangerous.

Olsen walked slowly back toward his shop, deep in forebodings. So he was turning people into nervous wrecks? Well, he had not intended to disturb anyone. His intention had been solely to save the mission and the lives of its participants. He was sorry that Willy was acting so uncharacteristically jumpy and tense. He thought that he had never seen such violent change in a man's character in so short a time. Suppose Willy made a mistake in midair and blew the robot up through his own nervousness? Olsen did not know what to do. Twenty-nine years of relatively sheltered life had left him unprepared for such a situation. He would gladly have taken a court-martial and a reduction in grade and even a dishonorable discharge if it would have saved the mission, but he was already heading toward one of those eventualities, and *still the mission was being flown.* It baffled him. Then he saw Joe Kennedy, tieless and sloppy in khakis, walking out of the hangar, and he hurried over on impulse, not even sure what he was going to say.

"Hello, Oley," Kennedy said affably.

"Joe, there's something I have to tell you," Olsen said, the words rushing out. "I think you're risking your neck unnecessarily, going on this mission. The system isn't working right. I want to make some changes to make it safer, but I can't get any cooperation."

"Gosh," Kennedy said, plainly surprised. "I don't know what to tell you, Oley. I appreciate what you're trying to do, but I don't have any say about things like that. I just volunteered to fly."

"Listen, Joe," Olsen said, trying to keep his voice as calm as possible, "you have a *big* say in this. You're the pilot. All you have to say is you're not flying the mission unless they make some changes."

"But I already volunteered."

"Sure, you volunteered, and you can unvolunteer, too, don't you see? You're risking your neck for nothing."

"How am I risking my neck?"

Olsen realized that he must soften his remarks. He could not tell Lieutenant Joseph Kennedy flat out that there was a fair possibility that the robot would blow up prematurely. Willy was already showing tension, and two men with the same fears might abort the mission through sheer terror. "Well, maybe not exactly risking your neck," Olsen said. "But I don't think the mission can be successful. I'm sure the plane'll malfunction before it gets to the target."

Kennedy said, "I can't do anything about that, Oley."

"You can go to the skipper and tell him to fix up your airplane."

Kennedy paused. "No," he said. "I don't think I will. I think I'm gonna fly it." He started to walk off, then turned and waved a friendly hand back toward the radio officer. "Thanks, anyway, Oley," he said. "I know you mean well. I appreciate it."

"I mean well," Olsen muttered to himself. "That's the nicest thing anybody's said to me." He headed for the shops, and he realized that the mission was going to be flown, and there was not a single thing he could do about it.

Crews placed on four hours' notice. Preliminary briefing at 0930. Weather forecast at 1031 was pessimistic. 1200 completed loading PB4Y drone. Radio search 1240–1605. No potentially harmful results noticed. Between 1400 and 1500 conducted final briefing, although the weather was bad, and at 1500 hours scrubbed mission.—Daily log of SAU No. 1, August 11, 1944

That night, Joe Kennedy stalked around the Nissen hut; plainly, he was in a petulant mood that was totally unlike his previous behavior. Simpson kept to himself, but every now and then Kennedy, in the manner of a typically disturbed person, would stomp down to his end of the hut and blurt out a few words of annoyance. Simpson tried to calm him, but at least an hour went by before Kennedy had stopped stalking and pacing and complaining, and by then the reason for his anger had slipped out in bits and pieces. Kennedy and his girlfriend had planned to spend the weekend with friends at a nearby estate. But now the mission had been postponed, and the girl was out there waiting. Someone had to get word to her. Kennedy had asked Bud Willy for a few hours' liberty, and Willy had flatly refused. "All you have to do is fall off your bike and sprain your ankle," Willy had said, "and the whole mission's off." Commander Smith had backed up his executive officer. Joe could go down the road to the crossroads and use the pay phone, but nothing more. Kennedy had hopped on a bicycle and called his sister's home and left word for someone to pass his message along. Then he had returned to the Nissen hut in a swivet.

After Kennedy finally said his prayers and turned in, still muttering imprecations to himself, Simpson sought out Olsen, and the two men took a walk to the officers' club to check on the status of the mission. "Far as I know, it's on for tomorrow," Ensign John Demlein, the radio controller in Lieutenant Harry Wherry's crew, told them. "Say, what's got into Joe Kennedy?"

"What do you mean?" Olsen asked.

"I was talking to him tonight, and he said something about being sorry he had volunteered for this mission. He never talked like that before."

"Did he seem nervous?" Simpson asked.

"No," Demlein said. "Not nervous. Mad, maybe, and a little wound up. I don't think he's got nerves, to tell you the truth."

The three men chatted for a few minutes, and then Olsen and Simpson headed back to the darkened Nissen hut. "Still feeling bad, Jimmy?" Olsen said.

"Yeah," Simpson said. "I'll feel bad for the rest of my life."

"Don't!" Olsen said. "You're a lucky guy, Jimmy. You're going to live through this thing."

"And Joe and Bud aren't?"

"I hope to God they are," Olsen said. "All night I'm going to be praying the same prayer. I'm gonna be praying that I'm wrong."

At 9 the next morning, Saturday, August 12, 1944, the whipped-cream mounds of clouds that had come over the field the evening before gave signs of dissolving. Behind them, the sky was growing brighter, and the "metro" data from Third Bomb Division indicated that the weather over western Europe would be generally CAVU from early afternoon on. Roy Forrest and Commander James Smith sat in Forrest's office studying the reports as they came in, and at 10:30 A.M. they placed the Navy combat crews on four-hour notice. By noon the last remains of the fat clouds were spinning away toward the east in thin tatters, and East Anglia was enjoying one of its rare days of hot sunshine. Men rolled up their sleeves, the sentry on Drone PB4Y No. 32271 blew perspiration from his nose tip as he tried to walk his post in a military manner, and for a change, the soldiers and sailors at Fersfield were freed from their constant preoccupations of coldness, dampness, and ennui. The untutored eye might have noticed no change in the day-to-day operations at the base, but every man knew there was a stirring in the air. The practice was over. The gray-white Liberator at the corner of the field seemed to hunker down on its big tires, and its wing tips barely vibrated in the hot light wind from the south. There was something new and solid about the aircraft, and one noticed that jeeps and other vehicles on routine runs around the base gave the four-engine plane a wider berth than usual. Under its camouflage netting, the ship was unmistakably a PB4Y, a B-24 in Army nomenclature, a heavy bomber with fat, squat fuselage and graceful, long, tapering wings, but there were subtle changes, the kinds that sometimes catch the eyes of suspicious antiaircraft crews. Two black broomsticks poked from where the tail turret once had been, but they did not look much like the twin .50-caliber machine guns that belonged there. Jimmy Simpson had painted them and installed them on the off-chance that an enemy fighter plane might make a run at the drone over the target and, seeing the twin barrels sticking from the tail, might pay the ship a little more respect. All other gun turrets had been removed and replaced with sheet aluminum, giving the Liberator a sleeker, more streamlined (and less familiar) silhouette.

Roy Forrest had been out inspecting the remodeled airplane early in the morning, and his first reaction was slight misgivings about the strangeness of the plane's new figure. "The British fire on anything that isn't in the aircraft identification manuals, and some that are," he had told a Navy lieutenant. "Let's hope this one looks harmless to them." Back at his office, he looked over a report that had been passed along from the Thirty-Fourth Bomb Group. The report, signed "Wackwitz," told how gunners at Clacton-on-Sea had fired "six to 12 bursts of low inaccurate barrage-type flak" on a formation of American bombers at 9 A.M. the day before. Clacton-on-Sea was to be Lieutenant Joseph Kennedy's third checkpoint. Forrest hoped that Eighth Air Force Headquarters had sent word to the British ack-ack officers to cease and desist with their cannonades if an American Navy PB4Y came cruising over the next day. One scrap of shrapnel from barrage-type weapons or, for that matter, a bit of lead from a capricious Tommy's rifle could send Joe Kennedy and Wilford John Willy and the whole Aphrodite program up in smoke. But as the morning grew older and the skies turned bright blue, Forrest stopped worrying. The PB4Y would not be flying alone; it would be in the middle of an air armada unmistakably composed of friendly aircraft. There would be two PV mother ships, a B-17 radio relay plane and another B-17 navigational ship, plus four P-51 Mustang fighters flying cover, two Mosquitoes and two P-38's functioning as weather and observation aircraft, several light liaison planes to spot the parachute jumpers, plus the inevitable spectators: Generals Partridge and Doolittle would probably show up in P-38's or P-47's, and there might be a B-17 or two loaded with officers from various headquarters out to see the show. Forrest realized that a British gunner who would fire an antiaircraft round into that flotilla would have to be insane. It would be different if clouds developed. The English gun crews sometimes fired at sounds in the sky or pips on a radar screen when the weather was bad. But today there would be no problems of aircraft identification, and Forrest dismissed the problem from his mind. There were other matters to be attended to, the most important of which was weather at the target. He was having his usual problems with the weather squadrons.

"Yeah, yeah," he said impatiently into the telephone. "I know it's irregular. Believe me, this whole damned project's irregular. But I need to know the weather on the deck, especially the winds. Flat down! Right on the ground, where the prairie dogs live. Now you go get it for me!"

At noon preliminary checkouts were begun, and an hour later the mission was definitely scheduled to fly at six o'clock, when the late afternoon sun would be flashing directly into the German gun crews' eyes. Still Forrest did not have the metro data he needed. "Goddamn it, Smitty," he barked at Commander James Smith, "those little weather nipshits are screwing up again. How about let's take a ride?"

"Let's go," Smith said.

The two officers went outside and climbed into Forrest's supercharged P-38, the lieutenant colonel into the cockpit and the naval commander in the observer's fishbowl of plexiglass in the "droopsnoot." In less time than it would have taken to argue with the weather recon officers, the two pilots had streaked across the Channel to the target, made their weather observations, and returned to Fersfield. "All clear!" Forrest told the operations officer when they landed. "It's as bright as Jacksonville, Texas. The winds are no factor. The Krauts are out sunning themselves on the terrace."

Final briefing began at 2 P.M. Just before the session, one of the project officers of Aphrodite took Joe Kennedy aside and said, "Lieutenant, I've heard rumors that your arming system isn't safe. What about it?"

"Forget it," Kennedy said, laughing. "I'm in no danger. I've got the best insurance policy in the world."

"What's that?" the project officer asked.

"My executive officer's flying with me."

"Does he know anything about the arming system?"

"Does he know anything?" Kennedy said with incredulity. "He practically grew up with this program. If he doesn't know anything about it, nobody does."

"Well, I'm glad you're confident," the Army officer said, "and I wish you every success in the world. We're all in this war together, although not everybody seems to know it." The two men shook hands and went inside for the briefing.

When the combat crews were assembled, the intelligence officer and the operations officer and Colonel Forrest and Commander Smith and several others spoke, but no one paid much attention. They had been through these briefings several times before; they could have flown the mission in their sleep, and the target just inside the French coast at Mimoyecques was so familiar to each of them that they could have reconstructed its shape in clay in a matter of minutes with blindfolds firmly in place. Nevertheless, the protocol had to be observed, and the session droned on for more than an hour. The plan was simple. The mother ships would take off first and climb to about 2,000 feet. The drone would follow and proceed on a checking course while Hugh Lyon's mother ship took it over Saxmundham, Beccles, Clacton-on-Sea, and West Manston, where the jump crew would slip out through the nose-wheel hatch. Lieutenant Harry Wherry's mother ship would fly in close and take control and steer the drone over the Channel to a point 6 miles from the enemy coast. Then, to avoid flak, Wherry would return control to Lieutenant Hugh Lyon's mother ship, flying 10 miles astern. Lyon's controller, Lieutenant (jg) John "Red" Anderson, would steer the robot into the target by television. If everything went perfectly, the mystery rocket site would be removed from the earth at 7 P.M. sharp, exactly as an eye is lifted from a potato.

When the briefing was over, Kennedy fell in with Ensign John Demlein, the controller in Lieutenant Harry Wherry's Lockheed Ventura, and they walked together toward the revetment where PB4Y No. 32271 was surrounded by sandbags and camouflage netting. Demlein and Kennedy were not old friends, but both were Catholics and they had attended masses at Fersfield and occasionally ridden out into the countryside for a break from the daily tedium. They were worlds apart socially, Kennedy the wealthy ambassador's son and Demlein the son of a New York City fireman, but somehow a friendship had sprung up. Demlein said, "Joe, you got your insurance policy paid up?"

Kennedy laughed. "Why the hell is everybody talking about insurance?" he said. "Nobody in my family needs any insurance money."

They walked toward the plane in silence, and then Kennedy stopped abruptly and handed Demlein a sheathed knife. "What the hell's this?" Demlein said.

"It's a paratrooper's knife. They gave it to me at the briefing."

"Well, maybe you'll get caught in your chute and you'll need it," Demlein said.

"Hell, I've got a penknife here that I've had all my life," Kennedy said, showing Demlein a Boy Scout knife with a bone handle. "I don't need a fancy paratrooper knife with a great big eight-inch blade to cut parachute risers. Here, take it! Keep it!"

"Well, if you're sure," Demlein said, and thanked his friend for the gift. Just before they parted, Demlein to head back toward the mother ship for last-minute checks and Kennedy to make a final preflight inspection of the drone, the two men stopped and shook hands. "Good luck, Joe," Demlein said.

"Thanks," Kennedy said, a broad smile on his face. "I'll need it."

On an impulse, Demlein said, "Say, how about inviting us to the wedding?" He believed that Kennedy was going to meet his girlfriend on the parachute drop and drive off for a secret marriage ceremony.

Kennedy hesitated, as though caught off guard. "You'll hear from me," he said briskly, and turned away.

Earl Olsen was puttering around in his shop, trying to keep busy. He had long since made the final check of the control gear in the mother ships and the drone; it was working perfectly. Before slipping out of the robot aircraft, he had considered snipping the jumper wire that would take the dangerous holding relay out of the system, but he thought about Willy's anger and the threatened court-martial and all the tension of the preceding days, and he had hopped out of the airplane and never looked back.

Now it was getting close to takeoff time, and he figured the best thing he could do would be to stay in his shop and mind his own business. The way matters stood, his mere appearance on the flight line might send his old friend Willy into a tirade, thereby endangering the mission even more than it was already endangered. So he stayed inside and worked on a radio receiver. At about five in the afternoon, an hour or so before scheduled takeoff, he heard the door to the shop open. He turned and saw Wilford Willy, in full jump paraphernalia, walk inside. Willy said, "Hello, Oley," as though nothing had ever come between them. "I want to ask you a favor."

"What's that, Bud?" Olsen said. He deliberately kept his voice as friendly and warm as possible; this was no time for personal quibbling or animosity.

"I want you to hook up the fuses," Willy said.

Olsen thought quickly. If there was any part of PB4Y No. 32271 that he wanted nothing whatever to do with at that moment, it was the ordnance system. Willy and he had almost gone to personal war over the subject; and now the same Willy was asking him to make the last-minute connections that would complete the arming system.

"Gosh, Bud, I don't know," Olsen said, still trying to figure out what to do. "That's the ordnance officer's job, isn't it?"

"Sure, it's the ordnance officer's job," Willy said. "But the ordnance officer's a new man around here. I don't know him, and I *do* know you, Oley, and I'll take my chances with you."

"Yesterday you were going to court-martial me," Olsen said.

"That was yesterday," Willy said softly. "When the mission's over, I *still* might court-martial you. But now I'm asking you a favor."

"Gee, I don't know, Bud," Olsen said. "I've never hooked up an ordnance panel in my life."

"So what? It's wires and plugs and circuits and voltages, and if there's anybody that knows about those things, it's you. Now how about it? Don't make me order you, Oley. Let's agree on this together."

Olsen picked up a tiny resistor and fingered it nervously. "How soon till takeoff?" he asked.

"Thirty minutes."

Olsen flung the resistor to the floor. "Okay, Bud, I'll do it on one condition, that Chief Orlowski comes along. He knows as much as I do about these things, and the two of us can check on each other."

A few minutes later Olsen and Orlowski were jeeping out to the loaded drone. "Tell me exactly what we're supposed to do," Orlowski said.

"Okay," Olsen said. "There are four inertia switches that will tumble on impact and complete the circuit to the fuses and blow the load all at once. Right now there's no connection whatever between the inertia switches and the fuses. We've got to make the connection."

"Simple enough," Orlowski said.

"Not as simple as you think," Olsen said. "If there's the

slightest current on the line, the whole thing can blow when we connect the plugs. That's what we've got to watch out for."

Jim Simpson was in the drone making last-minute adjustments to the autopilot and double-checking his typed list of directions taped to the panel between the pilot's seat and the empty space where the co-pilot's seat should have been. All three specialists realized that they were sitting on almost 11 tons of explosives, and social amenities were kept to a minimum. Olsen went to work with testing lights and galvanometers, checking every inch of wire, every resistor and capacitor and minuscule electronic part that had any relationship whatever with the arming panel. "Dead," Olson said. "It's a hundred percent dead. Now you try it."

Orlowski went over the same ground part by part. "Nothing," he said when he had finished. "There's no static voltage on the line."

"Okay," Olsen said. "Then we're ready to hook it up." He spotted Simpson still frittering with the autopilot knobs and dials. "Jimmy," Olsen called out, "get the hell out of here while we hook up the panel."

"Okay, Oley," Simpson said. "I'm leaving—good luck!"

Olsen waited until Simpson had joined Kennedy and Willy, waiting in a jeep at the far edge of the field while the hookup was being made. "Here goes!" Olsen said. His heart pounding, he shoved a jack into the cannon plug in one of the TNT booster blocks. Nothing happened, and he quickly inserted the other three jacks. Now a signal from the mother ship could remove the safety shutters from the fuses and make the final connection to the inertia switches, and the robot would be ready to go off on any high-G impact.

Olsen signaled out the pilot's window to Kennedy and Willy, a quarter mile away, and the two pilots and Jimmy Simpson drove up to the side of the drone. When the trio clambered aboard, Olsen heard Simpson say good-bye to Willy and then turn to the wealthy socialite who had befriended him. "So long and good luck, Joe," Simpson said, pumping his friend's hand. "I only wish I were going with you."

Kennedy said, "Thanks, Jim. Don't forget, you're going to make the next one with me." The handshake broke off, and Kennedy turned toward the pilot's seat. "Say, by the way," he added over his shoulder, "if I don't come back, you fellows can have the rest of my eggs." Everybody laughed; there were only two or three eggs left in the pirate's chest, and they all knew it.

Now Simpson stepped clear of the plane. Orlowski looked questioningly at Olsen, and the electronics officer said, "Chief, you take the jeep to the end of the runway and pick me up there. I'm staying with the plane till the last minute, just to make sure everything's all right."

"Aye, aye, sir," Orlowski said, and dropped through the exit-way to the ground. Olsen was amused by the farewell. His good friend Orlowski had never sounded more nautical or more respectful. Olsen guessed it was a reaction to the awesomeness of the moment.

Now he watched as Kennedy and Willy went through the mysterious rituals involved in starting up a four-engine aircraft. Once it had been a simple job. But in these modern four-engine bombers, with their double consoles and control pedestals and row after row of gauges and meters, the process of starting engines seemed as complex to Olsen as the calculus. Back and forth for what seemed an hour, Kennedy and Willy pushed and flipped at switches and controls and exchanged information, and when they had cleared away the last possibility of error (something about the trim tabs), Olsen saw Kennedy signal to a ground crewman outside, and at last the sharp whine of a starter motor split the late-afternoon air. The three-bladed propeller on the No. 3 engine, nearest to where co-pilot Willy was standing, began to tick over, and when it was whirling faster, Olsen saw Kennedy make a brisk motion with his hand. There were loud crackles and pops and a jet of black smoke, and then the engine was turning under its own power. No. 4, just outboard of No. 3, was started next, and then the ground crewmen wheeled the electric starting motor to the other side and kicked the remaining two engines into motion. Olsen noticed that Kennedy throttled back on the inboard engines and increased the power to No. 1 and No. 4, until the cabin was full of the roar and compression and the floor was vibrating. To Olsen, the plane seemed to be straining to move away, but it remained firmly in place, while Kennedy slowly pushed the two outboard throttles forward. "Stuck in the tar!" Kennedy shouted, and just then the PB4Y lurched away. Kennedy reduced power, and the heavy-laden aircraft bumped lightly on its shock absorbers and rolled toward the runway. Now and then Kennedy would kick at something, and the plane would jerk to one side or the other. "Potholes!" Kennedy shouted.

While they were taxiing, Olsen saw a PV flash by on the runway, and he knew that *Zootsuit Red,* piloted by Lieutenant Hugh "Rosy" Lyon, was taking off. Less than a minute later he saw *Zootsuit Pink,* Lieutenant Harry Wherry commanding, roar down the runway and lift into the sky. Now it was Kennedy's turn in a plane bearing the code name *Zootsuit Black.* Olsen wondered who had named the plane the color of death. At the end of the runway, Kennedy turned the PB4Y through 180 degrees, into the wind, and started slamming the power to one engine at a time, and Olsen knew that the Liberator would take off as soon as the last engine had been checked at full rpm's. He looked out the window and saw Orlowski sitting stonefacedly at the wheel of a jeep parked 20 yards away. "Goodbye, Joe," Olsen said. "Good luck." Kennedy turned his head and reached back and gripped Olsen's hand, and Olsen looked deep into the eyes of the man who was about to carry aloft the biggest airborne load of explosives in history. Kennedy looked excited, tense, keyed up, but he did not look scared. Olsen said to himself that he was glad Kennedy was flying this aircraft on which so much depended.

APHRODITE: DESPERATE MISSION   236

"Good luck, Bud," he said, reaching out for Willy's hand. The two old friends shook warmly, and Olsen noticed that his own hand was wet when he pulled it back. He thought that Willy looked unusually jittery, but as he clambered out of the airplane, he told himself that he might be imagining things, and even if Willy *was* unnerved, it only showed that he knew what was going on. In a way, Kennedy's cooler reaction seemed almost abnormal to the electronics officer. Some confused bravery with stupidity, but Olsen knew that Kennedy was anything but stupid. He could only conclude that the volunteer pilot was an uncommonly brave man, and so was Willy, for all his wet palms and nervous eyes darting about the cabin. Olsen found himself curiously touched by the scene, and he quickly climbed into the jeep beside Orlowski. "How'd they act?" the chief asked, but Olsen was unable to answer. He heard a tremendous roar, and when he opened his eyes, *Zootsuit Black* was halfway down the runway, gathering speed and momentum. A few seconds later the wheels left the asphalt and disappeared into the belly of the airplane. "Wow!" Orlowski said as the gray-white silhouette receded in the distance, climbing above the young pines until the last vestige of doubt about the takeoff was gone.

"The most beautiful takeoff I've ever seen," Orlowski said reverently.

"The most beautiful takeoff in history," Olsen said.

Orlowski drove the jeep at high speed to the shop, where a half dozen of Olsen's technicians were huddled in front of a small TV receiver that was tuned to the TV camera in the nose of the drone. Olsen and the chief elbowed their way through the men and saw that everything appeared normal. Groves of trees and small farms and now and then a tiny village flashed on the greenish phosphor screen, and Olsen knew that the precise track of the robot plane's flight was being duplicated in front of their eyes. After a few minutes, the picture went off, and there was a gasp from the men.

"That's all right," Olsen said quickly. "They're testing the control from the mother ship."

Within seconds, the picture had flickered back in shades of black and white and green; then it went off again. "There'll be no more picture till they get to the target," Olsen said to his men, "but by then they'll be out of our range. I guess you guys will just have to read about it in the papers." The men laughed, and Olsen nudged Orlowski and said, "C'mon, Chief, let's get a bite to eat." The two men walked across the hangar area toward the galley, ten minutes away, and just as they sat down to eat, they heard the unmistakable clatter of PV engines, out of sync as usual. They looked toward the east, in the direction of the sound, and saw the two mother ships returning.

As soon as Kennedy's *Zootsuit Black* had cleared the runway and started its steady ascent toward the 2,000-foot level, its wingmates from Army and Navy had relaxed. Someone in one of the planes had opened up his microphone on the air-to-air frequency and emitted a long, loud "Phewwwww!" For all the others knew, it might have been General Partridge or General Doolittle—both were up in their own fighter planes—or it might have been one of the colonels and brigadier generals in a B-17 observation plane, or one of the fighter pilots, or even one of the liaison pilots puddle-jumping down below on the deck. Whoever it was, he had spoken for all. The rest of the operation might succeed or fail, but at least it would be relatively simple and straightforward. The load of explosives was off and flying; it only had to be shepherded into the target. The control procedures would present no problems to Red Anderson and John Demlein; both men had steered the PB4Y around hundreds of miles of English countryside without a trace of trouble.

The first leg of the flight plan was supposed to take the armada from Fersfield to a point 4 miles east-southeast of the airfield at Saxmundham, a total distance of some 25 miles. Just before the drone reached this checkpoint, pilot Joe Kennedy's voice crackled into the headsets of Lieutenant Hugh "Rosy" Lyon and his controller, Lieutenant John "Red" Anderson. "Spade flush," the voice said, and repeated emphatically, *"Spade flush!"* This was the code signal for Lyon's mother ship, *Zootsuit Red,* to begin putting the drone through its final checks, and John Anderson scrunched down in front of the television receiver in the blacked-out waist of the PV and began to take control by means of a short metal stick and a telephone dial that triggered the radio emissions to the drone. He put the robot into a perfect left turn and leveled it off for a true course for the next checkpoint, the town of Beccles, 20 miles to the north. Then he turned the Ace on and off and saw with satisfaction that the robot aircraft obeyed perfectly. He dialed the signal that would turn Kennedy's television transmitter on and off and saw the picture respond to his touch on his screen. Then he dialed the TV back on, and the picture resumed with hardly a second's hesitation. There was no radio response from the drone, but Anderson knew this was according to plan. The fewer emissions from any of the planes, the fewer signals the Germans could trace and jam. The controller knew that Kennedy had been well briefed on the precise order of the tests, and unless something went wrong, the robot was to maintain strict radio silence.

Now the robot with the two mother ships in train had followed a navigational B-17 over the little villages of Theberton and Middleton and almost reached Blythburg, halfway to Beccles from the first turning point. The procedure called for controller Anderson to put the drone through a left turn, center, right turn, center, shallow climb, and shallow dive, and if the robot responded perfectly, Anderson was to turn over control to Harry Wherry's PV for the flight straight down over Clacton-on-Sea and to West Manston for the bailouts. From there the robot would fly a slight dogleg across the channel and into the target.

Rosy Lyon's vibrant voice came over the intercom. "Steady as she goes?" he asked.

"Steady as she goes!" Anderson answered. "How about a time check?"

The co-pilot answered: "Eighteen twenty-two. Dead on course. Dead on schedule."

Anderson grasped the metal rod on the control box and eased the robot into a shallow left turn. Suddenly the television picture in front of him flickered and died, and in the same instant he heard a loud gasp over the intercom. Before he could ask what was going on, he heard two powerful explosions and felt two thumps, as though a giant had pounded on the fuselage of the plane, and then he realized that the PV was falling away, out of control.

Harry Wherry's mother ship was about 400 yards behind the drone and several hundred feet above it, and since Anderson was still controlling from the other plane, several members of Wherry's crew were watching through the pilot's windshield. They saw the drone begin a slow turn to the left, but just as the left wing dipped a few degrees below the horizontal, there was a blinding flash of light, and the bright afternoon sky became incandescent. Where the drone had been there was now a yellow nucleus edged in smoke, with fire and flame going straight up and down from it, like a pair of giant Roman candles. In a split second the nucleus had turned into a greenish-white cylinder of fire, slightly compressed in the middle like an hourglass and flattened out on top.

"My God," Wherry said, and his co-pilot, Harry Fitzpatrick, said, "Holy Christ!" In that same instant the mother ship was hit by two massive jolts, and Wherry fought to gain control. The column burned brightly, almost as vividly as a welder's torch seen at close range, and just as suddenly, it was gone, leaving black smoke streaming away in the wind and a few small fires in the woods below. The men in Wherry's airplane blinked to restore their spotty eyesight.

"Look at Rosy!" Fitzpatrick shouted after a few seconds, and everyone could see the other mother ship slipping toward the ground at a high rate of speed.

"Pull out!" Wherry screamed. *"Pull out!"* The other PV was almost to the ground when the top wing snapped back to straight and level and the plane flew off over the smoking tree-tops. "They're okay," Wherry said. "Rosy's got it."

"I'm not sure the Mosquito's gonna make it," Fitzpatrick said. A Mosquito camera ship had flown through the center of fire and gone out the other side trailing smoke, and now it was circling and losing altitude.

"Did anybody see chutes?" Harry Wherry asked.

"Did you?" Fitzpatrick asked.

"No, not a trace," Wherry said. "I was just hoping that somebody else—"

"We saw the same things you saw, Harry," controller John Demlein said. He seemed to be struggling to control himself. "They're gone. Nothing could have lived through that blast."

"Let's go down and take a look," Wherry said, and he put the Lockheed Ventura through a series of turns until it was on the deck. There was nothing to be seen but a few wisps of smoke and some charred vegetation. Then a call came over the radio: *"Scranton! Scranton!"*

"That's it," Harry Wherry said. "We're through. Scranton means abandon mission." He shook his head slowly. "God-damn!" he said softly. "That was a word I thought we'd never hear." The mother ship turned toward Fersfield, and the inter-com was silent all the way home.

The two PVs landed three minutes apart and taxied into a crowd of the puzzled and confused. Neither Wherry nor Lyon, in the shock of the moment, had remembered to inform the

base about the explosion. No one knew how word had reached
Fersfield or who had transmitted the code word for abandon
mission. When controller Red Anderson climbed from Lyon's
mother ship, he found Commander Smith waiting. "Did you hit
the destruct button?" Smith asked.

Anderson could hardly believe his ears. He knew he had to
allow for the fact that eight or nine years of Navy radio-control
experimentation had just gone down the drain, and Smith, as
the steward of all this wasted work and motion, was under-
standably upset, but still Anderson thought his skipper should
not have asked the question or, if he had to ask it, should have
waited for a more private, propitious occasion.

"Of course, I didn't touch the destruct button," Anderson
said. "We'd barely started the control procedures."

Smith gripped the young lieutenant's arm. "Are you sure?"
he said.

Anderson found himself fighting back anger. "Skipper," he
said, "I just finished telling you I didn't touch the destruct button. You must think I'm some kind of lunatic. Go inside the
plane and look for yourself if you don't believe me." To Anderson, Commander Smith looked almost distraught.

The mother ships were examined on the spot, and it was determined that their arm and destruct buttons were securely
locked under their red plastic covers. Neither button could
have been touched without breaking seals. The explanation for
the blast would have to come from another direction.

As Anderson was walking away from the spot inspection, a
young Army officer whom he recogized from the officers' club
walked up and patted him on the back and said, "Well, Red,
you blew the whole thing, didn't you?"

Anderson turned and saw that the man was smiling. "You
dumb jerk!" he said. "Get out of here before I—"

"I was just trying to relieve the tension," the lieutenant said
meekly. Anderson hurried away.

A young sailor caught him as he was entering his quarters. "Sir," the sailor said, "the skipper wants to see everybody right away."

"Right now?" Anderson asked.

"Right away!" the sailor said.

Anderson walked to the unused dispensary where Commander Smith and Lieutenant Colonel Roy Forrest shared quarters. Men in flying fatigues milled about, talking in whispers. Anderson recognized the crews of the mother ships and several of the Navy ground officers. Smith paced the floor at the front of the group. His face was ashen, and he started to speak several times before finally beginning. "Gentlemen," he said, "this is an awful blow. It's an awful blow to all of us who knew Joe Kennedy and Bud Willy. And it's an awful blow to all of us who worked so hard in this program." He paused and turned his back to the men, and when he regained his composure, he turned and spoke louder. "But, gentlemen," he said, "I can promise you one thing. We're not finished. We're not giving up. We're going to get another drone, and we're going to lay it right on a target." He stopped again. "That's all I have to say for now," he said. "We'll talk again in the morning."

At 25,000 feet over mid-Channel, just above the effective reach of the enemy's coastal flak, a B-17 observation plane traced the same lazy circles in the sky that it had been tracing for an hour. On board were an Army crew and several naval observers, including Ensign James Simpson. Their assignment was to follow the drone's progress from mid-Channel to the target and report on its strike. But the drone was now thirty minutes late, and the VHF radio was silent, and everybody on board was getting itchy. To Jim Simpson, the observation flight had seemed ill-starred almost from the beginning. They had barely cleared the coast of England when someone had shouted: "Messerschmitts!" and Simpson looked out the waist hatch to see two stubby-winged fighter planes closing at high speed on the Flying Fortress. The intercom crackled with instructions to all hands to prepare to fight off the ME-109's. Simpson tried to man the machine gun in front of him, but the barrel was missing. The tail gunner reported that he had no ammunition. The bombardier said that the machine gun in the chin turret was jammed. "I guess that leaves me," the laconic voice of the pilot came through. "I've got my forty-five."

Simpson marveled at the pilot's coolness, but he marveled even more when the two fighter planes flashed up alongside the B-17, turned sharply on their sides, and flew formation with the bomber for a few minutes. To his amazement, Simpson saw that the fighter pilots were waving. His confusion lasted until the planes dipped their noses and disappeared. "Those Messerschmitts were Spitfires!" a voice said on the intercom. "Relax!"

After that inauspicious beginning to the observation flight, the B-17 had done nothing but wait. Now and then a flower of flak bloomed below them, and the pilot would move three or four miles away to take his chances on a new position. The sky was clear, and both mother ships and the drone would have to pass within six or eight miles. They would not slip by unobserved.

"Sir, it's forty minutes past zero hour," a voice said on the intercom.

"I know it," the pilot said, "and I can't figure out what the hell's going on."

At last the pilot informed everyone aboard that they were returning to Fersfield. "We'll reverse the route the baby's supposed to take," he said. "That way we'll intercept her in case she's still coming."

The B-17 descended toward England in what seemed to Simpson to be almost a power dive, and he estimated they were at about 4,000 feet when they made their landfall. All at once there were six or eight bursts of flak around them. The plane fell away on a wing, turned sharply back toward the Channel, and almost dumped Simpson out of his seat. "Hey, take it easy!" somebody said on the intercom, and the pilot said, "The Limeys are potshooting again!"

"Don't you have the code word?" somebody said.

"Yeah, I have it," the pilot said, "but I think it's yesterday's."

The B-17 flew parallel to the coast and made another landfall 50 miles to the north at Great Yarmouth, and this time there was no trouble. A few minutes later the plane banked sharply over the church tower at Diss and descended on the base. Before the plane had even rolled to a stop, Jim Simpson had spotted the unmistakable squat profiles of the PV mother ships up on the apron, and he knew that something must have gone wrong. When he climbed out of the door in the waist, he saw a jeep approaching at high speed. He recognized Olsen and Orlowski.

"What happened?" Simpson said.

"You haven't heard anything?" Olsen said.

"No," Simpson said. "What happened? We've been out over the target for an hour. Did they abort? Did they ditch in the Channel?"

"No," Olsen said, beckoning Simpson into the jeep. "The baby blew up."

Simpson felt as though he had been hit in the face. "You mean after they jumped?" he said.

"No, Jimmy," Olsen said. "I mean *before* they jumped. They're both dead."

Lieutenant Colonel Roy Forrest walked in circles below the control tower, talking out loud to himself and scuffing at the ground in anger and frustration. "Goddamn son of a bitch!" he said. "It was nobody's fault but mine. I'm the commanding officer. I'm the dumb bastard who could have insisted that they change that arming system. They said it was none of my business. It *was* my business. You're in command, or you're not." He walked faster and kicked more dirt. "You dumb shit, you!"

he said. "You stupid little nipshit bastard! Why didn't you have sense enough to scrub this whole thing? Oh, you dog!" He rounded the shack behind the tower and came out into the open once again and almost knocked down a trio of full colonels, climbing out of a transport plane. He recognized the little colonel from headquarters, the one who had acted as though Project Aphrodite were an overseas version of the Army-Navy Game. "I told you, Colonel," Forrest cried out. "I told you this would happen. I *knew*, and I didn't do a thing about it!"

"Forrest," the little colonel said, "shut your mouth!"

"But, sir—"

"Come here, Forrest!" the colonel snapped. "Stand at attention!"

"At attention?"

"Ten-hut!" the officer shouted.

Forrest snapped to. He supposed that this must be a first, a colonel ordering a lieutenant colonel into a quivering brace, and he wondered what was coming.

"Now you listen to me, Forrest," the colonel was saying, "and you listen hard! And don't you say a word till I'm finished talking to you. Is that clear?"

Forrest started to say, "Yes, sir," but the colonel was proceeding full steam ahead. "You are not to say a single word to a single soul about what happened today. Is that clear? *Is that clear?* And above all, you are not to say a single word about the arming system. We don't care to hear your opinions, and we don't need your hindsight. Is that clear?"

Once again Forrest started to answer, but the little colonel thrust his nose in Forrest's face and shouted, "Don't you say a word till I'm finished. Stand at attention! Now I'm telling you for the last time: Don't go walking around this control tower telling the whole world how you knew the mission was gonna fail! Do you hear me? Don't tell a soul! You're not to discuss this in any way, shape, or form. That's an order!"

Out of the corner of his eye, Forrest could see the three colonels starting to walk away. Then the short one returned and said through clenched teeth, "Forrest, if you have the sense you were born with, you'll keep quiet. If you don't keep quiet, I absolutely guarantee you a court-martial. *I guarantee it!* Is that clear?"

Forrest said nothing, and the colonel stalked off. When the three officers were out of sight, he unbraced himself and walked into the orderly room. Captain Loyd Humphries was sitting at a desk, typing. "What's the matter, Roy?" Humphries said. "You look like you were in the explosion, too."

"Sorry, Humpy," Forrest said sarcastically. "I'm not allowed to talk anymore. But if you want to know a military secret, I'll tell you a beaut. Somebody at headquarters is scared shitless."

"Of what?"

"Of a family named Kennedy."

That night the men of Mission Aphrodite fought their grief and their frustration in their own ways. Jimmy Smith accepted a dinner invitation from the commander of the Third Bomb Division, Major General Earle Partridge. "I know how you must feel, Commander," Partridge had said over the telephone. "Come on over here, and I'll feed you and try to cheer you up." Smith made his various preliminary reports by telephone and gratefully accepted the general's invitation.

Most of the men set about achieving unconsciousness by the quickest and most painless route. Earl Olsen went to the enlisted men's barracks, where he knew there would be old friends around, and began to pull at a bottle of bourbon. The bottle was gone in an hour, and Olsen, who barely drank in normal times, was stretched out in a coma. A radio technician named Hawkins picked him up like a sack of grain and deposited him in a bunk for the night.

Harry Fitzpatrick and John Demlein and a few of the other junior officers of the mother ship crews repaired to a Nissen hut with several bottles of gin and a case of grapefruit juice, but after a very short time they set the grapefruit juice aside and drank the ersatz English gin straight. No one knew when it started or who started it, but a shot rang out and a hole appeared in the corrugated metal roof. Soon the three men were hopelessly involved in trying to fire their service pistols through the previous holes, and the ceiling had begun to resemble a housewife's colander. Demlein was lying on the floor, holding his quavering .45 with both hands and sighting on a hole, when the door burst open and an Army provost marshal officer appeared. The three young officers waved their weapons and told the officer to clear out. "We'll see about this!" the provost marshal shouted as he started to close the door behind him. Demlein's pistol rang out, and a new hole appeared in the roof, and the visitor was gone. An hour or so and a gin bottle or two later, the young officers dropped off to sleep.

Ensign James Simpson, like Lieutenant Earl Olsen, had gone to the barracks. He drank with the enlisted men until he could feel the effects of the bourbon coursing through his system, and then he excused himself and went for a walk in the dark. The night was as clear as the day had been, and he found himself walking along the edge of the runway where his friends Kennedy and Willy had taken off just a few hours before. "Oh, God!" he said, in mingled reverence and profanity. "How could a thing like this happen?" He thought back over the years and years that the Navy had spent perfecting the equipment that had blown itself to dust in seconds. He thought about long hours he had spent shooting pool and playing Ping-pong and exchanging tall stories with Bud Willy, and about Willy's wife and three children back in Texas, and about his own intense conversations with the aristocratic lieutenant from New England, the most impressive man he had ever known, more impressive than a cargo hatch full of admirals. He walked past a slit trench dug into the side of the field for air-raid protection, and on an impulse he unsheathed his .38 side-arm and held it over his head. He muttered an epithet and emptied the magazine at the stars.

Earl Olsen awoke the next morning with his head throbbing like a fresh wound. Someone had shaken him, and when he looked up into the morning light, it felt as though acid had been thrown in his eyes.

"The skipper wants to see you right away," a voice said.

Olsen slowly steered his feet to the floor and began pressing at his rumpled uniform. *The skipper wants to see you right away.* Nothing good could come of that. Certainly the skipper had every right to be annoyed. A naval officer does not run to the bourbon the instant something goes wrong.

When he reached Commander Smith's quarters in the old dispensary, he saw that every officer in Special Attack Unit No. 1 was already there, and he knew they must have been waiting for him. "I'm sorry, sir," he said as he walked through the door. "I overslept."

"You overslept?" Smith said.

"Skipper, I apologize," Olsen said. Perhaps it would go easier on him if he made a clean breast of things. "I had a few drinks last night. I don't drink as a rule, and I guess I couldn't handle it."

"Forget it, Earl," Commander Smith said. "Everybody had a few drinks last night. How about telling us your story, from the beginning."

Olsen's head was splitting, and his mouth tasted like a pigsty, but as he repeated the history of the arming panel, starting with the day back in Philadelphia when it had been actuated accidentally three times, he found that one memory brought on another, and soon he was speaking clearly and forcefully. He told about his discussions with Willy and the argument about the holding relay and the improvised safety device, but he did not describe the rancorous nature of the exchanges, nor did he mention the threatened court-martial. "I realized that I'd have to go to everyone, to keep going to everyone, until I attracted somebody's attention," Olsen said. "That's when I went to you, Skipper."

A puzzled look came over Commander Smith's face. "Earl," he said, "I don't remember you saying anything to me."

Now it was Olsen's turn to be confused. The conversation had taken place only a few days before; Jim Simpson had been with him. Every word was clear in his mind. He studied Smith's face; the skipper's easy smile was gone. His face was blank and drawn. His eyes were red, and he looked as though he had not slept since the events of the day before. Olsen felt that he was talking to a man in the middle of a terrible crisis, a man who was deeply disturbed.

"Skipper," he said gently, "don't you remember a few days ago when I told you that I was concerned about the arming panel?" Smith did not respond. "Sir," Olsen went on, "it was right here in your office, and I came in and I said I thought I could correct the problem, and you referred me to Bud Willy, and you said whatever decision was reached between me and Bud was all right with you, that you didn't know enough about technical things. Don't you remember that, Skipper?"

Smith shook his head slowly from side to side. "I can't remember," he said. "Is that the end of your story?"

Olsen said, "Yes, sir, I guess that's all I have to say." He sat down in a quandary and rested his throbbing head in his hands.

"Skipper, may I say something?" a voice said from the rear of the room. Olsen recognized the soft Texas accent of Ensign Jim Simpson. "Sir," Simpson was saying, "I remember that conversation. Every word of it. I remember Earl telling you all these things before, Skipper. I was right here with him."

Olsen looked up. Commander Smith seemed honestly puzzled, his face wreathed in confusion. "Funny," the skipper said. "I can't remember it."

A few minutes later the meeting broke up. Commander Smith said that he had been ordered to Fleet Air Wing Seven Headquarters to make a full report, and he would be back in a few days. The men wandered off to their huts, and Olsen and Simpson walked together. When they were out of earshot of the others, Olsen said, "Jimmy, I know how much guts that took. It would have been very easy for you to keep your mouth shut. You're Regular Navy, and you've got your whole career to lose."

"I'm not worried about my whole career," Simpson said. "Maybe I know Jimmy Smith better than you do, or maybe I'm wrong. But I watched him all through that meeting this morning. He's in shock, Earl, an honest-to-God medical state of shock. He wasn't ducking out of anything when he said he couldn't remember talking to us. He *didn't* remember. You should have heard all the other things he didn't remember this morning. He's taken this whole thing personally—and hard."

"Then he's in no shape to go explain things to the admirals, is he?"

"He's not really going to make a report," Simpson said. "The report's being written right now by one of his aides. The skipper's going begging this morning."

"For what?"

"For a new drone," Simpson said. "For a new volunteer pilot. For another chance. And if I know him, he'll get it, too."

Those tiny portions of England known as Blythburg and Halesworth and Hinton Lodge and Newdelight Woods and the Westwood Marshes were trodden and retrodden on the day after the explosion, as American soldiers and officers searched for clues to the mishap. The ordnance officer and the bomb reconnaissance officer of the Third Bomb Division led groups to the scene and reported that the exact site of the explosion was "2½ miles northwest of Dunwich at Hinton Lodge." The routine report observed that "there were at least 60 houses in Blythburg and an unknown number of houses in Walberswick, Thonington and Hinton that received considerable damage, such as windows broken, plaster knocked from walls and ceiling. Parts of the plane are scattered over a large territory. One engine fell in Blythburg Lodge, three engines fell near Hinton Lodge." Another report told of severe damage to the estate of Sir R. B. M. Blois, between Blythburg and Walberswick, and still another listed the farm animals supposedly killed by the shock of the blast. The airplane's four engines were found to be totally beyond repair; they were abandoned where they lay, and portions of the wreckage that were too big to be put into jeeps were similarly left behind. There were no traces of human beings.

Inside his shop, Lieutenant Earl Olsen and several of his technicians worked hastily to set up a demonstration for the other members of SAU No. 1, all except Jimmy Smith, who was on his way to Plymouth. First they applied 28 volts to the same model solenoids that had been used in the doomed PB4Y. Within two and a half minutes the solenoids became too hot to touch. Then they applied a similar voltage to the arming circuit of the mark 143 fuse, the same fuse used in the drone. The experiment was repeated several times, and in every case "cook-off" and firing resulted in a minimum of two and a half minutes and a maximum of eight. "There's the answer," Olsen said. "We've done to this dummy circuit exactly what the holding relay would have done to the circuit in the drone. Anybody who knows electronics can tell you that there're a dozen different things that could have caused that holding relay to close. I don't think we need to look any further for our answer."

Under the direction of the senior officer present, Lieutenant Hugh Lyon, the nine officers worked up a discreet report which listed and considered some thirteen possible causes of the explosion, but pointed the finger plainly at the faulty arming panel. In an independent report, Commander Smith drew similar conclusions and recommended that the next drone be armed manually. There remained, however, a tedious month-long investigation ordered by the top brass. General Spaatz flew over in his own P-47. Captains and commanders and a few admirals descended upon the little airfield. Specially equipped airplanes were ordered to search the skies, looking for FM signals that might have triggered the explosion. They returned with reams of oscillograph records that showed nothing but wide-open channels on the FM bands. P-38's and other aircraft, their insides weighted down with special detection equipment, reflew the same course taken by Kennedy and Willy. But weeks of such probings produced no detectable interference or jamming on the Aphrodite wavelength. Every Royal Air Force counter-intelligence station in England was visited and its records checked and its personnel interviewed to see if any attempts had been made to jam the critical signal, but all that turned up was a station in Yorkshire that had heard the strange emissions and had considered jamming them, but had not yet got around to it. When everything else had been investigated, a complete dry run of the entire mission was held, and Hugh Lyon and Harry Wherry flew their mother ships four times around the course, twice on radio silence and twice making the same emissions they had made on August 12, while a P-38 radio search plane flitted about, trying to pick up clues to what had gone wrong. Again, nothing turned up, and at last the air testing was brought to a halt.

On the ground, the studies went on endlessly repeating themselves, apparently on orders of someone high up. A veteran electronics officer from Navy Radio Control Headquarters in the United States flew to England and analyzed the circuits and told Olsen that he had nothing new to add. A brigadier general from the U.S. Army Signal Corps showed up one day, took a five-minute look at the dummy arming panel, and said, "That's it. That's all the investigating you need to do. That's a stupid, ridiculous thing you've got there." He was gone within an hour. A committee of electronics specialists from companies like RCA and CBS arrived and analyzed the arming system from practical and theoretical standpoints, flipping out circular

slide rules and talking about vectors and milliamperes and co-
sines and logarithms, and concluded that Joe Kennedy and Bud
Willy had been killed by a faulty arming panel. One of the
men took Olsen aside before the delegation returned to London, and said, "Where was this thing designed?" Olsen told
them that it was put together hastily at the Naval Aircraft Factory at Philadelphia. "Well," the civilian said, "what kind of
people do they have over there? This whole thing is contrary to
the simplest electrical laws."

At last the final investigator completed his final investigation, and life at Fersfield returned to its usual abnormal nor-
mality. Commander Smith returned from Plymouth with the
news that SAU No. 1 was authorized to fly another mission, and
a new volunteer pilot would be along any day now from
VB-110, Joe Kennedy's old outfit at Dunkeswell. Smith
confided to a few of his close friends that he had recommended
Kennedy for the Congressional Medal of Honor, the nation's
highest military honor. Three weeks after the Navy's first Aphrodite mission, word came from the Navy's Board of Medals
and Awards. The Congressional Medal had been disallowed;
Joseph Patrick Kennedy, Jr., and Wilford John Willy would
receive the Navy Cross posthumously.

With the heroic and useless deaths of the two men before
them, the heterogeneous forces that made up Operation Aphrodite seemed to come together. Interservice friendships grew up,
and ideas began to flow back and forth between the technicians
of the Navy's Special Attack Unit and the technicians of Castor,
the group of Army robot specialists from Wright Field who had
succeeded the ill-starred double azon group. It was as though
the Army and Navy personnel had agreed implicitly that both
had experienced breakdowns and both had suffered losses; they
had been blooded together, and now the Army-Navy Game was
over. Even the grumpy little colonel at Third Bomb Division
Headquarters seemed to soften (perhaps under orders) after

his thunderous dressing down of Roy Forrest on the grass below the control tower. He sent word to the Navy that the Army was going forward with its own project, that the Army hoped the Navy would do the same, and that the Army stood ready to render any help or assistance its Navy comrades might require.

The new spirit of total cooperation extended through the ranks, spurred by the realization that three missions in eight days had failed miserably, that John Fisher and Joseph P. Kennedy and Wilford J. Willy were dead and a few other men still lying in the hospital, one of them recovering from an arm amputation. Knots of officers and enlisted men convened nightly to discuss their star-crossed project and brag about their own techniques and anticipate the day that was coming, when Aphrodite airplanes would cross the Channel and turn the German missile sites to powder. But as day followed day after the disastrous mission of August 12, a sweet-and-sour realization began to come over the men of Aphrodite. Allied troops were breaking through to the west of the Pas-de-Calais, where all four of the large sites lay within a few miles of one another. Any day now, infantrymen would reach the concrete slabs and neutralize them as effectively as the most accurate hit by an Aphrodite missile. The realization was sweet because it meant that the ground war was going ahead of schedule, and it was sour because it meant that the proud men of Aphrodite were soon to be deprived of their targets, their chance to "make good." Militarily, they would be all dressed up with no place to go.

The day came even sooner than expected. Before the Navy could complete the modification of a new PB4Y drone, Allied foot soldiers had swept through Siracourt, Mimoyecques, Watten and Wizernes, and intelligence officers had made an astonishing discovery. Underneath the thick cement lids of the mysterious sites there was little more than junk and debris. There was no sign that scientists or technicians had inhabited the empty living quarters below within recent weeks. Here and there were evidences of repair, but closer inspection revealed that most of the repairs were fakes—cosmetic touches applied to make it appear that the massive bunkers mattered to the Germans and that they were worth bombing repeatedly. So the capture of the large sites revealed what no one except a few intelligence officers had privately suspected: The Aphrodite project had been a nervous response to a threat that had long since been neutralized. To be sure, V-1 buzz bombs and the larger V-2 rockets were all too real and operational, causing thousands upon thousands of deaths in London and other English cities, but they were not being launched from the mysterious bunkers in the Pas-de-Calais, nor could they have been—the sites had been abandoned for months. With these discoveries, it became abundantly clear that during those earliest days of the project, when midnight telephone calls were flying back and forth and jump pilots hastily recruited and the menace to New York and London and even Pittsburgh discussed till all hours of the morning by the highest-ranking Allied officers, the mystery sites had already been as dead as tombstones. These first Allied soldiers to penetrate the dank acreages under the immense ferroconcrete domes were finding little except rats and cockroaches and tons of rubble. Where thousands of Nazi technicians were believed to have been working on secret weapons that could reverse the flow of the war, there was hardly a nut or a bolt left.

Eventually the ponderous machinery of Allied intelligence put together the seemingly impossible stories of the ends of the menacing sites. Watten had been bombed persistently long before Aphrodite, and unknown to the Allies, the Germans had been forced to abandon it and start a new rocket-launching site at Wizernes, which in turn had been ruined by British and American bombers. The site at Siracourt had suffered the same fate, and the one at Mimoyecques, Kennedy's and Willy's target, had housed a frantic scheme for pumping shells into London at the rate of several thousand per day, but the program had been handled so incompetently, it turned out, that a group of the highest-ranking German scientists had decided in May that the site must be abandoned and Hitler informed of the disaster. That was three months before the flight of the two Navy lieutenants.

How had the Allies been fooled? They had made the mistake of believing their eyes. The cement domes, even when they were buckled and pitted, had a businesslike appearance; anything could be going on beneath them—the preparation of poison gas, the arming of long-range rockets, the cultivation of bacilli. Workmen swarmed like ants around all four sites even after the heaviest bombing raids. At first, the work had continued under Hitler's orders; the *Führer* had refused with his typical stubbornness to accept the loss of the rocket launching sites that were to provide the decisive, secret weapon he had promised the German people. Later, after Hitler had realized that no large projectiles would ever be launched from the riddled works, he ordered skeleton crews to remain on the job, to give the appearance that the mystery sites were still functioning. Every bomb that fell on the large sites would not fall on Berlin, he pointed out, and for once he was correct. By the time the Allied ground troops had taken the sites several thousand tons of ordinary bombs had already ruined them ten times over, and seven Aphrodite missiles had been wasted on the "dead" targets.

To the planners at headquarters the news that Aphrodite had been conceived in response to a nonexistent threat came as a shock. But the information was not allowed to filter down to Fersfield, where several hundred officers and men yearned for a chance to prove themselves and their new weapon. The Aphrodite program could still prove potent in the Japanese theater, top military planners reasoned: Fully loaded war-wearies could be sent into Japanese strong points by television, softening the enemy up for attacks by landing forces. The program that owed its start to faulty intelligence evaluations might still make a major contribution to the winning of the war, and not only in the Far East. After all, certain inviting targets remained in the

European theater. Helgoland, the German submarine base hewn into the cliffs of an island in the North Sea, came immediately to mind; subs still cruised merrily in and out of the seemingly indestructible stronghold, despite hundreds of bombing raids. A direct hit by a few Aphrodite robots coming in at low altitude could put the whole place out of business. There were other inviting targets for unmanned aircraft loaded with explosives: ball-bearing plants, dams and canal locks, marshaling yards, refineries. And finally, there was a longer-range reason for maintaining the program. Once Adolf Hitler had brought Germany to the edge of victory by the indiscriminate bombing of cities like London and Coventry and Liverpool. If he happened upon another technique that might visit horror and destruction on England's civilian populace (the Nazis were known to be experimenting with atomic bombs), Aphrodite robots could be steered into cities like Berlin and Frankfurt in retaliation. A weapons system that had failed to pinpoint a single military target might well terrify the Germans out of their wits if it came thundering out of the night onto their cities.

So, its rationale reestablished, Aphrodite drew a second breath of life. Missions were scheduled as usual. The first one to be assigned was the Nazi U-boat pens at Helgoland, 300 miles across the North Sea. It was a naval target, cut into solid cliffs on an island, and Jimmy Smith and his Special Attack Unit No. 1 were eager to blow it out of the water.

Thirty-six hours after its second PB4Y drone was delivered, the Navy had completed the job of installing the control gear. This time there would be no jerry-built electronic arming system. The Navy would arm exactly as the Army had. The bail-out pilot would yank on a lanyard that would disconnect the safety devices and render the airplane live and ready to explode on impact. Earl Olsen objected to the new system; he said it would be simple to design a remote arming panel that would be both safe and effective. But the Navy was burned and shy of

such ideas, and so was the Eighth Air Force. Even before the ar-
rival of the new drone, the host headquarters had issued an
order that henceforth all Aphrodite robots, from whatever
branch of the service, must be armed manually.

The new robot was a war-weary, unlike the first one, which
had been fresh from the Consolidated factory. By the time the
Navy crews had finished working the war-weary one over, it was
in perfect working order. Its paint was chipped, and its windows were scratched here and there, but in those places where
it counted—in the controls and the landing gear and the engines—the plane was almost as good as new. Reconditioned engines were installed, and new tires replaced the old (everyone
in Aphrodite dreaded the possibility of a blowout on takeoff)
and brand-new cables were connected to the control surfaces in
the wings and the empennage so that there could be no question of a malfunction. Long aluminum tubes were snaked inside the fuselage from one end to the other, and the arming
wires were threaded through them as an extra safety precaution. Even if Winston Churchill had tromped through the
aircraft in his golf shoes, nothing would have gone off.

The new jump pilot arrived a week after the first Navy mission, and from the beginning of his tenure with SAU No. 1, it
was plain that he was going to question every procedure,
double-check every technique, and finally make his own decisions about that portion of the mission entrusted to him: lifting
the drone into the air. Lieutenant Ralph Spalding was every
inch the superior pilot that Joseph P. Kennedy had been. Both
men came from VB-110, the patrol squadron that had played a
major role in making the Bay of Biscay and the English Channel safe for Allied shipping. Both men had had more than their
share of combat experience, and both men knew the lumbering
PB4Y banana boat backward. Spalding, in addition, was an old
hand at Navy politicking and infighting. His father was a Navy
captain, and the young lieutenant had learned at his father's
knee. As soon as he arrived at Fersfield, he set about interview-

ing everyone involved in the disastrous first mission. Eventually
he came to Olsen, and he told the electronics officer that he was
getting pressure from various others who wanted to fly as
co-pilot.

"I'm not surprised," Olsen said. "So did Kennedy. Everybody
except the galley cook thought he was going with Joe."

Spalding asked for Olsen's advice, and the officer from Montana was frank. "Lieutenant," he said, "there's too much at
stake here for any pussyfooting around. We had one failure,
and there's a whole claque of guys back in Washington that
would love for us to have another failure and wipe out the
whole program. My advice would be for you to take the plane
off alone. Don't let anybody talk you into flying co-pilot. We'll
never know for sure what happened in that first flight, but I
know one thing: Bud Willy's presence in that airplane was no
asset to anybody. I knew Bud well, and I liked him a lot, but if
I'd have been Joe Kennedy, I'd have felt very uncomfortable
with the extra man along, whether it was Bud or anybody else."

Spalding thanked Olsen for his bluntness, and a few days
later word went out that Spalding would be flying alone. With
that key point settled, SAU No. 1 began planning the exact
strategies to be used on the long overwater attack on the heavily
defended submarine base. At the strategy sessions, Wilford J.
"Bud" Willy was sorely missed. He had been skipper Jimmy
Smith's strong right arm in planning the first mission, and even
his harshest critics had to agree that Willy was an instinctive
master of the science of attack. He knew how to compute headings and timings, and he had a natural talent for coordinating
fighters and bombers and recon planes and observers into one
smooth running unit. Most of all, he understood that an attack
plan had to provide for all sorts of contingencies: radio failure,
for example, or sudden weather changes, or mechanical failures
in the mothers or the drones.

Without their former executive officer, the men of SAU No.
1 spent long hours discussing and planning and debating and

arguing over the proper way to approach the Helgoland mission. For a time, it appeared that the mission was going to be flown with almost total simplicity, just like the thousands of successful training runs back at Traverse City, Michigan, and Clinton, Oklahoma, and Cape May, New Jersey. The drone would be steered to the target by a single mother ship, with the other mother ship flying high above as a standby. Olsen and Simpson argued for this simple system, but they were among the lowest-ranking officers in the program, and moreover, they were paddlefeet—ground officers—and easily ignored. As the planning sessions went on day after day, both Olsen and Simpson became convinced that the destruction of Helgoland was only partially on their comrades' minds. Both mother ship crews wanted to fly the mission—everybody wanted to get into the act again—and no one would give way to the others. Commander Jimmy Smith finally settled on an attack plan similar to the earlier one. Harry Wherry's mother ship would conduct the drone to within five miles of the target and then transfer control to Hugh Lyon's mother ship eight miles back. Lyon and his crack controller, Lieutenant John "Red" Anderson, would drive the attack home.

"Skipper, you're introducing an unnecessary step," Olsen said to Smith after the plan had been worked out. "If one mother has complete control of the baby and steers it straight across all that water, why shift off to another that may not be working as well?"

"Because I value the men under my command," Smith replied. "The first mother will be drawing flak. There's something like five hundred antiaircraft guns on Helgoland and more on flak barges anchored just off the island. To ask a mother ship to fly right over that stuff is downright irresponsible."

Olsen could see that the skipper's mind was made up. He wanted to point out that they were in a war, that flak was an ordinary hazard for a combat pilot, but he also realized that such statements were not for him to make. He would be safe on the ground while Harry Wherry was approaching all that spitting death, and if peeling off and transferring control to a trailing airplane would ensure the safety of the first mother crew, he would not argue against it. He was only certain of one thing: midair transfer of control injected another variable into the attack plan, and the more variables, the weaker the plan. He wanted to say all these things, but he remembered the bitterness and the hard feelings left over from the first mission, and he held his tongue.

With the method of attack settled on, there remained only one question: how to coordinate the flight of the robot with the flights of the mothers during the time that the air group was still assembling over England. The first mission had called for almost an hour of checking and rechecking, and no one knew what part these rigorous procedures might have played in the explosion that killed Kennedy and Willy. The informal board of inquiry that had been convened by the astute Hugh Lyon had taken note of this unknown quantity and suggested a simple procedure for any future flights: "After the plane has been placed in straight, level flight by the drone pilot, he will pass his information to the control plane. The control plane will not key any signals until the drone is over water unless it is absolutely necessary to keep the drone at general altitude and on general heading." In other words, there should be no check-out tests over England, and no control by the mother ship except when absolutely necessary. The benefits would be twofold: The flying time over heavily populated eastern England would be shortened markedly, and the radio signals available to the German jamming stations would be held to a minimum. On the other hand, the mother ships would be forced to take their chances with a robot that had not been fully checked out. In the end, the simple system was selected. The run across 300 miles of open water to Helgoland would be harrowing enough without adding an hour of testing and retesting over England.

With the attack plan in finished form, SAU No. 1 began the tedious waiting for the weather. The mission was scheduled several times, but billowing clouds or ground haze or squall lines over Fersfield or the North Sea target kept washing out the plans. The weather on September 3 was not much better, but everyone had become edgy, and on the night before, it had been announced that the mission would be flown if the weather did not grow worse. At dawn the weather was threatening, but Third Bomb Division Headquarters flashed the go-ahead signal, and the Navy's second-chance task force took off into a bluish haze. Lieutenant Ralph Spalding, a saddened and serious young man since learning that his regular crew had been killed back at Dunkeswell, managed a perfect takeoff and a perfect bailout and handed over to the mother ships a PB4Y that was trimmed and balanced and running straight and level toward the target.

Aboard the mother ships, there was temporary delirium when Spalding's parachute puffed open below the baby ship. Whatever happened now, they would have a fair chance to show what they could do to a target. If they failed, it would be their own fault, and they cheered and hollered over the intercoms when they realized that they would get their chance. There were more cheers when sixteen Army Air Corps P-51 Mustangs zoomed into sight just above, looping and barrel-rolling and showing their pilots' usual high spirits, and everyone knew that there would be fighter cover on the long round trip. Just before the task force left England, with the mother ships flying 200 feet over the drone at 2,000 feet, the rest of the task force joined up. There were two Mosquitoes, one for weather and one for photoreconnaissance, two more P-38 photo ships from another photoreconnaissance outfit, a P-38 radio-search ship that was maintaining a constant watch on the FM channels for possible jamming, and three Army B-17's, one for observation, one for relaying radio messages from the target area to headquarters, and one to provide navigational aid. But this time there were no diversionary bombing attacks preceding the mission, a fact which made Lieutenant Colonel Roy Forrest highly nervous. "The whole goddamn German interceptor force will be waiting for us," he said to Humpy Humphries just before they took off. "Just a little diversionary bombing over Bremerhaven or Wilhelmshaven would have taken the heat off us, but now we're going out there and asking for it." Forrest had asked for diversionary bomb support several times, but headquarters had told him that no bombers were available.

Just after passing over the English North Sea town of Great Yarmouth and heading across the water, the task force ran through a squall, and everyone was relieved to see all the planes appear on the other side of the squall line in the same formation. But now the group ran into a common overwater weather phenomenon. From the surface of the sea up to about 2,000 feet, there was a solid, gray undercast. From 2,000 feet to 6,000 or 7,000 feet, the sky was mostly clear, but above it was more solidly overcast. In between the two thick layers there were scattered clouds, and far out in front the sky appeared to be dotted with puffs of cloud all the way to the target. Some of the pilots turned up the volume on their receivers, thinking that they had missed the recall signal, but the procession of the planes continued to stream across the sky as though the weather were CAVU and the sun shining brightly above them. The mission might be aborted, but only under impossible flying conditions. The Navy men had waited three weeks for their chance, and they were not turning back now.

Inside the mother ships, the crews were happy but uncomfortable. For the first time in their careers, they were wearing flak suits, heavy outfits with slabs of metal sewn into pockets at strategic places. On their heads were steel flak helmets, and each man felt as though he had been handed an instant hangover. "Can't I take this goddamn thing off?" copilot Harry Fitzpatrick said to Harry Wherry, and Wherry answered, "Yeah, if you want to get killed. They got more flak guns at Helgoland than you got oil wells back in Oklahoma."

Aboard Hugh Lyon's mother ship, the men were grumbling mildly about the cumbersome suits, but Lyon sent word over the intercom that he did not wish to hear any further comments about it, that without the steel protection they might end up spending the rest of the war bobbing around the North Sea. Otherwise, the mission seemed to be proceeding normally. The undercast had broken slightly, and now and then the drone could be seen flying straight and level at Ace altitude of 300 feet, under control of Wherry's aircraft ahead. The crews were tense but optimistic; one more hour of straight and level flight and the heavy concrete pens at Helgoland would be shattered.

Back in the darkened waist of Hugh Lyon's PV, radio controller John "Red" Anderson was having trouble. Shortly after the plane had bumped and bounced its way through the squall line, Anderson's VHF (very high frequency) receiver had gone dead, and when he tried to key a few test emissions, he found that the transmitter was out, too. Probably the antenna had shorted in the heavy rainstorm. Anderson fussed and frittered with the equipment, but he was a pilot and a controller, not a radio technician, and nothing seemed to help. Now he knew that the mission was in serious jeopardy. When controller John Demlein's airplane reached a point five miles from the target, it was to transfer control to Anderson by voice code on VHF, and Anderson was to acknowledge by VHF. If Anderson failed to acknowledge, Demlein was to retain control and drive the attack home, but this would mean a few seconds of confusion at the most critical part of the process, with Wherry's airplane and the robot both enshrouded in flak and coming up on the cliffs of Helgoland at high speed. At all costs, such confusion had to be avoided, and Red Anderson thought he had the solution. He would fire a flare signal telling Wherry's crew that the VHF was out. He remembered that the attack plan called for the drone pilot to fire flares if his own radio failed; surely there must be a similar contingency plan for the mother ships. But there was none. Anderson searched his memory and rechecked the attack plan, but he could not find a word about what to do in the event of radio communications failure between the two mother ships. He would have to improvise.

He clambered out of the darkroom and into the pilot's compartment. "Rosy," he said, "our VHF is out."

"How do you know?" Lyon said. "We're supposed to be on radio silence till we reach the target."

"Yeah, I know, but after we went through that squall the receiver went dead, and I checked the transmitter, and it's out, too. That'll screw up everything. We'd better let Wherry know somehow."

"We've got time," Lyon said. There was still almost an hour of overwater flight ahead of them. "Let's make sure we're not getting panicky. Have you tried to fix the radio?"

"I've done everything I can. I think it shorted out at the antenna."

"How about flares?"

"There's nothing in the plan about flares. We'd just confuse the hell out of them."

"Yeah, I guess you're right," Lyon said. "Got any ideas?"

Anderson said that he thought he could get the information across to Wherry by blinking Morse signals on an Aldis lamp, and Lyon pushed the PV's throttle full forward and pulled up alongside the other mother ship. Wherry and his co-pilot, Harry Fitzpatrick, were clearly visible through the side window, and Anderson blinked the Aldis lamp to get their full attention and then sent slowly: N-O V-H-F. When there was no response, he blinked the message again, and this time the wings of Wherry's aircraft wobbled, and Lyon said, "He got it. There's his acknowledgment." Lyon waggled his own wings in return, and the two planes resumed their normal positions.

Anderson was still bothered. Somewhere in the back of his mind there was an old Navy dictum about responding to code messages "in kind." An Aldis lamp signal had to be answered by an Aldis lamp signal, a semaphore signal by another semaphore signal, and so forth. "Rosy," he said, "we've got to be absolutely sure he got our message. He's *got* to know it."

"He knows it," Lyon said. "That's why he waggled his wings."

"Okay," Anderson said, "if you say so." He was anything but certain that Lyon was right, but the pilot was the boss, and Anderson returned to his darkroom full of misgivings.

Aboard the other control airplane, Harry Wherry and his co-pilot, Harry Fitzpatrick, were discussing the odd actions of their old friend Red Anderson. "Imagine that!" Wherry said. "Red playing around with an Aldis lamp at a time like this."

"I wonder what he sent," Fitzpatrick said.

"You got me," Wherry said. "I can only read that stuff about two words a minute. That wasn't my strong suit at flying school."

Both Wherry and Fitzpatrick knew that ship-to-ship blinker signals and even air-to-air blinker signals were a favorite pastime in the Navy. At San Diego, Long Beach, or Norfolk, or any other naval harbor, you could stand on the shoreline after dark and see the sailors sending their messages back and forth. If you understood Morse code, you could read messages like "HOW U? . . . GOOD CHOW TONIGHT . . . GETTING MUCH? . . ." But the two pilots were slightly surprised that a serious and intense young man like Red Anderson would play the game in the middle of the most crucial mission of their lives.

"Well, you never know," Wherry said. "Some guys react differently to things."

"You don't suppose he had anything serious to say to us?" Fitzpatrick asked. "We could call him on the VHF and ask."

"Like hell!" Wherry said. "We're on radio silence. If they had anything serious to say, they wouldn't have buzzed off so fast." The two men turned their attention to the flight. The clouds had loosened up even more, and the mother ship had dropped to 300 feet. Now the drone was clearly visible 5 miles ahead, still flying straight and level for Helgoland. Soon they would be at the IP (initial point), where Ensign John Demlein would turn over control to Anderson 10 miles back at 2,000 feet, well out of flak range, and Wherry could flip the PV into a tight turn and follow the radio beacon back to England. "How's she going?" Wherry said on the intercom to Demlein in the darkroom.

"Couldn't be better," Demlein answered. "Too good to be true."

Now the cliffs of Helgoland began to tower over the robot and make visibility more difficult, but Demlein reported that he was maintaining perfect control. White puffs appeared in the television screen around the robot; they were bursts from flak barges anchored offshore. The drone flew through the flak, disappeared in a small cloud, and then began to come up on the sub pens. Exactly at the IP, Demlein broadcast the code word that would transfer control to Anderson. There was no answer. He repeated the transmission, but by now the drone was boring in. "Steady as she goes!" he said on the intercom to Wherry, to keep him from beginning the sharp turn away from the onrushing silhouette of the island. In his television monitor Demlein could see trees, vehicles, human beings racing across the sand, and small buildings. He saw open water, and then the mouth of the sub pens came into sight on his screen, and he could see that the robot was about 10 degrees off course to the right. He hit the control that would correct the course, but the drone responded only slightly, and the TV picture began to flicker and fade. "I think she's been hit!" he shouted on the interphone. He caught a glimpse of breakwater and pushed the dump control. Then he shouted, "Haul clear!" and felt the aircraft wheel around in a tight turn. He pulled aside the blackout curtains and saw the cliffs of Helgoland a few hundred feet off the wing. Harry Wherry had kept on course almost long enough to flatten the PV against the wall, and now he was pouring on full throttle to break out of the German flak zone. The plane had barely begun its turn when there was a tremendous explosion and the whole island of Helgoland seemed to jump out of the water.

"I don't know what we hit," Wherry said excitedly over the intercom. "Did anybody see?"

"No," Demlein said, patting gently at his tingling ears, "but whatever it was, it ain't no more!" He looked out the window and saw a mushroom-shaped cloud rising over the far edge of the island. The flak had stopped.

"Let's two-block the throttles and get out of here!" Fitzpatrick said.

Harry Wherry complied, and the gray-white Vega Ventura skipped about 50 feet over the waves at 250 knots. Over the radio, there were urgent requests and demands and exhortations for them to come back to join other planes in the task force, but Wherry turned down the volume and said, "I didn't hear anything, did you, Harry?" Harry Fitzpatrick said that all he could hear was the beckoning call of England.

Red Anderson had been sitting in his darkroom with his eyes fixed on the black screen of the television receiver and his hands clutching the control box. He was not certain that Wherry's airplane had got his blinker message, and he was not sure how Demlein would react when there was no answer to the control-transfer signal. In case the other aircraft transferred control and failed to wait for a voice acknowledgment—something that would be entirely possible in the confusion and excitement of the unit's first mission under fire—Anderson was prepared to take control of the drone himself and drive it into the sub pens. He waited and watched. The only sound was the heavy unsynchronized clatter of the PV's engines. He wanted to peek out the blackout curtains in the waist and find out where they were, but his eyes were fully attuned to the darkness, and he would not have time to readjust them when the TV screen went on. Suddenly the little screen blinked and began flashing green, and Anderson could see the cliffs of Helgoland in front of his face and, in quick succession, buildings, a stretch of open water, and the sky, all tilted at a slight angle. He worked madly at the remote controls to try to center the drone, but his maneuvering seemed to have no effect. When the flickering signal in front of him showed a long breakwater passing under the robot, Anderson figured that it was coming up on the sub pens, and since the drone was not reacting properly to signals anyway, he gave it the full dump signal. A few seconds later he heard gasps over the intercom and felt the plane turn, and he yanked his blackout curtains aside. About 20 miles to one side he could see a towering column of black smoke high in the sky. Rosy Lyon called on the interphone. "Red," he said, "you hit something, and I guarantee you it wasn't water. Now let's get out of here!" The PV skittered down almost to wave-top level and headed for England. "Aren't we supposed to wait for the fighter cover?" somebody said on the interphone.

"I don't see any fighter cover," Lyon said, and poured on the coal for home.

Flitting over the target in his "droopsnoot" P-38 with Captain Loyd Humphries tightly locked in the transparent nose in the observer's position, Lieutenant Colonel Roy Forrest sought to keep the air armada together for its own safety. He was astonished that the Luftwaffe had not crossed swords with the group all the way to Helgoland. Everyone knew that the German Air Force had taken its lumps and was no longer challenging Allied bomber formations en masse, but everyone also knew that there were heavy concentrations of ME-109's and Focke-Wulf 190's stationed at airports all along the northeastern coastline of Germany and Holland, only a few miles from the precise route of the Aphrodite task force. On the way in, Forrest had comforted himself with the hope that the twenty-five or so aircraft under his command might not present enough radar blips to excite the Germans into attacking, but the trip home would be another matter. There had been a mystery B-17 hovering in the wings during the attack on Helgoland, and by the time the group had completed the mission and formed up for the 300-mile return flight to Fersfield it had become obvious that the odd B-17 was a German spotter, radioing altitudes and headings for the benefit of the flak crews and the fighter-interceptors. German air intelligence had developed the canniness of a cornered alley cat about such matters, and Forrest feared that the Luftwaffe would carve up the air flotilla on the way home, when gas was low and perceptions loosened. The fighter cover of sixteen P-51 Mustangs was turning circles above at high altitudes, providing an air shield for the PV's and the random B-17's and the Mosquito and P-38 photo ships below. So long as they all stayed together, the Mustangs could shepherd them back to safety. But any aircraft that angled away from the formation would be in trouble. Within a few minutes Nazi fighters from the nearby Frisian Islands bases could take to the air, shoot them down, and dart back to safety. The menace was real; Forrest had confronted it many times in his long career as a bomber pilot.

"Got everybody spotted?" he said to Humphries on the intercom.

"Everybody except the mother ships," the observer answered. "They disappeared in the undercast."

"Headed which way?"

"Home. They lit out like a couple of young colts at an open gate."

Forrest flicked on his radio transmitter and issued code words for the formation to join up and head for home. The B-17's moved into sight, and the fighter cover signaled its assent, and the Mosquitoes and P-38 photo ships formed up, and everyone was ready except the two PV's. "Goddamn it!" Forrest said. "They're trying to make it alone! Why, those little nipshits!"

He turned up the power on his radio and began issuing urgent messages to the two mother ships. When code words produced no response, he began speaking crisp, simple ranch-type English. When that brought only silence, he gunned the P-38 "droopsnoot" out over the water and caught up with the two PV's. Both were on the deck, in the undercast, trying to remain below the German radar. "Get out of there!" Forrest radioed. "They'll clobber you down there!" Again there was no response, and Forrest said, "Do you read me? *Do you read me?* You are ordered to slow down and make S turns and 360's until the rest can catch up with you." The PV's kept on going.

Forrest decided that the airwaves over the North Sea were no place to teach the rudiments of combat formation flying to a couple of green Navy crews. "Look," he said, "I know you're reading me. Go ahead and disobey, you're doing it anyway. But for God's sake get on *top* of the clouds where you can maneuver if you have to." The silence continued, and through a break in the clouds to his left Forrest could make out the low silhouette of the Frisian Islands. He ordered four of the P-51's in the fighter cover to split off from the rest of the formation and fly above the runaway PV's to England, and then he returned to the main formation as it flew ponderously toward the west. No fighter opposition developed, and in a little over an hour the task force reached the coast of England, and the P-51's peeled off for their home base. "Many thanks, little friends," Forrest radioed, and the fighter ships waggled their wings and were gone.

"Roy?" Humphries' voice said on the intercom.

"Yeah."

"What're you gonna do about those Navy guys?"

"I'm gonna control my temper, Humpy," Forrest said. "I'm gonna sleep on it."

Humphries and Forrest walked past a group of the Navy fliers on their way from the apron to their quarters, and Humphries muttered softly, "Now remember what you said, Roy. You're gonna control your temper."

"Don't worry," Forrest said in a quivering voice. "I'm controlling it."

As they were moving alongside the others, a voice came from within the group. "Well, I guess our old PV's will outfly your sack of shit," it said.

Forrest slowed and almost stopped, but Humphries pulled him by the arm and said, "Temper, temper!"

Forrest contented himself with a loud aside. "Fine bunch of heroes!" he said. "Running home to Mama."

Later he summoned his friend, Commander James Smith, and passed along a message to the Navy pilots. "Goddamn it, Smitty!" he roared. "We've got a problem with your boys. They don't know who the hell's running this show. Now so far I've been telling you *why,* but now I'm telling you *what!* Do you understand that, sir?"

"Yes, I understand, Roy," Smith said, looking slightly chagrined. "Now how about calming down and telling me what they did?"

"They ran away from their fighter cover, that's what the little nipshits did."

"Well, they told me they were outrunning everything so they thought they might as well keep on going," Smith said.

"I don't give a rat's ass what they thought," Forrest said. "They're not paid to think. They're paid to take orders. I came right alongside both of them and ordered them to come back and join the formation, and they practically thumbed their noses at me. Now, Smitty, I want you to get this message across to them and get it right. I happen to know a little bit more about this goddamn enemy than they know, and this project is my responsibility, and right or wrong we're gonna do it my way! Those little nipshits of yours are gonna follow orders, or they're gonna be court-martialed. Now will you make that clear to them, sir?"

"Yeah," Smith said. "I'll make it clear."

The photographs of the Navy's strike on Helgoland were rushed into the developing rooms, and the morning after the mission everyone waited around to find out what had been hit. There was a lot of talk about the missed signals from mother ship to mother ship. Harry Wherry admitted manfully that he had misunderstood the Morse signal by Aldis lamp, and everyone agreed that the attack plan should have included something unmistakable, such as a bright flare, to indicate VHF failure. Demlein and Anderson discussed the control of the robot, but it was impossible to determine which of the two controllers had dived the robot into the island. The radio-control receivers in the baby would accept accurate signals from any source, and both men had been transmitting feverishly. Technicians like Olsen and Simpson, removed from the discussion, reckoned that the drone had accepted a portion of control from each mother ship and that the main cause of the confusion was an attack plan that had tried to get everybody into the act. In one respect the mission had turned out similar to Kennedy's: No one would ever know for sure exactly what had gone wrong. Exploded robots told no tales. The only certainties were that the Kennedy mission had been a total failure, but this second Navy attempt had at least produced an explosion in the vicinity of a legitimate target. The question remained: Where?

At last word reached Fersfield from intelligence. Special Attack Unit No. 1, United States Navy, had destroyed a coal pile. The force of the blast had scattered coal powder all over the island of Helgoland and dug a crater about 60 feet in diameter and about 12 feet deep. There was minor damage to small buildings a few hundred yards away on the edge of an airfield and some windows broken at even greater distances, but nothing of strategic importance (except coal) had been disturbed. Aphrodite Mission No. 4, like Aphrodite Missions Nos. 1, 2, and 3 had flopped. Not long afterward Lieutenant

Ralph Spalding took off in another PB4Y for the United States and was lost with all hands when the plane slammed into the side of a mountain.

With the combat failures, the antidrone forces in the Navy Department in Washington had the ammunition they needed to kill the program that they had regarded for so long as wild-eyed and visionary. It was a case of old enmities surfacing. In the course of fighting for their program for almost a decade, conscientious officers like Jimmy Smith and Commander Delmar Fahrney and Commander Robert Jones and Commodore Oscar Smith had made some enemies, and now the enemies moved in for the kill. In response to an urgent cable, Smith flew to Washington and argued for five days before top Navy brass, but his arguments came smack up against two essential facts: Navy Mission No. 1 and Navy Mission No. 2. It was not bad enough that the Navy had squandered millions of dollars on the program down through the years, the critics argued, but they had to pick a Boston socialite with important political connections for one of their first casualties. The repercussions of Joe Kennedy's death were still reverberating around the capital. Franklin D. Roosevelt had asked for a report. Secretary of the Navy James Forrestal had written a personal letter to the bereaved father, and those involved in the matter were walking on eggs lest the irascible Joseph P. Kennedy, Sr., find out the true circumstances of his son's death. Plans were made to name a destroyer after the brave pilot, but everyone knew that the elder Kennedy would not be consoled by such an obvious sop. Joseph Patrick Kennedy, Jr., firstborn son of Rose and Joseph Kennedy, Sr., had been his father's favorite. Moreover, he had been a fine officer, with a long and creditable combat record and his death seemed totally unnecessary to the Aphrodite critics now heavily laden with hindsight.

Patient and alone, Commander Jimmy Smith fought back. He described again what the radio-control project had accomplished with smaller drones like Vultee trainers and specially built TDR's and TDM's and even F6F Hellcats. He reminded the officers of demonstrations that they had witnessed themselves, when controllers had made drones perform all sorts of tricks in midair, and then steered them into the center of bull's-eyes on bombing ranges. He told about the midnight calls when SAU No. 1 was formed and readied almost instantly for combat and presented with a four-engine bomber to control instead of the smaller aircraft that had been used in the program for years. He told about the enterprise and skill of the Navy technicians who made the adaptations to the PB4Y in a few short days, and finally he told about the missions themselves, one in which the plane had blown up inexplicably and another in which the target had been missed by a matter of yards because of an equipment failure. Surely this could not be considered the end of the program; surely there was a bright future for these prototype American guided missiles.

The loyal skipper of SAU No. 1 went from office to office and officer to officer, talking himself hoarse, and when he saw that his message was not getting across, he reduced his argument to writing and sent it through official channels. About the second mission, he wrote: "The mission was very successful from an experimental operational view . . . the accomplishment of this mission indicated a high state of training and ability on the part of the personnel comprising the special air unit on its first combat mission into enemy territory . . . it is therefore recommended that the PB4Y drone control plane team be directed operationally against Japan at the earliest possible date."

But no Navy PB4Y drone ever flew against Japan. Even while Jimmy Smith was arguing in Washington, SAU No. 1 was being broken up in England. By the time Smith had made all his points, the argument had become meaningless. The pilots and controllers of Special Attack Unit No. 1 had been shipped to places like Brazil and Africa and the Aleutians. A few technicians were returned to Traverse City, but most of the men were posted to other duty in other fields. Commander Jimmy Smith was sent to sea as captain of the USS *Chincoteague,* a seaplane tender. The dogged little Missourian took the assignment philosophically. "A naval officer always like to go to sea," he told a friend. Everyone agreed that he had done his best. Now the Navy program was as dead as Joe Kennedy and Wilford Willy. Some argued that the entire Aphrodite project should be allowed to die naturally—indeed, that it was dead already. But like many another moribund military program, in times of war as well as peace, it had built-in momentum and continued to roll.

3. Castor

AT Fersfield, Roy Forrest surveyed his domain. Jim Rand and double azon were gone, although five mother ship crews remained on the station. The Navy had cleared out, and the only sign of its recent tenancy was a few inches of bourbon in the bottoms of bottles stashed away in the corners of their empty huts. The Castor technicians from Wright Field had reported to Forrest that they were prepared to fly a mission at any time, using the mother ships brought to the base by Major Rand almost three months earlier. Forrest hoped that they would get the chance. With all the high-level sniping at the whole Aphrodite program, Forrest would not have been surprised to see the project axed at any minute. He wondered, in fact, what kept it going after its first missions had been failures and its primary targets had been overrun by ground troops, and then he remembered the conversation back at headquarters several months earlier. "This is the Old Man's baby," someone had said. "This is the Old Man's favorite toy." And the old man had turned out to be General Henry H. Arnold, boss of the Army Air Corps.

Roy Forrest told himself that the Aphrodite program might exist for the sole delight and edification of the commanding officer of the Air Corps, and then again it might exist for more cogent reasons, military reasons that made absolute sense. He was not privy to all the thinking at Elveden Hall and High Wycombe and Spaatzhouse.

Determined as he was to conduct the program at its maximum effectiveness, regardless of the past history and regardless of the loss of targets, he took special interest in an intelligence bulletin he received one day about the German battleship *Tirpitz.* The mere existence of the enemy capital ship, lying inside a mesh of antitorpedo nets in Alten Fjord near the northern tip of Norway, forced the British to divert three battleships to guard convoys going through the area toward Murmansk in the Soviet Union. The British had been trying for two years to knock out the *Tirpitz,* but there she lay in the comfortable harbor, her broad steel hull apparently immune to the bold attacks by air and submarine.

Forrest called in one of his most inventive aides, Major Ralph Hayes of Detroit. "What about it, Ralph?" Forrest asked. "Can we knock her out?" Hayes began poring over maps and studying ordnance circulars and making phone calls. When at last he said, "We can do it," Forrest ordered him to work up a formal attack plan.

Hayes conferred with the British and received assurances that an Aphrodite mission could take off from Lossiemouth, far in the north of Scotland. But in London, American ordnance officers said they doubted any known bombs would do the trick. Undaunted, the indefatigable Hayes called on British munitions experts and learned that they had hydrostatic bombs that could be set to go off at a certain depth of water. "If you could get enough of these to explode simultaneously under the hull of the ship, the blast would lift her up and break her in two," a British ordnance officer said. "The problem would lie in getting enough of them into one of your B-17's, and then dumping your aircraft just short of the *Tirpitz,* so it will sink to the bottom and go off."

The problem was even more challenging than Hayes and the British had imagined. The hydrostatic bombs were more like torpedoes, and they were far too bulky for the forklift loading devices that snaked under the open bomb bays of B-17 and shoved their lethal loads up into the open bomb bay. Moreover, the bomb bay of a B-17 would not hold enough hydrostatic bombs to do the job, even if they *could* be lifted by the available equipment. Forrest and Hayes put their heads together late one night, but even the inspiration of a bottle of English gin did not solve the problem. "What we need is a good old-fashioned cherry picker," Forrest said. "Then we could lower those bombs into the plane."

"What the hell's a cherry picker?" Hayes asked, and Forrest told him it was a simple hoisting device used back in the States for changing engines in automobiles.

"Let me think about that one for a while," Hayes said, and began tracing lines on the small tablet he always carried. After a few minutes he pushed a drawing toward Forrest.

"You're drunk!" the commanding officer said as he looked down at a sketch of a B-17 with the entire top of the pilot's cabin and radio compartment removed.

"I don't know how the hell *you* can tell that *I'm* drunk," Hayes said, "but drunk or sober, I'll bet this will work. All we have to do is get the technicians to slice the top off the fuselage. Then we use one of your cherry-picker things to lift the hydrostatic bombs into the air and gently lower them into the airplane. That way we can fill the bomb bay and the whole rest of the plane. They say we need about twenty-six thousand pounds of bombs to blow the *Tirpitz*. This will handle it."

Forrest took another look at the outlandish drawing. "By God, Hayes," he said, "I may be drunk myself, but I think you've got something."

The next day the two officers conferred with a Boeing technical representative and determined exactly what parts of the fuselage roof could be removed without taking out structural strength. Then they asked their mechanical experts to do the job. After a few days, they had the only open-cockpit four-engine bomber in the European theater.

"Why, it's a roadster," the admiring Forrest said, and the

description stuck. Every pilot on the base wanted to fly the roadster, and while Hayes and Forrest were negotiating with the British for bombs and a target date, the pilots all but lined up for rides. The first men to test the open-cockpit bomber came back with warnings that the airstream would blow their caps off, and subsequent flights were made with hats tied down by scarves borrowed from girlfriends. "Fun is fun," Forrest told the assembled pilots one afternoon, "but it has come to my attention that several banana boat pilots have been sent into the flakhouse on account of you guys. They told the flight surgeon they were buzzed by open B-17's flown by women in babushkas. Now you guys have got to cut that out!" When the laughter died down, Forrest singled out one of the prospective jump pilots. "Waters," he said, "I don't want to hear any more reports about you tagging onto B-24 formations and standing up and saluting either. You have a very curious sense of humor, Waters."

At last the hydrostatic bombs were delivered to Fersfield, and the ticklish task of loading the roadster was begun. When the last bomb was lowered into the bomb bay and strapped down, and every available inch of open space was filled with other hydrostatic bombs of varying sizes, word came from the British that permission to fly from Lossiemouth had been withdrawn. The Royal Air Force and the Royal Navy's Fleet Air Arm had heard about the proposed mission; they would take care of their own targets, and no assistance would be required from the Americans. Not long afterward, the British newspapers reported the crippling of the *Tirpitz* by 12,000-pound "tallboy" bombs. "Well," said the disappointed Forrest, "they said they'd do it, and they did it. Can't complain about that."

Lieutenant Colonel Dale Anderson, technical chief of the Castor program, was a brilliant officer with a capacity for work barely matched by the ill-starred Jim Rand. Described by Pappy Tooman as "a real good man but not a good enough backbiter to get along in the military," Anderson had his own ideas about the Aphrodite missions and how they should be flown.

To Forrest, Castor seemed the best chance to turn the failures of the project into successes. He had heard all sorts of stories about the savvy of Anderson and the rest of the Castor team, which included Peter Murray, the civilian electronics genius, and skilled technicians who had been working together on remote control for five or six years. Once, Forrest was told, a team of generals and War Department officials had gone out to Muroc Dry Lake in California to watch Anderson put on a show, and the grand finale had astounded them all. Anderson had lifted one airplane into the air by remote control, then sent an explosive-loaded robot on an intercept-and-destroy mission while the visiting delegates snickered up their sleeves at his audacity. In about three minutes, the chase robot had pulled alongside the target robot; Anderson punched a button, and the amazed spectators saw both drones go up in smoke.

On his few visits to the shops at Fersfield now occupied exclusively by Anderson and his Castor technicians, Forrest had been impressed by their obvious proficiency and freewheeling imagination. The Castor drones had everything that double azon and the Navy had had, television and radio remote-control gear, plus improvisations of their own. The drones were equipped with electronic navigation gear, so that the mother ship would not lose control of them even in bad weather. Attached to the belly of each drone was a remodeled P-47 auxiliary gas tank, full of liquid that produced smoke. Such devices were not new in the program, but Forrest found that this smoke could be keyed off and on by radio impulses from the mother ship. Thus it could be saved for the run on the target, and the smoke would provide a tracer effect and increase the accuracy of the strike. Forrest was highly impressed, and even more so when he learned that the Castor robots had remote throttle control, and even a repeat-back magnesyn compass so that the mother ship controller could look at his television receiver and determine the exact heading of the drone from the drone's own compass.

There was one more advantage enjoyed by the Castor team, Forrest thought as he sat on the edge of his bed and pondered the future of his command. The Castor team had studied the results of the earlier missions and learned from them. Now they knew, for example, not to load the robots too far above the horizontal center of gravity. They had a better idea of the uses and limitations of Ace. They would not attempt the sort of remote-control arming device that had killed Joe Kennedy and Bud Willy. The program had history and continuity and some operational experience now, and every mistake could be turned to good use. The Castor program was the Allied repository of all the accumulated knowledge of the strange new science of guided missiles, and Forrest retained the highest hopes for it. It seemed to him that the ingredients for a successful strike were present at last.

Anderson shared that belief. At thirty-four, short and trim, with a close-cropped graying haircut, he reckoned himself the athletic equal of most of the men on the base and was determined to fly as jump pilot on the first Castor mission. He had been a pilot since winning his wings at Randolph Field in 1936, and he knew the bailout technique. Despite the fact that Aphrodite had been having parachute troubles, Anderson had no fears. He thought he knew what was wrong. A static line was useful when fifteen or twenty paratroopers had to line up in a slow-moving C-46 or C-47 and drop at regular intervals, but it was a severe liability when the pilot was inexperienced at parachuting, had to drop through a narrow hatchway next to a whirling propeller, and fall into a slipstream that could reach as high as 200 mph. Moreover, the trailing static lines flapped against the drone's fuselage as the flight continued, and Anderson was convinced that more than one control problem had been the result of antennas bent and battered to pieces by the heavy static cord. If the pilot would pull his own rip cord, both problems would be solved.

"I don't know, Andy," Roy Forrest had said when they discussed the proposed solution. "The static lines are policy for the operation, just like the manual arming. I don't think I'd want to ask one of my pilots to pull a rip cord. Suppose he hits his head on the hatch and he goes into the slipstream unconscious? We almost had a couple like that in the early missions."

"Suppose I said that one of your Eighth Air Force pilots wouldn't have to do it, that I'd provide you a pilot from our technical group?" Anderson said.

"I think I'd still have to stick with the static line," Forrest said, "and I'd have to turn down your volunteer anyway. I like the program the way it is. You supply the brains, and we supply the men."

"Roy," Anderson said, "I was thinking of being the jump pilot myself, to make sure that everything goes right."

"*You!*" Forrest said loudly. "The man the whole show depends on? You must be crazy to suggest something like that. If Partridge or Doolittle ever found out I let you do a damn fool thing like that, they'd have me on the clipper in the mess hall for the rest of the war, and they'd be right."

"They don't have to know," Anderson insisted.

"They ain't gonna know," Forrest said, "because you ain't gonna do it."

The argument continued off and on for several days, but Forrest refused to budge. Finally he made two compromises: against the policy of the program, Anderson would be allowed to fly, but as a controller, not as a jump pilot. He would replace one of the Eighth Air Force controllers who had been undergoing daily training in the new equipment. As for the static line, it would be altered slightly. A long thin wire was stretched from the front to the back of the airplane along the belly, and each bailout pilot would reach under and clip his static line to it. After the line had accomplished its job of opening the parachute, it would slide down the wire on a ring loop and trail in the wake of the robot, where there would be nothing for it to hit.

Anderson did not like the second part of the compromise, but he finally gave in. The mission was set on that basis. The target would be Helgoland, and the task force would be restricted to a primary mother ship, a backup mother ship, a single robot, and the various support aircraft. Anderson was disappointed; he had wanted a maximum effort, with four babies on the target, but headquarters seemed to have become curiously disinterested in the program, and he would have to settle for this rather simple plan. His technicians were disappointed, too, but he told them that a small effort was better than none. Like the Navy's drone program, the Army version had had to struggle for years on limited budgets and second-rate equipment and derision. The men were accustomed to small efforts. At least, after five years of preparation, they would be going into combat.

Donald Salles, twenty-four years old, short and chunky and handsome, a distant relative of an early President of Brazil, slapped his cards down, cried, "Gin!" and began adding up the score. "Makes it over fifteen thousand, Lindy," he said. "Looks like the trip to London's gonna be on you."

"I'm not worried," said his opponent, twenty-five-year-old Richard "Lindy" Lindahl, a commercial flower grower from the Midwest and a former lead pilot for the 388th Bomb Group. "The game's young. The way things are going, we won't be flying this mission till the war's over."

The two men had been playing gin rummy almost nonstop ever since coming to Fersfield and completing their rudimentary jump training. Now there was nothing to do but wait, and they had played something like 500 hands before Salles had moved into his 15,000-point lead. At a penny a point, the winnings would support both of them on the five-day pass they had been promised after their jumps. Salles had dealt another hand when an enlisted man came running into their hut. "Sir," he said, "there's a mission on for tomorrow."

"Sure, there is," Salles said, having been through the entire procedure several times before. "They set us up the night before, and the next day we get stood down. We've been stood down so many times I don't even think about it anymore."

"No, sir," the enlisted man said. "This time it's definite."

The next morning the ceiling and visibility were zero, and Salles' prediction came true. The following day was September 11, and without the least warning, the mission was scheduled for the afternoon. The ops officer explained that headquarters was getting more and more reluctant to schedule fighter support for Aphrodite missions, but suddenly some fighters had become available, and it would be wise to take advantage of them. The briefing was held at 1 P.M. in the large room just below the control tower, and Salles listened lethargically. Most of the talk concerned the target and approach routes and flak possibilities, and the two jump pilots knew that their jobs would be long over by that time. When the briefing was finished, a beefy navigator from one of the mother ship crews walked over to the two men and said jovially, "Well, today's the day we get rid of you!" It had been a long-standing joke in the project that the only escape was to bail out; otherwise, one remained with the program forever, like Pappy Tooman and Jack Lansing and Foster Falkenstine and some of the other pilots.

Lindahl said, "Maybe you won't get rid of us so easily. We might come back and make another jump."

"Yeah," said the navigator, "and Hitler might be an Eagle Scout, too. What're you guys gonna do on your pass?"

"We're going to London," Salles said, "on him!"

The two comrades walked out to their loaded drone and preflighted it, circling the ancient aircraft several times until they were positive that everything was in order. Lindahl was joking and relaxed, and it occurred to Salles that it would be a great relief to both of them to get the mission over. He checked his own nervousness, holding the fingers of opposite hands until they almost touched, and he noticed that they were barely trembling. "Hey, Lindy," he said, "do you suppose there's something the matter with us? Shouldn't we be afraid?"

"Speak for yourself," Lindahl said. "I'm the world's greatest faker."

The starting procedures were normal, and as Lindahl steered the loaded drone along the rumpled taxiway, Salles looked out the co-pilot's window and realized for the first time how alone they were. "Look at those bastards leaving the flight line!" he said to Lindahl. "They're running like rats." A few men were visible against the upper rail of the two-story control tower, but the instant Lindahl turned the B-17 into the wind at the end of the runway and began to rev up his engines, they too vanished to air-raid shelters. Then a loud siren went off, and the two men were on their own.

"Well, what do you say?" Lindahl shouted over the roar of the engines. "Should we lepers go out and play?"

Salles held thumbs up, and the B-17 lurched into motion and picked up speed until the end of the runway was clearly in sight. Lindahl eased back on the control column, and the black asphalt fell away. "Hey, I can see the sugar beets!" Salles said, looking down at the patch of tilled earth that began where the runway left off.

"I think there's a whole bushelful in the undercarriage," Lindahl said. The plane was climbing steadily. The first takeoff of the Castor program had been perfect, and Salles turned to see that Lindahl was smiling.

"What's so funny?" Salles said.

"I was just thinking about what I'm gonna do," Lindahl said.

"Jumping from this thing is funny?"

"No," Lindahl said, "but buzzing the tower is!"

Salles watched him kick the robot into a climbing turn and slowly work his way up to about 1,000 feet before leveling off

and heading back for Fersfield. He knew about Lindahl's
pranks, and he was not in the least concerned. The fake would
end momentarily. But then he noticed that Lindahl had put the
drone into a shallow dive and the airspeed indicator had passed
220 miles an hour. "Hey, what're you doing?" he shouted.

"I told you," Lindahl said. "I'm buzzing the tower!"

The B-17 and its ten tons of Torpex cleared the control tower
by several hundred feet, and as it roared over the top, Salles
saw men jumping to the ground. "Jesus, Lindy," he said, "I
think I saw Colonel Forrest."

"He needs the exercise," Lindahl said, and pulled the
bomber back to altitude and the trail of the navigation ship
they were following.

Salles put on his headsets and concentrated on the ground-to-
air radio frequency. "They'll be calling up any second now," he
said, "chewing our asses out."

"Who'll be calling?" Lindahl said, laughing. "There's nobody in the tower to call!"

Salles realized that the pilot was right. The chewing out
would have to wait for later. He slipped down into the crawl
space to begin setting up the autopilot, wondering if he would
have the courage to jump out, but he found that there was so
much fiddling to do with the knobs and controls of the gadget
that he was too busy to worry about anything. "Won't that be
something to tell the grandkids?" he said to himself. "Going on
a mission like this and being so calm about it!" The time had
come to jump, and he was halfway through the tunnel to the
navigator's hatch when he looked up and saw Lindahl easing
himself down from the pilot's compartment. "Here," Lindahl
said, handing Salles a chest pack. "You forgot something. I
know you're a cool character, but you'd better put it on."

Salles accepted the safety chute sheepishly and watched as
Lindahl headed back into the compartment above. "Okay, let's
go!" Lindahl called, and Salles said, "Okay, see you down below!" He dropped into the slipstream and felt the static line

catch and fall away, and then there was a jarring jolt, and several hundred square feet of white silk were billowing gently over his head. "What a snap!" he found himself saying, and then he wondered about his buddy. The force of the slipstream had spun Salles around, and he yanked on the risers to try to stabilize his fall so he could look back and watch Lindahl, but by the time he brought the oscillations under control his friend was nowhere to be seen. Maybe the robot had flown out of his line of vision, or maybe there was trouble with the autopilot. He hoped not. It was no simple job to fly a B-17 and adjust the relocated autopilot at the same time.

The day was gentle and the breezes were mild, and Donald Salles did not even lose his footing when he landed softly in the middle of a field. Within seconds he was surrounded by British farmworkers, and several young girls offered to gather up his parachute for him. Salles laughed. He knew what the girls had in mind. For the last four years, every wedding dress in England had been made of parachute silk. "Go ahead," he said, exhilarated by his successful jump. "Take it away! It's yours." One of the farmers invited him into a nearby house for a glass of bitters, and he enjoyed several pints with his new friends before a jeep drove up to retrieve him and return him to Fersfield. "What about Lindy?" he said to the driver. "Did you pick him up yet?"

"No, sir," the driver said. "We're not sure where he is. Nobody saw his chute."

Lieutenant Colonel Dale Anderson had been test flying one of the robots when word came by radio that the metro data was good and fighters were available and Castor would fly its first mission practically at once. It was 11:30 in the morning when he received the message, and briefing was scheduled for 1 P.M. "Isn't that just like the Army?" he said to his co-pilot as he put the robot into a tight turn and headed back for Fersfield. "We work for years and years getting everything going perfectly, and then they give us an hour and a half notice of a mission!"

At the briefing, Anderson requested that the strike time of 1800 be advanced an hour, rushing things even more, but he had talked to the meteorological officer and learned that the unexpectedly good weather at Helgoland was not likely to hold through the evening. Since clear skies were vital to the television control, the change was made, and everyone ran out of the briefing room to get ready for the 3 P.M. takeoffs. Somehow the departure timings were made good, give or take a few minutes, and at exactly eight minutes after three, the last airplane of the task force lifted its wheels and headed out to sea. It was the P-38 Lightning, piloted by Lieutenant Colonel Roy Forrest with Captain Loyd Humphries once again shoehorned into the "droopsnoot."

It took less than fifteen minutes for the jump crew to set up the autopilot, and when the robot was flying straight and level and responding perfectly to Anderson's control, he transmitted the code word authorizing the crew to jump. One man went out almost immediately and disappeared into the checkerboard of farms below, his chute turning into a white speck and finally disappearing altogether. From the mother ship, piloted by Pappy Tooman and flying only a few hundred feet astern of the baby, Anderson and the other crew members could see a pair of legs dangle out of the navigator's hatch and remain dangling for twenty or thirty seconds. "He's sure in no hurry," Tooman said on the intercom. "Maybe he's waiting for better weather."

"Maybe he's making sure he brought along some toilet paper," another voice said, and just then the jumper's body was seen to detach itself from the airplane. As in all the Aphrodite jumps, the spectator's first impression was of a man being shot from a gun at the circus. The body did not seem to fall so much as it seemed to be propelled in a straight line from the front to the back of the aircraft. Just as it passed the tail wheel there seemed to be a slight hesitation, and then the jumper's body slowly began to tumble in a full erect position.

Roy Forrest was flying his P-38 500 yards behind the robot when the parachute jumping began, and when he saw the slight hesitation and the tumbling of Richard Lindahl's body, he realized that the primary chute had failed. He gunned the P-38 up closer and waited for the pilot to pull his chest pack. The jumping had begun at 2,500 feet, and there was still time. "He's not doing it!" Loyd Humphries said on the interphones, and Forrest stood the twin-boomed fighter plane on its nose to get a better look. Down below the still-erect body of the parachutist was falling to earth. "Do it, son," Forrest screamed. "Do it! Open the goddamn thing!" But the body kept on falling, and Forrest and Humphries saw Lindahl hit the ground, bounce once and lie still.

The task force had droned out over the North Sea, and Forrest gunned the P-38 to catch up. Still shaken by the long fall of the jump pilot, he checked the skies up and down and saw that the fighter cover was in perfect position. A cluster of P-51 Mustangs hovered at 12,000 feet, and more fighters were visible as dots in the sky at 28,000. The relatively defenseless mother ships and the completely defenseless robot would be flying within 8 or 10 miles of the Frisian Islands, where the Germans had several fighter bases, and these "little friends" flying high above might deter the weakened Luftwaffe from making an attack. But at the target nothing was going to stop the Germans from throwing up a fearsome wall of flak, and Forrest knew it. Intelligence had reported that the September 3 Navy mission had apparently made the Germans jumpy, and several detachments of antiaircraft personnel had been rushed to the sub base. German Air Force intelligence was not stupid; they must have deduced the nature of the September 3 attack, and on this follow-up mission just eight days later the flak crews could be counted on to lay a withering curtain of cross fire in the direction of the drone and the mothers. Forrest cursed softly to himself. The simple solution to that problem would have been to send a few dozen bombers across the island of Helgoland an hour before the Aphrodite mission. Several thousand antipersonnel bombs could have silenced those gun batteries, at least long enough for the robot to thread its way into the sub pens, but Third Bomb Headquarters had denied Forrest's request for the softening-up mission. The bombers were busy elsewhere. It seemed to the officer from Texas that any time he needed something nowadays, such as diversionary bombers or even spare parts, it was unavailable. Times had changed, and the program was being treated like a stepchild.

A voice crackled in his earphones and interrupted his thoughts. "Look!" somebody was saying. "Who's that?"

Forrest craned his neck for a look at the assembled aircraft below him, and then he did a double take. There were supposed to be five B-17's in all: a primary mother ship, a standby mother ship, the drone, a radio relay aircraft, and an observation plane. But Forrest thought he saw six.

"Hey, Humpy," he said, "count those B-17's for me."

"I already did," Humphries said in his Arizona twang. "There's six. An extry just came up from the rear and tagged on."

"Who is he?"

"How the hell would I know? Let me check his markings."

"The markings don't make a shit," Forrest said. "The Germans have paint, just like us."

Forrest rummaged around and found the crystal that would enable him to talk to the fighter escort by radio. He snapped it in place and called the P-51 squadron commander. "See that?" Forrest said.

"Sure do," the fighter pilot answered. "Son of a bitch moved in as though he owns the place."

"Take a few friends, and move in tight on him," Forrest ordered, "but don't do anything drastic till you hear from me."

"Roger," the P-51 pilot answered, and Forrest saw three of

the twin-engine Lightnings peel out of formation and form around the intruder.

"How's he look?" Forrest called.

"Nothing special," the squadron commander answered. "Ordinary 17, Eighth Air Force markings."

"Waist gun hatches closed?" Forrest asked.

"Closed on both sides," the fighter pilot said, "and we can see a couple of faces at each hatch."

Up to now, the appearance of the mystery B-17 was an old story to Roy Forrest, as indeed it must have been to all the experienced pilots in the group. (One had appeared briefly on the second Navy run on Helgoland.) In the course of the war, the Germans had reconditioned dozens of B-17's that had been shot down over the Continent, and some of them had been sent back into battle on behalf of the enemy. Forrest had lost several planeloads of friends to a ghost Flying Fortress that had tagged onto a bombing mission and started blazing away when the planes were helpless on their bomb runs. Lately, these B-17 gunships had become more rare. Now the Germans were sending the Trojan planes into Allied bomber formations for the sole purpose of radioing back altitudes and airspeeds and headings to the flak crews below. The German B-17's would make no hostile moves; they would appear to be harmless and friendly, and before anyone knew what had happened, they would dive out of sight and a murderous pattern of pinpoint flak would appear.

"Now get this straight," Forrest radioed. "I don't like the looks of that airplane. Keep an eye on her! If you see those waist hatches open and those fifties swing into position, shoot her down! No ifs, ands, or buts!"

"Roger," the fighter chief replied.

"And one more thing," Forrest said. "If she drops out of the formation and heads for the Continent, follow her down, and if she gets into a landing pattern, shoot her out of the sky. If she turns back toward the UK, follow her and watch her land and don't do anything further, except tell me later where she landed."

So far as Forrest was concerned, the mystery ship was now neutralized. He took a last look before proceeding to other matters. The B-17 was flying on the same heading as the task force, but now it had dropped back to about 1,200 yards in the rear. Sometimes it would pull up closer, surrounded by the loose phalanx of P-51's, but then it would drop back, apparently content to trail the task force. "All right, you old whore," Forrest said to himself. "I'm leaving you now, and if you're not a good girl, you're dead!" He gunned the P-38 and flew on ahead to see how the others were doing.

In the primary mother ship, canny old Pappy Tooman had seen the intruder and had drawn exactly the same conclusions as Forrest, but when he saw the three Mustangs form up around the mystery plane, he relaxed and concentrated on his task, which so far as he was concerned was the perfect execution of the mission. Nothing less would do, and he had high hopes, despite the program's dismal record. He knew enough about the radio-control process to recognize the mastery of the quiet little lieutenant colonel sitting in the nose in front of his TV screen and his row of switches and controls. "How's she set up?" Tooman asked, when they crossed the midpoint and began to draw near to the Frisians on the right.

"Perfect," Anderson said. "The jump crew did a good job."

"They're good boys," Tooman said. "I hope they're all right."

"I'm not sure. I only saw one chute open. You heard anything?"

"No, we won't know anything till we get back."

The total flying time from the last landfall at Orford Ness to the initial point about 10 miles west of Helgoland was just under two hours, and on the last third of the flight the task force would be within 8 or 10 miles of the Frisians. Normally, this would mean light flak and the possibility of a fighter attack, but with sixteen P-51's flying cover and the German Air Force severely undermanned, Tooman and his crew were not overly concerned, and the task force was flying "loosey goosey" as it approached the target. Both robot and mother ship were at 2,500 feet, with the mother a mile or two in trail, when Anderson requested that they drive closer for a look at the baby. "I think the cowl flaps might be open on one side," Anderson said, and Tooman shoved the throttles ahead and pulled up until they were flying wing tip to wing tip with the drone and its load of Torpex. A loud derisive noise came over the interphones, and Tooman interpreted this as a comment by one of his crewmen about the proximity of the two planes.

"Who did that?" Tooman said, but the only response was a repetition. "Okay, knock it off," Tooman snapped. "If you don't like what we're doing, get out and walk. That water down there's a nice comfortable thirty-six degrees."

"Everything's okay," Anderson said. "Cowl flaps on both sides are tucked in. I must have been imagining things." The mother ship slackened speed to about 115 miles an hour, barely off a stall, until the robot had opened up a 2-mile gap between them. They were flying along straight and level, with the IP almost reached and the Frisians lying low and shadowy off to the right. Suddenly they were bracketed by a half dozen puffs of dense black smoke, and the B-17 rocked from side to side from the force of several near-misses. Tooman kicked the rudder and slammed the control column forward with all his strength, and the Fortress slipped into a turning dive straight down toward the sea. The G forces had flung some of the crew members around, and Tooman could hear them grumbling again on the interphones. One of the machine-gun turrets had spun so quickly that it had broken through its safety stop, and now it was whirling in full circles. Cool air came rushing in through a broken waist port, and it carried the acrid smell of gunpowder. Tooman kept the B-17 diving until it was just over the waves, and then he leveled off and continued on course for the target.

"They're shooting at us!" the surprised voice of Lieutenant Colonel Dale Anderson came over the intercom.

"Yeah," Tooman said calmly. "That's the way they play at this war, Colonel."

"But they were shooting at the baby, too," Anderson said. "They *can't* do that."

Tooman had to laugh. "Don't worry, Colonel," Tooman said. "If they hit it, we'll go back and get another one."

A new voice came over the interphone, and Tooman thought he recognized his waist gunner. "Why the hell don't you tell a guy when you make a move like that?" the voice was saying.

"The next time I'll send you a telegram," Tooman said. "In the meantime how about being at ease?"

"I don't like this," another voice was saying. "I just don't like to fall this fast. No, sir, I don't like to fall this fast."

"If we take a hit from that kind of stuff," Tooman said, "you'll fall a hell of a lot faster. Now button up! We're getting close." Tooman thought about the black smoke that had appeared without warning in such heavy density, and he knew that it came from no ordinary ack-ack guns. The bursts were twice too big for 88-mm howitzers, and they came twice too fast for ordinary antiaircraft weapons. The only conclusion Tooman could reach was that the Germans had moored a light or heavy cruiser inside the Frisian Islands breakwaters and waited until the Aphrodite task force was square in their sights before letting go with every gun on board, including four- and eight-gun batteries. They must have been tracking the task force for several miles. Then Tooman thought about the mystery B-17. "Hey, Karrels," he said to the tail gunner. "Where's that 17 that was following us?"

"Still following us," said the gunner.

"That explains a lot," Tooman said. He wondered how much longer Roy Forrest was going to put up with that flying fifth column. They had been lucky the first time, but now they were coming up on Helgoland, and already the little twinkles of yellow light were pointing out the dozens of gun emplacements climbing up the cliffside. With accurate information on altitude, airspeeds, and headings, those gunners could knock down the whole formation, starting with the drone. "Well, it was fun while it lasted," Tooman said to himself, and prepared for the run on the target.

When the mother ship had executed its abrupt fallaway evasive maneuver, Dale Anderson had almost been flipped squarely through the plexiglass windows in the bombardier's compartment. After he had got up and brushed himself off, he looked out the window toward the drone and discovered that it was gone. Calmly and methodically, he keyed on the controls that would turn on the smoke, and within a few seconds he picked up the robot about five miles ahead and slightly off course. He could see that the drone was at the IP, and he knew that the time had come to turn the robot from its easterly course to the 320 degrees that would take it squarely into the sub pens. He was too far back to accomplish the maneuver visually, so he keyed the control that would cause a picture of the robot's magnesyn compass to be transmitted to the television screen in front of him. The signal blinked in clear and vivid, and Anderson read the compass heading. Still working with the methodical skill of a man who had been remote-controlling airplanes for years, he turned the robot through 120 degrees until its own compass readings showed that it was squarely on course to the target. He flipped on the Ace and lowered the baby ship to an altitude of 250 feet and locked it in. "Hold your altitude," he instructed Tooman. "And drop back about two or three miles." Anderson was now in full command of the mother ship, just as a bombardier takes over a normal bomber on the final run, and Tooman obeyed with his usual crisp efficiency. "Try a little more altitude," Anderson said, "the picture's fading."

Tooman climbed, and Anderson said, "Hold it! Picture's perfect."

Now the robot was 10 miles from the target and steady on course. In his TV screen, Anderson could see the cliffs and sharp hillsides of the island looming up ahead, and they seemed to be covered with an eddying gray dust. He realized that he was looking at the smoke from hundreds of antiaircraft guns going off simultaneously. Then he began to see big puffs of smoke around the robot, and geysers of water poking up around the baby's wings. "They're lobbing shells, trying to trip her in a splash!" he said to himself. He had never heard of such a technique. Now his screen was showing a speckled pattern of spurting lights, and the entire cliffside of Helgoland seemed to be erupting fire. The mother ship had fallen about six miles behind the drone, and he was just as pleased. Despite the heavy fire, the drone was responding perfectly, and since there was no flak this far to the rear, Tooman was able to maintain a slow, controlled, steady course on which it was easy to carry out the control maneuvers.

Anderson fixed his eyes on the screen and moved his hand to the control that would turn the Ace off. Now there was nothing in the screen but cliffside and water and sub pens, and the baby was still dead on course. When the first breakwater of the submarine harbor passed into his screen and disappeared out the bottom, Anderson turned Ace off and grabbed the dump switches. The second breakwater appeared in the screen, and straight ahead the openings of the sub pens loomed huge and unmistakable through the arcs of fire and smoke. "Now!" Anderson said to himself, and he applied full down elevator. For an instant, the sub pens grew even larger, but then they started to slide out of the left side of the television screen. He quickly applied a corrective signal to the diving drone, but the sub pens sped across the screen even faster and finally disappeared altogether. Then Anderson got a glimpse of the east breakwater of the island sliding in and out of the screen in the same manner, and his picture went out. He looked up to see a towering pillar of thick smoke soaring into the sky until it reached nearly 10,000 feet.

Tooman whipped the mother ship around in a tight turn, but someone said over the interphone, "Take it easy! All those guns stopped!" Anderson looked out the glass front of the aircraft and saw that the island was silent. Where hundreds of positions had been shooting yellow arcs of light a few seconds before, now there was nothing but the climbing corridor of smoke. He pictured the gunners walking around holding their ears, some of them lying flat on their backs from the force of the blast, and maybe some of them even dead. But killing and deafening German antiaircraft gunners was not Aphrodite's mission, and Anderson was inconsolably upset. For the life of him he could not imagine what had gone wrong. One second the drone was heading right into the mouths of the pens, and in the next it was falling away and blowing up. He sat and stared morosely into space, as Tooman made a few circumnavigations of the island. They flew back through the smoke and made a low pass right across the mouth of the sub pens. Now Anderson could see where the drone had exploded harmlessly against the side of the cliffs. It was less than 150 feet from the target.

A voice was coming over the interphones. "Colonel," it said, "Colonel! Can't you hear me?"

Anderson shook himself back into awareness and said, "Yes, I can hear you."

"You did a great job," Pappy Tooman was saying. "You did the best job yet."

While the B-17 slowly gained altitude to form up with the other aircraft for the flight home, Tooman patiently described what he had seen from the pilot's seat. He told Anderson that the drone had been on course for the mouths of the sub pens when fire had broken out in the right wing, probably as a result of a flak hit. Even with the wing swept by flame, the B-17 continued its steady dive toward the target for twenty or thirty seconds, while more puffs of smoke and splashing water obscured it. When the baby was only 1,000 feet from the target, an engine appeared to quit on the right side, and the plane began a slow turn. It continued to veer off until it exploded just short of the cliffs to the right of the target. Tooman said that the explosion had started out as a bright white nucleus and then changed through a yellowish orange and then a greenish orange before turning black and dense and billowing.

"High order then?" Anderson said. "Everything went off at once?"

"No question," Tooman said. "A low-order explosion would have been black from the beginning. So it was close. You almost did it."

Anderson said softly, "Yeah. Too bad we're not playing horseshoes," and lifted off his headset. The B-17 had climbed to about 5,000 feet, and behind them he could see the squat island of Helgoland receding in the distance, looking like a spent clinker. No sparks came from it now. He could barely make out the outline of a Mosquito diving over the sub pens. Probably it was taking pictures for the photorecon unit. Too bad about the miss. Ten more seconds of straight and level flight, and the Mosquito would have had something to photograph. Now it was just providing the final confirmation of failure.

Ahead, Anderson could see the profiles of P-51's, stunting and gamboling in the sky. Probably they were under the impression that the mission had succeeded, Anderson thought. Or maybe they just didn't care. Their job was to fly cover and stay alive, and they had done both. Now they were swooping up to great altitudes, jettisoning their wing tanks, and rolling over and chasing them down to the deck with machine guns blazing. One of the paper composition tanks took a direct hit and went up in a puff of yellow light, and the P-51 pulled out of its dive and flew away, wings waggling with braggadocio. Anderson watched disconsolately. Under different circumstances, he would have found the air show interesting, even humorous. Now he just wished they all would get home as quickly as possible. Ahead and off to one side he saw a Flying Fortress that looked strange to him, but then he recognized it as the one that had trailed them across the North Sea. As he watched, the mystery bomber veered south on a rough heading toward London, and three P-51's rolled and looped around it, providing an escort until the lumbering ship and its frolicsome companions disappeared in the haze of late afternoon.

When Roy Forrest returned from the mission, cursing and grumbling about the Aphrodite program and its insoluble problems and its just plain rotten luck, the phone was ringing in his office. He picked it up and recognized the voice of a staff major at Eighth Air Force Headquarters. "Tough one, Roy," the major was saying. "The big brass saw it all, and they said your men did a great job."

Forrest shook himself. "If we did a great job," Forrest said, "we'd have hit the target."

"Well, you almost *did* hit the target," the major said. "One of the generals radioed in that he saw a scar in the side of the cliffs, and it's about fifty yards from the sub pens."

Forrest found himself growing confused. The strike had been only a few minutes more than three hours ago. How had any general been able to see the marks of the explosion on the side of the cliffs? The photo reconnaissance unit planes probably had not even landed yet.

"What're you talking about?" Forrest said. "How could anybody know all about the strike this fast?"

"Why, Roy," the major said, "don't you remember we called you before the mission and told you a planeload of brass was coming over to observe? Didn't you see a B-17 from Pinetree trailing you all the way?"

Forrest smacked his forehead. "So that's it!" he said. "And you say you told me about it before we took off?"

"No," the major said. "*I* didn't tell you about it, but I know *somebody* did. The boss left specific orders that you were to be told."

"Well, let me tell you something, Major," Forrest said, his voice booming into the crackly English phone. "You didn't inform me, and nobody else informed me, sir, and make no mistake about it! Now who were those stupid goddamn clods that came out there in a B-17 without my knowledge and came within a pinch of coon manure of getting their asses shot down in the North Sea?"

The major reeled off a list of lieutenant colonels and a few generals. It seemed to Forrest that almost everybody except Jimmy Doolittle and Hap Arnold had been crammed into the B-17. When the last name was read off, Forrest said, "Major, are you a religious man? 'Cause if you are, then you'd better get your ass to the nearest chapel and pray thanks to God that this wasn't a very hot day."

"Why?"

"Because if one of those desk pilots that you just read their names to me had taken a notion to let a little ventilation into that B-17—if one of those brass hat monkeys had opened one of those waist windows a quarter of an inch, the whole goddamned plane would have been shot out of the sky *automatically,* and nobody would have been able to stop it. And that list you just read me would have been for funeral services!"

Forrest cut off the conversation and flung his feet up on his desk for one of the last times. The Aphrodite program was going from bad to worse, he told himself, and headquarters was failing to pay it the most elemental respect. Small wonder. Combat forces needed one factor: targets. And all the targets that had seemed so important three months before were gone. Helgoland had no great significance even if they could hit it. The submarine war was in its last days. Perhaps the program could be put to good use in the Japanese theater; Forrest had reason to believe that headquarters had selected Helgoland as a target

solely because of its similarity to missions that could later be
flown against Japan, with a long overwater flight climaxed by a
strike on an island or a coastal installation. But that meant that
Aphrodite, despite its avowed classification as a high-priority
instrument of the Allied war effort, was still in a training status.

No, it made little difference how he approached the problem.
Roy Forrest could not fool himself into believing that he was
any longer a part of an important operation. He thought about
his wife and the fourteen-month-old daughter he had never
seen, and the comrades he had lost in two long years that seemed
like twenty in the European theater, and how pleasant it would
be to bow gently out of World War II, now that there was no
longer any question about the issue. His bones told him that
Aphrodite had outlived whatever useful purpose it had had.
One of the colonels in Curtis Lemay's outfit had suggested
that they go to the Pacific together to take part in the B-29 operation, but Forrest was not excited by the prospect. He had
bombed enough places, enough people; he had had enough war.
He picked up the phone and asked to be rotated to Texas.

Donald Salles jumped out of the jeep that had returned him
to Fersfield and ran into the operations office. "Where's Lindy?"
he said, and an ops captain named John Sande told him that
Richard Lindahl was dead. A loop of static line had caught
around his shoulder, and at the end of the first thirty-seven feet
of his jump he had taken a 19-G jerk and died of a broken back.
There was one consolation: He had been dead almost from the
instant he left the plane, and he had felt nothing.

Salles bicycled back to his quarters, shoved a few changes of
uniform into a small bag, and cycled through the gate for the
eight-mile ride to Knettishall and Comanche Joe's, the longest
military bar in England. He had been promised a five-day
pass, and so far as he was concerned, it had just started. The
score sheet back at the base still showed his 15,000-point lead
over Lindahl, but now he would have to finance the short vaca-

CASTOR 305

tion on his own. He figured he could always find quarters at
Knettishall and relax around the officers' club at night, and although he was a light drinker, he craved a few days of oblivion.
At Comanche Joe's he threw down a few shots of scotch and
decided to blow all his money in a poker game. The trip to
London was dead anyway. An hour after he had played his first
hand he had tripled his bankroll. He tried everything to lose.
He raised "on the come" when he had no prospect of winning
and lucked out frequently. The other players made him change
his seat several times, but the luck stayed with him. Officers were
cutting in and out of the game, and Salles impoverished them.
Once his opponents made a formal request for him to adjourn
to the bar to change his luck, and when he came back, he won
some more. By nine o'clock he had run a short bankroll into
$500, and he decided he might as well catch the last train to
London. He and Lindahl had planned an uproarious visit to
the English capital after their mission together, and now that
he was alone he thought that maybe he could find a few small
pleasures by himself. He was wrong. He spent five days and
every penny in his wallet, and he had a terrible time.

Roy Forrest's bones proved to be right. The Aphrodite project dragged on for eight months after Forrest flew home in a
B-17 with his old group commander, Colonel Bill David, but
nothing was accomplished that was worth the trouble. A new
commanding officer took over at Fersfield and immediately announced that certain changes would be made. For one, the jump
pilots would undergo extensive parachuting training. To show
the way, the new CO and an officer from the paratroops staged
demonstration jumps before the assembled personnel of the
project. The CO pulled the wrong risers and came down between two hangers, bouncing off the walls like a Ping-pong
ball, and the paratroop lieutenant drifted over the field and out
of sight and was not seen again until the next day. The jump
pilots were told to practice leaping from the backs of moving

trucks, but so many of them banged themselves up that this program was abandoned, and parachuting matters were left more or less as they had been under Forrest's direction.

As though to guarantee that no missile would ever endanger a target, the Eighth Air Force refused Dale Anderson permission to fly any more missions. The man who had come within an eyelash of demolishing the sub pens at Helgoland was informed that henceforth the Eighth Air Force would provide the personnel, that his own hide was too valuable to risk in combat. Anderson returned to his shops and his slide rule, and veteran Third Bomb Division pilots were brought in and trained as controllers. Some of them learned rapidly and performed with skill, but the fine art of guiding war-weary B-17's with the quixotic electronic equipment of the 1940's proved too much for any of them to overcome.

Missions produced catastrophic results. On one of the early ones under the new management, a mother ship pilot and his controller argued all the way across the North Sea about whether the mission should be aborted; the weather was almost ceiling zero, and in order to maintain control, the mother had to fly wing tip to wing tip with the drone at an altitude of 50 feet, barely above the high seas. When the pilot announced that he was aborting and turning back to England, the controller warned that the slightest change in direction would cause him to dive the baby and blow them all up together. The mission was continued, and the controller managed to knock out some 12,500 square yards of the lower town of Helgoland, which was not a military target. Two weeks later a pair of babies went back to Helgoland, but both were lost in the haze on their attack runs. One crashed in the North Sea; the other leveled out in typical B-17 fashion and flew all the way to Sweden, where it blew up on landing and caused American diplomatic officials a few anxious moments. The Swedes, who had been hit more than once by runaway missiles from Hitler's rocket works at Peenemünde, were touchy about such matters; but instead of a scorching complaint, Swedish military officials sent a polite note to the effect that a lost B-17 had crashed and exploded in southern Sweden, and unfortunately there was no trace of the crewmen. Not long after, a loaded drone was being controlled toward a small town in north Germany when it slowly began losing altitude and mushed into a plowed field without exploding. The weather closed in, and fighters and attack bombers returned to the scene the next morning to destroy the robot before the entire Aphrodite program could be compromised. (To the same end, ground crews in England had been dispatched to the scene of John Fisher's crash to recover the airplane's antenna, thus eliminating any chance of the top-secret wavelength's getting into the hands of the enemy. Otherwise, loaded robots could be turned around by Nazi radio technicians and steered back to London.) The fighters and bombers over Germany found nothing. The search-and-destroy missions continued for three weeks, to no avail, and it was not until the end of the war that Allied intelligence found out what had happened. A contingent of German troops, stationed in the neighborhood, and surrounded the downed airplane and ordered the crew out. When there was no response, they battered in the door of the B-17 and entered with drawn pistols. A few seconds later, peasants in a nearby farmhouse heard an explosion and ran to the field to see a smoldering pit, 10 or 12 feet deep. Intelligence officers went back and checked the old records of the search-and-destroy missions and found that several of the pilots had reported a gravel pit at the approximate place where the drone was supposed to have landed. No one had noticed, however, that the gravel pit was new.

After a few more failures the Aphrodite program became the subject of discussions on the highest levels. The Army Air Corps had turned away from strategic targets like Helgoland and sent a few of the missiles into German cities, ostensibly to wreck large industrial areas and marshaling yards, but in fact to strike terror into the civilian populace. As usual, the missiles had exploded wide of the targets. But General H. H. Arnold, Aphrodite's best friend in high or low position, remained enthusiastic about the possibilities of the weapon. He wrote General Spaatz in England and suggested the wholesale use of war-weary airplanes "as an irritant and possibly a means of breaking down the morale of the people of interior Germany." Arnold admitted that there were British objections to the idea and added: "From my point of view, however, I can see very little difference between the British night area bombing and our taking a war-weary airplane, launching it at, say, 50 or 60 miles away from Cologne, and letting it fall somewhere in the city limits of Cologne. . . . My idea would be to turn them loose to land all over Germany, so that the Germans would be just as much afraid of our war-weary planes on account of not knowing just where they were going to hit as are the people of England from the buzz-bombs and rockets." When not even a sobering reply from the perspicacious Spaatz ("We have not had much success in hitting the target") could dampen Arnold's optimism, grandiose plans were laid to inflict Aphrodite robots on the cities of Germany at the rate of twenty-five a month.

At first, the British gave partial approval of the plan, but on January 27, 1945, General Spaatz sent an urgent message to General Doolittle: "APHRODITE BABIES MUST NOT BE LAUNCHED AGAINST THE ENEMY UNTIL FURTHER ORDERS."

Later, a high-level memo explained what had happened: The British Chiefs of Staff and the British Defense Committee had withdrawn their approval; "[they] feel that the employment of these bombers will expose London, which is a unique target and already under attack by long range rocket, to similar attacks by German war-weary bombers," the report said. Under urging by the military, Franklin D. Roosevelt broached the subject directly to Winston Churchill at the Yalta Conference in early February, and Churchill said he would reconsider when he returned to London. Roosevelt died on April 12, 1945, and shortly afterward the new President, Harry S. Truman, received a personal letter from the British Prime Minister. It pointed out in vivid terms that the British had already endured great misery and hardship on the home front and that the use of American war-wearies against Germany might backfire and bring even more hardship upon his countrymen, especially upon the Londoners who had already suffered tremendous losses in the Battle of Britain and the V-1 and V-2 campaigns. On the other hand, Churchill said, he realized the military correctness of the American plans, and therefore he was reluctantly removing the official objections to Aphrodite.

Because of the tone of the letter, Truman ordered that Aphrodite be suspended in Europe. The atom bomb would be operational any day; there was no need to continue experimenting with a weapon that might expose the British to a final measure of retributive suffering, especially when the weapon had been used nineteen times and had scored an equal number of misses. Truman's order effectively ended the Aphrodite project. Various generals memoed one another that the technique might be useful later against Japan, but everyone who knew about the Manhattan Project and the atom bomb realized that Aphrodite had become redundant.

During these final death rites of the program, an uncomfortable nucleus of mother crews and baby pilots and ground personnel had been kept together while their old squadron comrades were being rotated by the thousands back to the United States. Morale plummeted. The crews were rusty and bored and properly annoyed, and some of them began to show it by challenging civilians, drinking heavily, getting into trouble with women, and performing unseemly maneuvers such as driving their jeeps into trees and ditches, landing their airplanes with the wheels up, and taxiing into the mud of the farmer's patch at the end of the runway. Now and then one of the pilots would slip away and fly as air crew on a regular bombing mission or volunteer to go across the Channel and return a salvageable bomber to England. But most of the time there was no useful activity whatever. To work off steam, officers would engage in such games as butting heads in the mess hall, or jumping from a fast-moving vehicle on a dare, or squaring off to fight until one or the other was laid out cold. These were high-spirited, prideful airmen, carefully hand-selected, and they could not be held down indefinitely on a dreary East Anglian air base. Their lives were a constant battle against boredom and cold. The English still guarded the coke pile as though it contained the crown jewels, and with the coming of deep winter the fight to augment the daily one-pound ration had almost become a matter of survival. When at last the word came down that the base would be closed, the British departed, and the crews broke up the remaining buildings one by one for firewood. At the end there was little left but the tire-scarred asphalt and the broken hulls of cannibalized bombers. Thus the Aphrodite station at Fersfield became one of the first military establishments to self-destruct

It seemed a fitting end.

EPILOGUE

Where are they now?

Henry James Rand did not stay long in the hospital. As he tells the story on himself: "I was there about two weeks, and one day when I refused to play baseball, the colonel in charge of combat fatigue said I was crazy. By that time I'd repaired all the PA systems and the radios in the hospital, just to keep busy, but he said I was psychotic because I wouldn't play baseball. So my old boss, General George McClellan, called up and said he needed me in France. Too many Allied planes were bombing and strafing our own men, and the Air Corps wanted me to work on a radio warning system that could be installed in the front lines to automatically show the aircraft exactly where the lines began and ended. I said okay, but I was stuck in the flak-house because the colonel said I was nuts and I needed another six months of psychiatric care. So General McClellan said, 'Put the colonel on the phone!' General McClellan said, 'So you think he's nuts?' and the colonel said, 'Yes.' and General Mc-Clellan said, 'Well, for Christ's sake, he's *always* been nuts. Don't you change him!' A few days later I was assigned to OSS and sent to France, and I stayed there till the war was over."

After the war, Dr. (of science) Rand continued his wheeling and dealing career as an inventor, an improviser, and a fabricator, and founded the H. J. Rand Development Company in Cleveland, a firm that existed to exploit Rand's own ideas. His interest in cancer research, the project that had sent him to

Germany in the first place, never waned, and his firm has continued to fight the disease. Hundreds of victims of throat cancer
are able to speak with a device that H. J. Rand Development
manufactures: a sort of artificial voice box controlled by the
mouth and powered by miniature batteries. From cancer research, the firm branched into other aspects of medicine. The
device that helped to keep General Dwight D. Eisenhower alive
through multiple heart attacks came from the Rand plant in
Cleveland.

General James H. Doolittle, who made the call to Rand that
started the double azon phase of Aphrodite, is now seventy-three
years old and almost as active as ever. As a director of various
corporations, he ranges between his office in Los Angeles and
points around the world and lists himself in *Who's Who* simply
as "aviator." General Earle Partridge, who had good reason to
beg off the job of running Aphrodite but got it anyway, lives in
an active retirement similar to Doolittle's. At sixty-nine, he
maintains a half dozen directorships, serves as an adviser to
the Air Force Academy (near his home in Colorado Springs,
Colorado) and thinks a week is poorly spent that does not include a dozen or two hours of flying time.

Fain Pool, the jump pilot with a reputation for skill at formation flying, planned retirement in 1970, after twenty-eight years
in the Air Force. His last tour of duty was as a lieutenant colonel
in charge of operations and training at McCord Air Force Base
in Tacoma, Washington. It was a desk job, but Pool accepted it
only on condition that he could make frequent trips at the controls of a C-124 Starlifter. Frank Houston, the reluctant jump
pilot, lives near Pool, on Lake Washington, south of Seattle, but
he is neither retired nor threatening retirement. Before World
War II was over, Houston counted up the points from his various medals and dashed back to the United States to apply for a
job as an airline pilot. Now he is a senior pilot for Northwest
Airlines, flying jets on much the same route that his old friend
Fain Pool used to take to places like Tokyo, Manila, and Saigon.

Another jump pilot, the affable Joe Andrecheck, retired from the Air Force as a lieutenant colonel and now lives in Orlando, Florida.

Carroll "Joe" Bender, the pilot who borrowed Earle Partridge's *Silver Queen* and made some of the first important tests of the Aphrodite program, retired from the Air Force as a major and now teaches school in Los Angeles. Ralph Hayes, the intrepid major and engineering officer nicknamed Smoky when he toggled the smoke tanks on as he buzzed a field and scared the ground personnel half to death, works as project engineer at a manufacturing firm near Chicago.

The autopilot expert who could not make the gadget function on his mission, Philip Enterline of Kittanning, Pennsylvania, now teaches sociology at the University of Pittsburgh. He is a PhD. Frank Houston's autopilot man, Willard Smith, returned to his native Doylestown, Pennsylvania, went into the television business, and now owns a TV repair shop. His spare time is still taken up with the reading of philosophy and other humanistic sciences, and he remains as skeptical as ever of the thought processes of the military.

John "Jack" Lansing, the mother ship pilot who frequently tangled with the pugnacious Major Rand, is a vice-president of Pacific Light and Power Company. Wilfred Ferguson "Pappy" Tooman is still in charge of a crew, this one a crack intercontinental troubleshooting crew for the telephone company, and mother ship pilot Foster Falkenstine owns a real estate firm in the Maryland suburbs of Washington, D.C.

Roy Forrest, commander of Aphrodite, works as an administrative assistant at the giant construction company of Brown and Root, Inc., in Houston. His speech is as salty as ever, except when ladies are present, and then he is the soul of South Texas gentility. His friend, Loyd Humphries, "Captain Humpy" to the men of Aphrodite, works as a geologist several hundred miles away in Forth Worth.

Lieutenant Colonel Dale Anderson, the technical expert from

Wright Field, stayed in the service on radio control and guided missile projects and finally retired as a full colonel. Now he teaches mathematics in the Los Angeles area and builds airplanes in his living room and garage in his spare time. Donald Salles, the jump pilot who survived Colonel Anderson's mission against Helgoland, works as an FAA control supervisor in the Washington, D.C., area. His poker luck has returned to normal.

The Navy men have enjoyed similarly varied careers. Mother ship pilot Hugh "Rosy" Lyon serves the Office of Naval Intelligence as a captain and lives with his family on the island of Coronado, near his office in San Diego. The other mother ship pilot, Harry Wherry, works in Indianapolis as a salesman when he is not running off to swim and frolic in the West Indies with his family. The delightful sense of humor and goodwill that carried him through his travails in the Aphrodite program have never deserted him, and he looks back on the program as "a headache but never a bore." For all his battles with Lieutenant Wilford "Bud" Willy, Wherry still mourns his loss. "Willy was one of the great guys," Wherry insists. "He was just like the rest of us: in over his head and trying to make the best of it." As for the two controllers in the Navy project, John "Red" Anderson and John Demlein, Anderson holds a doctorate in chemistry and several important patents; Demlein owns an industrial roofing company in Syracuse, New York.

James Simpson, the "raw ensign" of the program, retired from the Navy and then reenlisted, and now is in Vietnam, rounding out thirty years of service. He is as slight and nearsighted as ever, but no one kids him about his rank these days. He is a lieutenant commander. His former skipper, Jimmy Smith, retired as a captain after thirty years and now teaches mathematics in San Antonio, Texas.

Earl Olsen, as quiet and wholesomely "square" as ever, is in charge of the Systems Integration Laboratory at the Navy Missile Center, Point Mugu, California, a job that perforce makes him a key figure in the missile program. He still looks back on the Aphrodite project as "one of the great tragedies of my life.

"I've thought about it for years," he said. "I've told the story to close friends, and I've asked them what they would have done. It's always worried me. How could I have saved Joe Kennedy's life and Bud Willy's life? There must have been a way. But sometimes I think that the only way would have been for me to make such a commotion that there would have been a court-martial, and even that might not have done it. I could have snipped that jumper without telling anybody, but I'd certainly have been caught, and I'd certainly have been court-martialed for that, too. But that's probably what I should have done. I'd have survived it, and so would the others."

All the world knows the later history of the family that survived the heroic Joseph P. Kennedy, Jr., but the exact details of the death of the twenty-nine-year-old "star of our family," as his father once described him, were kept secret from the family. James Forrestal wrote a touching letter to the elder Kennedy shortly after the tragedy, and the files in the case, themselves unrevealing and distorted in many places, were locked up tight. The Kennedy family comforted itself with a letter from a naval officer who had gone to college with Joe, Jr. "As you no doubt are aware," the young lieutenant wrote to Joseph P. Kennedy, Sr., "the mission was an extremely important one of an experimental nature and exceedingly dangerous. It was on Joe's part, I am sure, a carefully calculated risk, one which he undertook—not lightly, but because he knew that if it succeeded, his work would have a tremendous effect on the war at that stage and because he knew no one else had the qualifications—and most of all, the guts—to carry it through successfully. You may not have heard that he *was* successful and that through Joe's courage and devotion to what he thought was right, a great many lives have been saved."

Later the Navy Cross and young Joe's three Air Medals and various other decorations were passed on to the family, and

Destroyer No. 850, launched in the fall of 1945, was renamed *Joseph P. Kennedy, Jr.,* and young Robert F. Kennedy was ordered to join her complement as a seaman.

Joe Kennedy, Jr., left behind a family that did not need his GI insurance, but Wilford "Bud" Willy's family was destitute. Just before going overseas, Willy had moved his pregnant wife and two small sons into a neat house in Fort Worth. He had sixteen years in the Navy, and in a few years he planned to retire with his family. On the morning of August 13, 1944, Willy's handsome wife, Edna, was stepping out her front door with the couple's newborn baby girl in her arms, on the way to church for the baptismal ceremonies, when a Western Union messenger arrived with a collect telegram. Thus Mrs. Willy learned that her husband was missing in action. A few days later his death was confirmed, and she was told that there were no remains, not even a wallet or a ring or a hat. With three small children to support, Mrs. Willy did not know which way to turn, but she went to work and before long was holding her own.

The Kennedys began a lifelong correspondence with the gritty young woman who had met Willy back in New Jersey and borne his three children, and when college time came, both the sons were sent to the schools of their choice, with all expenses paid by the Kennedy family. When the older son was having a rough time at Notre Dame, Joseph P. Kennedy, Sr., wrote: "I wish I had a nickel for every time I failed at something." The correspondence continued. When the elder Kennedy suffered a stroke and partial paralysis, Rose Kennedy kept in touch with the Willy family by mail.

Lyndon B. Johnson put the Kennedy-Willy wartime relationship to political use during the campaign of 1960, when he ran for Vice President with the young Senator John F. Kennedy. The big issue was Catholicism, and Johnson stormed up and down Texas telling crowds: "When Joe Kennedy and Wilford Willy went out to die so that you could live, nobody asked them what church they went to!" Sometimes Mrs. Willy would be in the audience, at Johnson's request, and he would ask her to stand up and be recognized.

Three years after the successful campaign, President John F. Kennedy sent an invitation to the Willy family to join him at breakfast at the Hotel Texas in Fort Worth. There he put his arm around eighteen-year-old Karen Willy as though he had known her all his life. "I've heard a lot about you, young lady," the President said to the child whom Bud Willy never saw, "and I want you to remember something. Your father was just as much a hero as my brother was. There were no two finer people." That afternoon John Kennedy was dead.

AUTHOR'S AFTERWORD

I acknowledge a deep debt to the Department of Defense for permitting me to become the only person ever to see the full and complete top-secret files—Army, Navy, Air Force and Luftwaffe—on Operation Aphrodite. Mrs. Marguerite Kennedy, chief of the Archives Branch of the U.S. Air Force Historical Division, exhibited a patience which passeth understanding in guiding me through a labyrinth of secret and classified Air Force documents never before examined by any writer. Colonel L. J. Churchville, chief of the Public Information Division of the Air Force's Office of Information, was helpful, as were Dr. D. C. Allard and Commander Joseph Marshall of the United States Navy's historical sections. Retired Air Force General Earle Partridge gave generously of his knowledge and sketched in important areas of the story not covered by the official files. I thank them all.

But mostly I wish to thank the journeymen of Aphrodite, the former privates and buck sergeants and second lieutenants and chief petty officers and lieutenant commanders who sat up till all hours of the nights in Seattle and San Diego and Tallahassee and Detroit and Boston and Boise over coffee and Cokes and sometimes stronger stuff and told the story of this desperate mission as only "working stiffs" could know it. They created this book; I was only their secretary.

Rollinsville, Colorado   JACK OLSEN

INDEX

Kennedy, Joseph P., Sr., 274, 316
Kennedy, Robert F., 316
Kennedy, Rose, 316

Landings, disabled aircraft, 64-66
Lansing, John "Jack," 58-61, 287, 313
Liberator (B-24), 50-51, 56, 63
  converted. *See* Drones
  Navy radio-control system, 175
Lightnings (P-38), 96, 139, 262, 269 ff., 291 ff.
Lindahl, Richard "Lindy," 286-90, 292, 304-5
Living conditions, 49-50, 73-74, 78-83
London
  bombing of, 18, 26, 29, 47-48, 141, 191, 255
  rocket threat, 67-68, 85, 137, 151, 255
Lyon, Hugh "Rosy," 194, 195, 215, 229, 314
  explosion report, 251, 252, 261
  Helgoland mission, 260, 264-66, 269
  third operational mission, 235, 238-41

Maquis, supplies for, 32
McClellan, George, 311
McGuire, Master Sergeant, 33
Mimoyecques, France, launching site, 95, 140, 150, 215, 229-30; abandonment, 254-56
Morale, 77, 86, 148, 160, 309-10
Morrison, Herbert, 85
Mosquito photo planes, 96, 270, 301
Most, Elmer, 94, 97, 100; operational mission, 110, 145
Mother ships, 23, 25-26, 53
  Castor (Army) program, 286 ff.
  communications failure, 264-68, 273
  control checkout, 261
  divided control, 260-61, 273
  first operational mission, 94-95, 109 ff.

flak suits, 263-64
  Helgoland mission: Castor, 286 ff.; Navy, 260 ff.
  Navy, 176, 215, 229, 237 ff., 260 ff.
  runaway, 269-72
  second operational mission, 163 ff.
  third operational mission, 227, 229, 238 ff.
Murray, Peter R., 174, 283
Mustang (P-51), 62, 262, 270-71, 292 ff.
Mustard gas, 19

Napalm, 52, 158-59
Naval Aircraft Factory, Philadelphia, 175, 181, 196, 201, 253
New York City, rocket threat to, 18, 30-31, 137, 151, 255
Norway, 19
No. 4 robot plane, 140-41, 143
No. 342 robot plane, 98-109, 111-16
No. 461 robot plane, 124-35
No. 835 robot plane, 109-11

Observation planes, 96, 109, 242-44, 262-63, 269-72, 302-3
Odom, Thetus, 34
Officers' clubs, 82-84
Olsen, Earl, 213-14, 234-37, 314-15
  electronic arming system criticism, 195-209, 210, 215, 219-25, 248-53
  Helgoland mission, 260-61, 273
  Kennedy death, 244, 246, 248-51
  manual arming criticism, 257
  ordnance fusing, 231-33
Operation Ferret, 187
Orlowski, Navy Chief, 234-37, 244
  arming system, 196-200, 201, 207
  ordnance fusing, 232-33

P-38 Lightnings, 96, 139, 262, 270, 269 ff., 291 ff.
P-47 Thunderbolt, 62
P-51 Mustangs, 62, 262, 270-71, 292 ff.
Pacific War, 83-84, 87, 256, 275, 303-4